Latin and the F
Languages in tl
Middle Ages

Edited by
Roger Wright

The Pennsylvania State University Press
University Park, Pennsylvania

First published in 1991 by Routledge

First paperback edition published in 1996 by The Pennsylvania State University Press, University Park, PA 16802-1003

Library of Congress Cataloging-in-Publication Data

Latin and the Romance languages in the early Middle Ages / edited by
    Roger Wright. —1st paperback ed.
        p.   cm.
    Reprint. Previously published: London ; New York : Routledge, 1991
    Based on a workshop at the ninth International Conference on
    Historical Linguistics at Rutgers University, Aug. 14–18, 1989.
    Includes bibliographical references and index.
    ISBN 0-271-01569-1
    1. Romance languages—history. 2. Latin language—Influence on Romance.
  3. Latin language, Medieval and modern—History. I. Wright, Roger.
PC45.L38 1996
440' 09'02—dc20   95-41360
                                                   CIP

Contents

Preface to the Paperback Edition

Latin and the Romance Languages in the Early Middle Ages, the papers of an international "workshop" with the same title held at Rutgers University in 1989, was published by Routledge in 1991, in hardback only (ISBN-0-415-05606-3). The circumstances of this workshop, and the nature of the papers, are explained in the Introduction. The first printing completely sold out in early 1994, and the rights reverted to me. The present volume is a direct reprint (but for the correction of three minor mistakes). I am very grateful to Penn State Press for arranging this paperback version, at a price more accessible to most of the Latinists, Romanists, historians, philologists, and historical linguists who are interested in the topic. Even six years after the workshop, the ideas and information contained in this volume are still at the cutting edge of the field, and the contributors represent a high proportion of the present experts in the topic.

There have been several reviews of the first edition, mostly favorable, and some are remarkably long, such as those that follow: *Zeitschrift für Romanische Philologie* 107 (1991), 674–83 [Johannes Kramer]; *Revue de Linguistique Romane* 56 (1992), 207–22 [Pavao Tekavcic];*Vox Romanica* 51 (1992), 248–49 [Bengt Löfstedt]; *Studies in Language* 16.2 (1992), 448–67 [Yakov Malkiel]; *Diachronica* 9.2 (1992), 259–85 [Kees Versteegh]; *Medium Aevum* 61.2 (1992), 326–28 [David Pattison]; *Neuphilologische Mitteilungen* 94 (1993), 231–33 [Outi Merisalo]; *Romance Philology* 46.3 (1993), 322–27 [Suzanne Fleischman]; *Modern Language Review* 88.4 (1993), 923–26 [Ralph Penny]; *Speculum* 68.3 (1993), 912 [Laurie Shepard]; *Comparative Romance Linguistics Newsletter* 42.2 (1993), 5–11 [Steven Dworkin]; *Revista de Filología Española* 73.3 (1993) [Ramón Santiago]; *Journal of Hispanic Research* 2.2 (1994), 279–88 [Steven Dworkin].

The papers have aroused considerable reassessment and discussion, whether or not readers agree with the perspectives here expressed, and we hope that this reprint can continue to stimulate informed attention to an academic area of great intrinsic interest that requires interdisciplinary expertise of many kinds to see in focus.

Liverpool, June 1995

Notes on contributors

Paul M. Lloyd is Professor of Romance Languages at the University of Pennsylvania, USA. His publications include *Verb–Complement Compounds in Spanish* (Tübingen: Niemeyer, 1968) and *From Latin to Spanish (vol. I)* (Philadelphia: The American Philosophical Society, 1987).

Tore Janson is Professor of Latin at Gothenburg University, Sweden. His research interests cover Latin literature and language, historical linguistics and Bantu languages. His publications include *Prose Rhythm in Medieval Latin from the Ninth to the Thirteenth Century* (Stockholm: Almqvist & Wiksell, 1975) and *Mechanisms of Language Change in Latin* (Stockholm: Almqvist & Wiksell, 1979).

József Herman is former Director of the Linguistic Research Institute at the Hungarian Academy, now working at the Università degli Studi di Venezia, Italy. He is a well-known authority on Late Latin epigraphy; a wide selection of his articles is now available in *Du Latin aux langues romanes* (Tübingen: Niemeyer, 1989).

Alberto Varvaro is Professor of Romance Philology at the University of Naples, Italy. His many studies on Romance philology include *Storia, problemi e metodi della linguistica romanza* (Naples: Liguori, 1968; Spanish translation, Barcelona: Sirmio, 1988).

Thomas D. Cravens is Assistant Professor of Italian at the University of Wisconsin, Madison, USA. He has published numerous articles on Romance historical phonology, morphology, and semantics, and is currently engaged in research on various aspects of Central Italian linguistic history.

Harm Pinkster is Professor of Latin in the Klassiek Seminarium of the University of Amsterdam, The Netherlands. He has written many studies applying modern linguistic theory to Imperial Latin texts; in particular, *Latin Syntax and Semantics* (London: Routledge, 1990).

John N. Green is Professor of Romance Linguistics at the University of Bradford, England. He jointly edited the four-volume *Trends in Romance Linguistics and Philology* (The Hague: Mouton, 1980–2), and prepares the 'Romance Linguistics' section of the annual bibliography *The Year's Work in Modern Language Studies*. His own research specializes in the syntax of Romance languages and lexically affiliated creoles.

Roger Wright is Senior Lecturer in Spanish in the Department of Hispanic Studies, The University of Liverpool, England. His publications include *Late Latin and Early Romance in Spain and Carolingian France* (Liverpool: Cairns, 1982).

Marc Van Uytfanghe is Professor of Proto-Romance, Late and Medieval Latin in the Universities of Ghent and Antwerp, Belgium. His research interests cover the linguistic, cultural, and religious history of Late Antiquity and the Early Middle Ages; he is co-author (with Gabriel Sanders) of the invaluable *Bibliographie signalétique du latin des chrétiens* (Turnhout: Brepols, 1989).

Rosamond McKitterick is University Lecturer in History and Fellow of Newnham College at the University of Cambridge, England. She has published *The Frankish Church and the Carolingian Reforms (789–895)* (London: Royal Historical Society, 1977), *The Frankish Kingdoms under the Carolingians 751–987* (London: Longman, 1983), and *The Carolingians and the Written Word* (Cambridge: Cambridge University Press, 1989).

Katrien Heene works in the Department of Post-Classical and Medieval Latin at the University of Ghent, Belgium, studying Carolingian hagiographic works, the image of womanhood presented there, and the extent to which they were comprehensible.

Michel Banniard is Professor of Medieval French Language at the University of Toulouse-II, France. He has recently published *Genèse culturelle de l'Europe (V^e–VIIIe siècle)* (Paris, Le Seuil, 1989) and *Viva Voce: communication écrite et communication orale du IVe siècle au IXe siècle en Occident Latin* (Paris, Etudes Augustiniennes, 1990).

Birte Stengaard is Professor of Spanish at the University of Oslo, Norway. Her book on the semantic development in the Iberian peninsula of SEDERE,

STARE, and IACERE was published in 1991 as a supplement of the *Zeitschrift für Romanische Philologie.*

Carmen Pensado is 'profesora titular' in the Department of Romance Philology at the University of Salamanca, Spain. She has published *El orden histórico de los procesos fonológicos* (Salamanca: Salamanca University Press, 1983) and *Cronología relativa del castellano* (Salamanca: Salamanca University Press, 1984).

Thomas J. Walsh is Chairman of the Spanish Department at Georgetown University, Washington DC, USA. He has worked on several problems of Romance etymology and historical phonetics, including the probably apocryphal *-IARE suffix and the aspiration of [-s] in dialectal Spanish.

Robert Blake is Professor of Spanish and Chair of the Department of Spanish and Classics at the University of California at Davis, USA. He has published several studies of the practical conventions used by medieval Spanish scribes and modern applied linguistics.

António Emiliano is responsible for the 'Linguística Inglesa' courses at the New University of Lisbon, Portugal. He is currently completing a doctorate on the scribal and graphematic conventions employed in the thirteenth-century Portugal–León border area.

Marcel Danesi is in the Department of Italian at the University of Toronto, Canada. He is simultaneously a specialist in Italian linguistics and in cognitive semiotics, and his publications include *Teaching a Heritage Language to Dialect-Speaking Students* (Ontario: Ontario University Press, 1986).

1 Introduction: Latin and Romance, a thousand years of incertitude

Roger Wright

The Ninth International Conference on Historical Linguistics (ICHL) took place in Rutgers University, New Brunswick, New Jersey, USA, from 14 to 18 August 1989. The committee of the International Society for Historical Linguistics have adopted a policy of including in their biennial conference programmes special 'workshop' sessions on topics of current interest within the history of particular languages and language groups, and for this conference it was decided (at the suggestion of Professor Paul Lloyd) to hold one on 'Latin and the Romance Languages in the Early Middle Ages'. I was asked to invite speakers and organize the session.

This topic is in principle of central concern to Latinists, Romanists, philologists, general linguists, medieval historians, and textual critics, in addition to historical linguists. Accordingly, some forty invitations to participate were sent to distinguished scholars in all these fields. In the event, the session included sixteen papers. It was genuinely both interdisciplinary and international; there were four participants from the USA, two each from Belgium and Britain and one each from Sweden, Hungary, Italy, The Netherlands, Norway, Spain, Portugal, and Canada. These papers are printed here in the order in which they were delivered, which is roughly that of chronological order of subject matter. The other papers in this volume (those by McKitterick and Banniard) were submitted by scholars who were unable to come but offered their paper to the volume anyway.

The ICHL conferences are a remarkable mixture of friendly co-operation and intellectual stimulation. Scholars working on a whole variety of different language histories meet there to share discoveries, ideas, suggestions, information, approaches, and methods, so this 'workshop' session was not out of place. Even so, there was a foreseeable danger that such an international and interdisciplinary gathering might fragment into splinter groups and mutual incomprehension. But nothing could have been further from the truth. The meeting of minds developed during these two days from initial wariness until at the end the atmosphere was charged with real intellectual excitement. This was not because we had reached a consensus, for we had not, but because we were presented with many new ideas and unforeseen approaches by colleagues from other backgrounds, which often produced echoes in our own areas of expertise. The results of the several encounters may take years to evaluate.

The issues that were expected in advance to arise can be summarized as follows: given that the inhabitants of the Roman Empire spoke Latin, that spoken Latin developed eventually into the Romance vernaculars, and that in the Late Middle Ages Latin and the Romance languages were both used separately and kept conceptually distinct – all of which is uncontroversial – what do we think was happening in the meanwhile? How and why did this distinction ever arise? In the thousand years between Aelius Donatus and Dante Alighieri, when and where is there evidence available to suggest that Romance speakers either did, or did not, think that Latin and Romance were separate languages? What did writers and grammarians of different times say explicitly and suggest implicitly? Can modern sociolinguistic and pragmatic theories help us understand the variations necessarily arising in this period? Are the linguistic data attested in surviving written texts always, sometimes, or never a useful guide to contemporary speech habits? Could it be that spoken Imperial Latin was anyway more like the Romance languages than we usually give it credit for? Why and how were the earliest 'Romance' written texts elaborated? All of these questions have been raised in recent years, and most were in the minds of the participants as they prepared their contributions; but many new suggestions and themes also turned up in the papers and in the ensuing lively discussions, so it seems worthwhile to introduce some of them briefly here.

We have to distinguish clearly between linguistic change and metalinguistic change (see the papers by Lloyd, Janson, Wright, and Danesi), or, to put it in a slightly different perspective, between what was actually happening in the Early Romance-speaking communities and what they thought was happening (Herman, Varvaro, Van Uytfanghe, Pensado, Walsh). We should consider carefully how, if at all, varying sociolinguistic levels and registers could have been reflected in contemporary texts (Herman, Varvaro,

Cravens, Green). Given that the prescriptions of the grammarians were partial and non-descriptive, we should look again closely at early texts from perspectives that the grammarians of the time knew nothing of, such as the pragmatics of word order (Pinkster) and the distinction between phonetic allophones and phonemic restructuring (Cravens, Walsh). Since the development and divergence of what we now call the Romance languages is (to all historical linguists in whatever field) obvious, natural, and only to be expected, one of the interesting questions now is no longer the nonsensical old one of 'When did Latin cease to be spoken?' (because it never has, and a quarter of the world's population still speak it, under different names) but 'When did a separate non-Romance Medieval Latin begin?' (Van Uytfanghe, Heene, Wright). Why was there ever a need to come up with new written 'Romance' systems at all, and how did it happen? (Janson, Cravens, Emiliano). Could the listening public, at various places and times, understand what was read aloud to them? (Lloyd, Herman, Heene, Blake, Walsh). Does the Carolingian textual evidence support the view that spoken Latin was at that time incomprehensible to the illiterate in the way that Merovingian evidence does not? (Van Uytfanghe, Heene, McKitterick). Need apparent illiteracy imply lack of intelligence? (Herman, Wright, Stengaard). Is the argument over whether tenth- and eleventh-century Spanish texts represent 'barbarous Latin' or 'written Romance' solvable on empirical grounds? (Stengaard, Pensado, Blake, Walsh). Should we distinguish Romance writing from Romance spelling, the latter being elaborated first? (an attractive suggestion from Emiliano). Is it sensible for us to suggest that people could be using more than one language for different social purposes – e.g. Latin and Romance – without realizing it? (Herman, Pensado, and Walsh thought perhaps so; Lloyd, Janson, and Wright thought probably not). Here, as in other connections, are cross-linguistic comparisons valid? (Janson, Cravens, Banniard). Can a modern appreciation of the complexities of the time help us to understand such perennially enigmatic texts as the Riojan glosses? (Green, Emiliano, and in particular Stengaard, who sees the combinations of different types of gloss here as all in aid of vernacular 'rephrasing'). How can we solve the apparent contradiction to the effect that the educated encountered archaic morphology and syntax when reading and writing without it having left many traces in literate Romance speech? (Green, Blake). An allied question is: could word order disambiguate in compensation for loss of case endings? (Blake thought so, Walsh thought not). What are the consequences of the written word's gradually becoming ideographic (logographic) rather than alphabetical in nature? This theme, introduced first in passing by Varvaro, unexpectedly became the focus of considerable discussion. It may not be clear from the published text of Blake's paper, but in reading his tenth- and eleventh-century examples aloud he used some of the written words as ideographs for formally unrelated synonyms; *agro* as [kampo], for example. It was suggested that this was merely interlingual translation (between Latin and Castilian), but he defended his ideographic interpretation stoutly. Soon afterwards, Emiliano's paper presented a similar view with great force. In discussion the English examples of *lb* as [pawnd] and *e.g.* as [fəɹɪgzámpəl] were adduced. If this idea proves acceptable, the date at which Latin and Romance have to be seen as different languages could well be right at the later end of the millennium-long spectrum of suggested dates; for even the Carolingian 'reforms' took a long time to become widely established (Van Uytfanghe, McKitterick), and Dante himself is less of a modern-style Romance linguist than he tends to be presented as (Danesi). I thought I would have to defend my date (c. 800) against those who prefer it earlier, but in the event I seem to be more often criticized for suggesting the conceptual break comes too early. If this all seems confusing, we can take heart from the comments made by Herman and Van Uytfanghe that the confusion lies as much in the subject matter as in the modern scholars. (Even so, readers should be warned that modern theoretical linguists tend not to be consistent with each other over what we mean by the word 'diglossia'; contributors to this volume have made their own meaning clear in context.)

So many good ideas were presented in such a short time, that we were inevitably left considering questions rather than answers; there was no time for a digested consensus to form. This open-endedness is an admirable thing. Twenty years ago Romance philology sometimes seemed to be a closed field with few loose ends; but now it once again seems a lively and fascinating area with many unsolved problems, proposals, and suggestions to debate; the interpenetration of textual philology with historical-linguistic theory has proved highly fertile. Some traditional Latinists and historians are also beginning to understand the relevance of these issues; the next stage in widening our collective understanding of the relationship between Latin and the Romance languages in the Early Middle Ages will have to be to try and explain the excitement and the problematic nature of the field to those traditional Latinists and medieval historians who still cannot see the point of it: some of them assume still that Latin is Latin is Latin, of whatever date and place, and that the development of the Early Romance languages is wholly irrelevant to their concerns. But to historical linguists it is self-evident that Imperial Latin only has direct spoken continuity with Medieval Romance, post-Classical written Latin being a separate entity of problematic origin and an unclear relationship with either of the others; and those medievalists who still believe that what the historical Romance linguists say is of no relevance or consequence to them should realize from this collection of papers that the ball is now in their court to explain why not.

Part I

'Late' Latin and 'Proto'-Romance (before AD 800)

'Proto'-Romance speech, as reconstructed by modern historical linguists, is not very like the texts that survive from the centuries when it is supposed to have been in general use. This dissimilarity has led many modern scholars to envisage the literate strata of very early Medieval Romance-speaking Europe as being essentially bilingual (Latin–Romance) in the same way as they were in eighth-century Germanic-speaking areas (Germanic–Latin). The chapters in Part I consider the plausibility of this hypothesis. As Herman and Varvaro show here, people at the time seem not to have been aware of this postulated bilingualism. Herman sees no great problem in this, in that people can be in practice bilingual without realizing that they are. Lloyd, on the other hand, argues (on theoretical grounds) that languages can only seriously be regarded as being different entities from each other if their actual speakers think they are different languages; and Janson argues (also on theoretical grounds, and with a modern parallel) that identification of the existence of separate languages, where once there was thought to be one complex single language, follows rather than precedes the establishment of separate written norms. Varvaro, approaching from the perspectives of modern sociolinguistics, allies this question to that of the divergence of the Romance languages, seeing the latter as intimately connected with the decreasing salience of the universal formal style to which every dialect shifts in normal monolingual continua. The other three papers in this section consider the question from the viewpoints of three main areas of linguistic theory: phonology (Cravens), syntax (Pinkster), and morphology (Green). Cravens suggests, adducing parallels from modern Italy and the United States, that the ostensibly small number of mis-spellings we find attested are in fact impressively large, and certainly enough to discount the need to postulate the existence of a separate literate phonology that had not undergone phonetic evolutions. Pinkster analyses the relative order of Verb, Subject, and Object from an essentially functional (pragmatic) viewpoint, arguing that both in Latin and in subsequently attested Old Romance there is no clear structural canonical order, with the implication that whether or not we wish to visualize two coexisting languages in the very early Romance Middle Ages, there were probably not in evidence two starkly contrasting word-order patterns. Green concentrates on the synthetic passive verbal morphology in an attempt to decide which written forms were merely learnt and which could also have existed in speech as sociolinguistic markers, reformulating the concepts of register and style to suit a complex but still essentially monolingual society. In so far as there is a consensus of views in this section, it is that (at the time concerned) differences between styles, registers, and regions were great but compatible with the feeling that theirs was one monolingual speech community; although perhaps, as Herman suggests, they may have been wrong to feel that way.

2 On the names of languages (and other things)

Paul M. Lloyd

My concern in this chapter is mostly with some general problems of names and naming and how they apply to the topic that we are discussing in the present volume: namely, how did the Romance languages come to be distinguished from Latin? One point of view that has been at least implied, if not directly stated, in numerous works on the subject is the notion that in the Romance sections of western Europe, speakers finally 'recognized' or 'realized' that Latin and Romance were different languages about the time that Charlemagne attempted to reform the Latin of the church, and perhaps as a consequence of that reform. Elcock, for example, believed that from AD 813 'the knowledgeable man in France was to be consciously bilingual; and the priest was credited with two languages to use and confuse' (1975: 343). A more recent work describes the declaration of the Council of Tours in 813 in this fashion: 'The message is clear. French Romance had been born and this is its baptismal certificate' (Pei 1976: 87.) In a more recent study we find a similar declaration regarding the language of Merovingian charters: 'on revient à l'explication traditionnelle qu'il y avait deux langues, celle des hommes de culture et celle des personnes dépourvues de toute connaissance littéraire' (Calboli 1987: 21). Just how far back the two languages go is not agreed on by all. Some have been inclined to place the 'birth' of the Romance languages much earlier in time. According to another scholar, 'au moment même où les indigènes des provinces romaines ont commencé à parler latin, dans chacune de celles-ci a pris naissance une langue romane nouvelle (sous des influences locales)' (Witloch 1984: 41, summarizing the opinions of Maxmilian Křepinský). Just how one knows that there were necessarily two 'languages', rather than two forms of one 'language' or two 'dialects' is never demonstrated. It seems rather to be assumed as though it were a self-evident fact that needs no demonstration.

This point brings us to a more general problem of names. According to one interpretation of Bertrand Russell's principle of names, in order for something to have a name, regardless of any other considerations, 'the subject must have a capacity to distinguish the object of his judgement from all other things'. There must be 'sufficient conditions for being able to discriminate an object from all other things: for example, when one can perceive it at the present time; when one can recognize it if presented with it; and when one knows distinguishing facts about it' (Evans 1982: 89).

The traditional philosophical attitude towards general names or terms is that a name is fundamentally a description of its referent and thus refers to whatever fits the characteristics that the term or name means. As Bach puts it: 'The name "N" is semantically equivalent to the description of the bearer of "N" (1987: 135). That is, 'the meaning of, say, "lemon", is given by specifying a conjunction of *properties*' (Putnam 1977: 103). 'The conjunction of properties associated with a term [such as "lemon"] . . . is often called the intension of the term "lemon". This intension determines what it is to be a lemon' (Schwartz 1977: 14). The application of these properties to specific items is known as the *extension* of a term.[1] Specific denotation requires that the item identified by a term should fill the description of that term.

However, in some variants of this theory, there is no necessity for a 'conjunction' of properties associated with each term; that is, the same number and kind of properties do not necessarily have to be found for each object denoted by a term. For some philosophers, it is sufficient that something denoted should have a certain number of the properties associated with it; something is to be called by a name if it has 'enough features from a cluster of properties' associated with it.

> Each meaningful term has some meaning, concept, intension or cluster of features associated with it. . . . The meaning determines the extension in the sense that something is in the extension of the term if and only if it has the characteristics included in the meaning, concept, intension, or, in the case of the cluster theory, enough of the features.
>
> (Schwartz 1977: 15)

Thus, intension determines extension.

Recently, a new theory of reference has come to the fore in philosophy. This theory holds that 'names have no intension in the traditional sense' (Schwartz 1977: 13). Proper names, for example, have no sense but are rather labels or tags for objects and their 'reference is determined not by any conceptual content in the name but by tracing back along some sort of causal chain leading originally from the object to a speaker's use of its name' (Salmon 1981: 11). According to this theory, it is held that the names of objects are similar to proper names, particularly those terms that refer to natural kinds of things. Their extensions are not determined by concepts or descriptions, but like proper names, have their reference established by something like a causal chain.[2]

These two philosophical theories may not necessarily exclude one another, as Schwartz (1977) points out. Some terms may refer to 'natural kinds', e.g., *gold, water, tiger*, while other terms are attributive; that is, they refer not to specific objects but rather to 'whatever satisfies a certain concept' (38). Thus a term like *bachelor* means any unmarried male of marriageable age, and does not represent any kind of empirical discovery about the nature of unmarried males. If the definition should be changed to include women, it would not be the result of any empirical discoveries, but rather of the extension of the basic meaning 'unmarried' to all humans, by eliminating the second attribute of 'male'.

This brief excursus into philosophy may seem otiose to some, but I believe that there may be something in this sort of speculation that is applicable to the question of matters of labels, even labels of those things, such as human languages, which are not solid objects in the real world.

Stimulated by the preceding speculations, we might well ask whether the name of a language refers to a natural kind of thing or is rather definitional in nature. In other words, do people label a particular form of speech a 'language', and give it a proper name when they recognize it to be such because it is described or characterized by a cluster of features which are necessary for one to recognize it? Or is a form of speech termed a language simply because of the decision of a speech community to call it such? Wright (1982) claims that until the adoption of the new form of pronunciation for written texts in Latin, and the subsequent development of a new system of spelling to represent the vernacular more directly, in Romance-speaking Europe people were not conscious of the existence of two separate languages. It has been held by some that Wright abuses the label of 'Latin' to include both the written form of the Latin/Romance of western Europe and the vernacular language, as two forms of the 'same' language. In the words of one critic: 'W. draws the unwarranted inference that Latin and vernacular were the same language' (Walsh 1986–7: 212). The first question to be asked at this point might well be: why is such an inference unwarranted? It would seem to me that we might be better advised to try to determine, if possible, what Late Latin/Romance speakers themselves thought of what they spoke and what they read and wrote (or rather those few who knew how to read and write). In short, we should not assume that the point of view of much later generations, i.e. that Romance and Latin were distinct languages, must necessarily have been that of those of the seventh, eighth, and ninth centuries.

In contrast with the references cited earlier, H.F. Muller (1923) showed that until the ninth century the term *lingua romana* apparently had exactly the same meaning as *lingua latina*: 'there is no evidence . . . to bear out the contention that the expression *lingua romana* refers to the existence in the VIIth century of a language different from Latin, as far as the people were conscious of it' (13). Further, he stated, 'we could adduce many proofs of the absence of consciousness on the part of the people that they were using a language different from Latin. This *feeling* prevented them consequently from giving a special name to a language, which, to them, was nonexistent' (17–18) (italics added). Wright (forthcoming) similarly points out that the word *Latinus* was used to refer to both the written and spoken forms of language in non-Catalan Spain before AD 1080.

Yet even Muller was evidently convinced that 'after the Carolingian Renaissance, people *realized* its [i.e., the vernacular's] separate identity' (15) (italics added).[3] In short, Muller seemed to be claiming that the origin of the limitation of the term *lingua romana* to something distinct from *lingua latina* was the result of some sort of 'feeling' or 'realization' that the differences between the vernacular and the written language were so great that they could no longer be called one language.

Here again we must ask: can this really be true? Can it be that something about the forms of speech (including written language) suddenly triggers in the consciousness of speakers (or at least some speakers) the realization that what they *speak* is a different 'language' from what they write? From a modern point of view it might seem obvious that those people must have recognized that the difference between the two forms of language made them two languages. And yet, when one considers the variety of languages or forms of speech (including writing) around the world that have been classified as the same language, I think we should not be too certain that the (to us) very obvious differences between speech and writing during Merovingian and Carolingian times must have made people aware that they spoke one language and wrote another, entirely different, one.

Of course, I do not claim to be making any kind of original discovery if I assert that within certain very broad limits, calling a particular form of speech a 'language' is the result, not of recognition of it as a something separate and distinct in the outside world, or as different in some way or ways from other forms of speech or writing, but rather the result of attribution, rather than discovery.

There are limits, of course. Two forms of speech may have almost identical grammars and phonetic systems, and yet never be classified as two forms of the same language if the inventory of morphemes of each is totally or almost totally different. One may think of the case of Kannada, a Dravidian language, and Marathi, an Indo-European tongue, both spoken in central India and completely unrelated genetically and yet each having a grammatical structure that allows bilinguals to translate almost morpheme for morpheme from one into the other (Gumperz 1967: 53–4). No one is likely to claim that these two forms of speech are simply variant forms of the same language. On the other hand, when it comes to genetically related forms of speech, the matter is rather different. Although it has been said many times, it seems that it never can be repeated too often that the difference between 'language', 'dialect', and 'register' is not one that can be demonstrated with clear and unarguable proofs. One well-known sociolinguist, Joshua Fishman, even states:

> A theory which tends to minimize the distinction between languages and varieties is desirable for several reasons. It implies that *social* consensus (rather than inherently linguistic desiderata) differentiates between the two and that separate varieties can become (and have become) separate languages given certain social encouragement to do so, just as purportedly separate languages have become fused into one, on the ground that they were merely different varieties of the same language.
>
> (Fishman 1967: 33)

It should be clear that a recognition that there are differences between varying forms of speech, or differences between speaking and writing, really has nothing to do with whether people think of those varying forms as different languages, different dialects, or simply unimportant variations. It has often been pointed out that

Cicero, Quintilian, and others were well aware that the language they used in conversation and informal letters was unlike the forms of speech utilized in arguing law cases.[4] And yet, we can find no indication that they believed that they spoke one language and wrote another.

It may be useful to make some comparisons with other language families. For example, Chinese is considered a single language, although from the point of view of those coming from outside Chinese studies, it appears to be much more like a family of languages using a single written norm. Much of Chinese classical literature is unintelligible to those not trained specially in the classics, and yet no one doubts that Classical Chinese literature is written in Chinese.

A case even more similar to that of Romance Europe in the seventh to ninth centuries could well be that of Modern Arabic. When I began the study of Arabic, for example, I discovered that the various spoken 'dialects' found in the Arabic world are not all mutually intelligible.[5] Spoken literary Arabic is, in fact, unintelligible to many illiterate speakers of Arabic dialects,[6] and yet Arabic is accepted as 'one' language. Someone learning literary Arabic must learn three separate case endings for nouns which must be written, and yet when pronouncing words aloud, these endings appear only in the speech of the educated, having disappeared from the vernacular long ago, and then in an inconsistent and highly variable manner (El-Hassan 1977: 120–2).[7] Similarly, the classical passive, although absent from illiterate vernacular, appears frequently in the speech of educated people (El-Hassan 1977: 122–3). In fact, although Arabic is often cited as a perfect case of 'diglossia', the true complexity of the manifold varieties of speech found throughout the Arabic-speaking world makes the notion of any division into a 'high' versus a 'low' form of language, as in the classic conception of diglossia (Ferguson 1959), vastly oversimplified.[8] As Mitchell remarks: 'educated Arabic conversation constantly oscillates between written and vernacular and written–vernacular hybridization within the scope of a sentence, phrase, or even word' (1986: 11). Is it not conceivable that the situation in early medieval Romance Europe was very similar to that of Modern Arabic, with a complex variety of realizations in speaking, of partly 'Latin', i.e. written language, and spoken 'Romance' in a dynamic and constantly shifting fashion, in which 'the receptive awareness of speakers is much greater than their productive performances suggest' (Mitchell 1986: 10)? Yet modern scholars insist that this enormously complex pattern of

linguistic features is and 'will remain *one* Arabic' (Jernudd and
Ibrahim 1986: 5; italics mine).

To cite the opposite kind of example: would any linguist from
outside the Romance field think that Spanish (Castilian) and
Portuguese are different 'languages' were it not for the fact that
speakers of Spanish and Portuguese insist that they definitely are
languages and not simply slightly varying dialects of one single
language?

As I hope to have indicated above, the term 'language' is not a
label referring to a naturally delimited referent in the real world. As
Pulgram said: 'the boundary between "Latin" and "Romance" . . .
does not occur in nature, any more than do manmade subdivisions
in other continua. . . . No scale exists on which to measure the
relative linguistic values of available criteria' (1975: 52–3). Is it not
then a reasonable conclusion that the use of the term *lingua romana*
to indicate the vernacular as consciously distinct from *lingua latina*
(regardless of whether, or how, it may have been pronounced) is the
result not of any 'realization' or 'feeling' that they were two
different languages, or because 'Romance' finally had attained a
sufficient number of properties to allow it to be classified as a
separate language (or languages), but is rather a reflection of the
invention of a new system of representing the spoken form of
Latin/Romance which was clearly distinct from the traditional
spelling system? In other words, was it not, rather, the result of a
social consensus that Romance came to be considered a different
language from Latin?

In conclusion, it seems to me that very few scholars have
attempted to escape the perspective of later times and to determine,
as far as they may, just how speakers of Romance/Latin regarded
the various forms of speech and writing of their day and see if they
themselves interpreted the variety of linguistic phenomena they
observed as one 'language' or not. Difficult as it may be to put
oneself back into the mental state of a long-dead people from a
vanished age, especially one so distant and so different from our
own, I believe it to be the most essential of our tasks. We cannot
assume that our perspective must have been the same as theirs.
Undoubtedly, we can never truly understand how those people
thought and felt; the weight of subsequent history bears too heavily
upon our minds, since, after all, we cannot help knowing how it all
turned out. Nevertheless, it is still a fundamental task of historians,
including language historians, if we are ever to be able to
comprehend the circumstances and the factors that led to the

conception that 'Romance' and 'Latin' were different languages, or in other words, what might best be called the 'invention' of 'the Romance languages'.

NOTES

1 Of course, there may be more involved than just this. In the descriptional theory of Gottlob Frege, 'every singular term has in addition to its *denotation*, or the object denoted by the term, a *Sinn* or sense, which is the manner in which the term presents its denotation to the listener or reader' (Salmon 1981: 9). Thus the contrasting terms 'the inventor of bifocals' and 'the author of *Poor Richard's Almanac*' both have the same denotation, namely Benjamin Franklin, but are presented with different senses.

2 'It is in general not the case that the reference of a name is determined by some uniquely identifying marks, some unique properties satisfied by the referent and known or believed to be true of that referent by the speaker' (Kripke 1980: 106).

3 Müller (1986) shows that the correct way to interpret the Edict of the Council of Tours is to distinguish first *rustica lingua* as having the general meaning 'vernacular speech', which is then specified as either *Romana* or *Theotisca*.

4 Cicero's remarks in one of his letters are often quoted: 'Verumtamen quid tibi ego in epistolis videor? Nonne plebeio sermone agere tecum? Quid enim simile habet epistola aut iudicio aut contioni . . . Epistola vero quotidianis verbis texere solemus' (*Epistulae ad familiares*, IX, 21.1). Quintilian states: 'Nam mihi aliam quandam videtur habere naturam sermo vulgaris, aliam viri eloquentis oratio' (*Institutio oratoria* 12, 10, 40). Taken out of context, both quotes may seem to imply that the 'sermo vulgaris' is a different 'language' from that of more formal uses. In context, however, it seems clear that both Cicero and Quintilian are referring principally to style and vocabulary. As Quintilian remarks: 'si res modo indicare satis esset, nihil ultra verborum proprietatem elaboraret; sed cum debeat delectare, movere, in plurimas animum audientis species impellere, utetur his quoque adiutoriis quae sunt ab eadem nobis concessa natura'.

5 This contention is disputed by Ezzat (1974), basing himself on the experience of university students in Beirut from various Arab countries. His experience, however, is strictly based on educated persons having long experience with literary Arabic.

6 My colleague and teacher of Arabic, Roger Allen, informed our Arabic class that in the coffee houses of Egypt, for example, when the news broadcasts are received from Radio Cairo in Modern Standard Arabic, someone educated in this 'language' must sit by the radio and translate (*transferre*?) into the local vernacular so that all the patrons can understand what is being said.

7 Regarding the case endings, Jernudd and Ibrahim (1986: 5) remark: 'even the Arab academies have given up on useless and artificial enforcement and recognize that the written language works well without them.

Inflectional punishment of school children may continue, but such practice now realistically only serves to further undermine this morphological system.'

8 The question of the term 'diglossia' has been much discussed, and most students have found themselves dissatisfied with Ferguson's original definitions. With regard to Arabic, Mitchell concludes that

> the notion of 'diglossia' does not provide an adequate descriptive framework for ESA [Educated Standard Arabic]. It has to be seen as a first approximation to a statement of the distribution of varieties of Arabic among a set of language functions, and it is not, therefore, strictly germane to the needs of grammar writing.
>
> (1980: 104)

Drettas, examining its application to Greek, likewise concludes that 'la construction fergusonienne n'est pas applicable sans de nombreux aménagements aux situations mêmes qui lui servaient de fondement empirique' (1981: 92). Van Uytfanghe claims that the term must be limited to two different 'registers' of a single language and not to two different 'languages' (1983: 399). Fasold proposes that the term should refer to 'the two ends of the formality–intimacy continuum of language use, rather than to two linguistic varieties' (1984: 53), while D'Souza (1988) thinks that the term has been used indiscriminately to refer to almost all linguistic situations, and is therefore not especially useful. It is clear that 'diglossia' was actually a crude first approximation to an approach to the problems of language variety in linguistic communities.

BIBLIOGRAPHY

Bach, Kent (1987) *Thought and Reference*, Oxford: Clarendon.

Calboli, Gualtiero (1987) 'Aspects du latin mérovingien', in József Herman (ed.), *Latin vulgaire – latin tardif. Actes du Ier Colloque international sur le latin vulgaire et tardif. (Pécs, 2–5 Septembre 1985)*, Tübingen: Niemeyer, 19–35.

Drettas, Georges (1981) 'La *Diglossie*: un pèlerinage aux sources', *Bulletin de la Société de Linguistique de Paris* 76: 61–98.

D'Souza, Jean (1988) 'Diglossia in the South Asian sociolinguistic area', *Instituut voor Toegepaste Lingvistiek* 79–80: 25–59.

Elcock, W. D. (1975) *The Romance Languages*, revised and with a new introduction by John N. Green, London: Faber & Faber.

El-Hassan, S. A. (1977) 'Educated spoken Arabic in Egypt and the Levant: a critical review of diglossia and related concepts', *Archivum Linguisticum* (n.s.) 8: 112–32.

Evans, Gareth (1982) *The Varieties of Reference*, ed. John McDoud, New York: Oxford University Press.

Ezzat, Ali (1974) *Intelligibility Among Arabic Dialects*, Beirut: Beirut Arab University.

Fasold, Ralph W. (1984) *The Sociolinguistics of Society* (Language in Society, 5), Oxford and New York: Blackwell.

Ferguson, Charles A. (1959) 'Diglossia', *Word* 15: 325–40; reprinted in Dell

18   *Paul M. Lloyd*

Hymes (ed.), *Language in Culture and Society*, New York: Harper & Row, 1974, 429–39.

Fishman, Joshua (1967) 'Bilingualism with and without diglossia; diglossia with and without bilingualism', *Journal of Social Issues* 23, 2: 29–38.

Gumperz, John J. (1967) 'On the linguistic markers of bilingual communication', *Journal of Social Issues* 23, 2: 48–57.

Jernudd, Björn H., and Ibrahim, Muhammad H. (eds) (1986) *Aspects of Arabic Sociolinguistics* (*International Journal of the Sociology of Language*, 61), Berlin: Mouton de Gruyter.

Kripke, Saul (1980) *Naming and Necessity*, Cambridge, MA: Harvard University Press.

Mitchell, T. F. (1980) 'Dimensions of style in a grammar of educated spoken Arabic', *Archivum Linguisticum* (n.s.) 11: 89–106.

—— (1986) 'What is educated spoken Arabic?', in Björn H. Jernudd and Muhammad H. Ibrahim (eds), *Aspects of Arabic Sociolinguistics* (*International Journal of the Sociology of Language*, 61), Berlin: Mouton de Gruyter, 7–32.

Muller, H. F. (1923) 'On the use of the expression *lingua romana* from the first to the ninth century', *ZRPh* 43: 9–19.

Müller, Karl-Ludwig (1986) 'LATINUS und ROMANUS als Sprachbezeichnungen im frühen Mittelalter. Zu den Anfängen eines romanischen Sprachbewußtseins', in Armin Burkhardt and Karl-Hermann Körner (eds), *Pragmantax. Akten des 20. linguistischen Kolloquiums Braunschweig 1985*, Tübingen: Niemeyer, 393–406.

Pei, Mario (1976) *The Story of Latin and the Romance Languages*, New York: Harper & Row.

Pulgram, Ernst (1975) *Latin–Romance Phonology: Prosodics and Metrics* (Ars Grammatica, 4), Munich: Wilhelm Fink.

Putnam, Hilary (1977) 'Is semantics possible?', in S.P. Schwartz (ed.), *Naming, Necessity and Natural Kinds*, Ithaca and London: Cornell University Press, 102–18.

Salmon, Nathan U. (1981) *Reference and Essence*, Princeton, NJ: Princeton University Press.

Schwartz, S. P. (ed.) (1977) *Naming, Necessity and Natural Kinds*, Ithaca and London: Cornell University Press.

Van Uytfanghe, Marc (1983) 'Histoire du latin, protohistoire des langues romanes et histoire de la communication', *Francia* 11: 579–613.

Walsh, Thomas J. (1986–7) 'Latin and Romance in the early Middle Ages', *Romance Philology* 40: 199–214.

Witloch, Zdenek (1984) 'La Naissance des langues romanes, le latin vulgaire et le latin classique', *Philologica Pragensia* 27: 41–7.

Wright, Roger (1982) *Late Latin and Early Romance in Spain and Carolingian France*, (ARCA Classical and Medieval Texts, Papers and Monographs, 8), Liverpool: Cairns.

—— (forthcoming) 'Early medieval Spanish, Latin and *ladino*', *Colloquium Hierosolymitanum*, Jerusalem.

3 Language change and metalinguistic change: Latin to Romance and other cases

Tore Janson

Why do people in Spain and France not talk Latin? After all, people in England still speak English, even though the appearance of that language is not too far removed in time from the introduction of Latin into south-western Europe. The Greeks still speak Greek, just like they did even before Roman times. People in northern Africa speak Arabic, just as they did 1,500 years ago.

The question seems to me to be a legitimate one. It will be discussed here as an example of historical change that concerns language but cannot properly be called language change.

It is clear that the question has to do primarily with language naming, and only secondarily, if at all, with language usage. The people in Morocco and Libya, for example, agree that Arabic is the language of their respective countries. This does not mean, however, that the language is spoken in the same way in the two countries, and even less that the spoken language is close to the form of Arabic upon which the common written language is based. As for Greek, both the written and the spoken language of today are different from their ancient counterparts, but still the Greeks choose to use the term 'elliniki' for all periods and styles, just as English people use the term 'English' both for the language now in use and for that of the periods called Old English and Middle English.

Thus, the difference between, say, Spain and Morocco is not necessarily that language change has progressed at a different pace or in a different way. The crucial point is that at some time the inhabitants of Spain discarded an old language name as denotation for their mode of communication, whereas nothing similar has happened in Morocco since the Arabic invasion.

Obviously, there are connections between changes of language names and language changes. Some of these will be discussed presently. However, the first point to be made is that the two kinds of events are easily distinguishable and should be distinguished. (For further discussion of this, see Chapter 2 in this volume.)

Further, language naming is only one important instance of a more general type of event: namely, that of changes in the ways to talk and write about languages. These are clearly not changes in language usage or in the language system, but in the attitudes towards the language. I will use the term 'metalinguistic changes' for this whole group of events.

Among metalinguistic changes, changes in language name constitute an important subgroup. In this chapter, interest will be devoted only to these. However, it should be noted that other events also belong to this kind. Examples are changes in the perception and evaluation of dialects and sociolects, as well as changes in the attitudes towards borrowed words and other innovations in a language. Generally, metalinguistic changes are changes in the verbally expressed norms and judgements on language.

Within Romance linguistics, the question about the period of transition has been raised repeatedly. A precise formulation is the title of two well-known articles, Lot 1931 and Norberg 1966 [1974]: 'A quelle époque a-t-on cessé de parler latin?' Such a question may actually mean different things. It may refer to the primary metalinguistic problem of when the users began to call their language something other than Latin. It is possible to investigate that, of course. On the other hand, it may refer to a more subtle metalinguistic problem: namely, what name the modern researcher wishes to apply to the language of a certain time and area. That is not a matter for investigation. Rather, the scholar has to make a choice. The choice should be based partly on facts about language usage, which can be investigated, but other factors inevitably come into play.

Thus, the question of transition from Latin to Romance involves two historical processes, that of language changes and that of changes in language names; and in addition a terminological problem: namely, what names to use in the modern discussion. I bypass the last question and leave it to others to debate such things as whether the spoken language of sixth-century Gaul should be called Romance or Latin, or whether people in twelfth-century Italy should be decreed to have spoken Italian, even though the word *italiano* is not attested until the next century. The reason why much interest has been devoted to such problems is not the trivial matter of classification but the fact that they have to do with such important things as the boundaries between scholarly disciplines and sometimes with the extremely sensitive matter of modern nationhood and ethnicity. For a recent survey of such questions, see Smith (1986).

It is now time to approach the question of the relationship between language change and change in language naming. For a long time it was regarded as obvious that there existed a fairly direct causal relationship, so that when the language had changed enough, a new name appeared. Norberg (1966 [1974: 3]) states: 'Le latin parlé n'est jamais mort mais il a changé, d'une génération à l'autre, de telle façon qu'un beau jour on a trouvé qu'il était pratique de l'appeler roman et de réserver le nom de latin à la langue écrite.' He also shows that very significant linguistic changes took place in Gaul in the seventh century, which, of course, is an important fact.

However, several other languages, such as English, have kept their name in spite of drastic language change, and so the connection is not necessary. It may also be noted that there are cases when a new language name appears without much language change, such as when the term *norsk*, or *Norwegian*, gained acceptance as a language name a few centuries ago. Thus, the fact that a language changes is not in itself a necessary or a sufficient cause for a change in language name.

It is the aim of this chapter to make some general, and by necessity rather sweeping statements concerning how and why new names are adopted. To that end, I will first consider the historical circumstances of Romance language naming and then compare it with an instance of language naming at another time and in another area.

To begin with, it is well known that there is absolutely no evidence for any language name other than Latin in the Romance area before the ninth century. Naturally, this does not prove that no such names were ever used. It is conceivable that people even at this time began to think and talk about their languages as something different from Latin, even though no hint of that is left in our sources. The first question is how probable that is.

For my part, I regard it as extremely unlikely. In the seventh and eighth centuries, western Europe was a politically fragmented region with an overwhelmingly rural and local economy. People lived their lives in their villages without many contacts with the world outside. Probably there was considerable dialectal diversification. Thus, what existed was a standardized written language, used by a very small literate elite and associated with the enormously prestigious name of Latin, and in addition a large number of locally spoken language forms without any prestige at all. In my view, these forms may possibly have been named by the name of the village or district, when need arose, but more probably never received a name at all.

This may seem less than convincing to persons who speak and write a prestigious and well-defined language. However, it is a fact that users of speech forms with low prestige and no established written form may well lack an established name for their particular way of speaking. This is true, for example, for many of the creole languages of the world: the names found in the linguistic literature are very often late inventions by linguists. Information about this can be found in handbooks like Holm (1989). It is true that most people, if pressed, will agree that they speak the language of their own town or district. But that is at most the name of a dialect, not of a language. Not all languages have names.

For the ninth century and onwards there is considerable evidence about names. One of the merits of the remarkable book by Roger Wright on Late Latin and Early Romance (Wright 1982) is that new light is shed on the process of language naming, especially in Gaul. I accept his main conclusions, and thus subscribe to the view that the appearance of the term *rustica Romana lingua* in 813 is intimately connected with the reform of spelling and pronunciation introduced by Alcuin a short time before. Previously, there seems to have existed no distinction in name between the spoken language and written Latin; rather, Latin was simply the written form of the spoken language, and was pronounced in no other way when read aloud. And even during the ninth century, when terms like *lingua Romana* are met several times, it seems that the notion of a special linguistic form is connected not so much with a general difference between written Latin and spoken vernacular as with the difference between the learned pronunciation of written Latin and the ordinary way of talking. Clearly, there are no texts from this century or the following one that allow us to draw the conclusion that there existed a notion of two quite separate languages, Latin on the one hand and Romance or French on the other. As Wright has shown, that development belongs to the eleventh century.

The establishment of this fact is very important. It means that the process of establishing new language names does not belong to Carolingian times, but to the long period of expansion that followed after the disastrous tenth century. Further, judging from the facts presented by Wright, it seems likely that the naming process was not a two-stage process. What happened was hardly that a distinction between *roman* and Latin was first established over the whole area, and that the different names for Romance languages were created later. Rather, in each part of the Romance area, the distinction between Latin and Romance appears almost simultaneously with a name and a written language for that part, and this happens at widely different times in different areas. The most important developments occurred in the period between the years 1000 and 1300.

During those three hundred years, the economy of Europe became more diversified and more advanced, and there was a steady rise of activity in most fields of human culture. Politically, this is a period during which the power of central secular authorities, like kings and courts, was very much augmented. Several states rose to significant powers. This is a time when trade and administration made it possible and necessary for people to keep in touch throughout large regions. Also, the fabric of society changed profoundly, with accruement of wealth and influence to new hands. In that situation, it is reasonable that one may need a name for the language spoken in a region, or even by a social group, especially if it was culturally and politically important.

However, as a matter of fact the new names do not appear only or even primarily as names of spoken languages. For it is clear from well-known facts, and has been shown in detail for Gaul and Spain by Wright, that the process of naming is intimately connected with the establishment of new written languages. It can even be argued that the new written forms appear before the new names. For it seems to be generally true that reasonably standardized ways of writing become established at a time when the name of the language is still not definitely fixed. Thus, for example, in France the term that eventually dominated, *français*, for a long time had competition from *roman*. In Italy, Dante never used the word *italiano* but actually preferred the term *latino* for what we call Italian.

This leads to the question of where the names came from. Did there exist names in general use for the languages of different areas, and were these names subsequently applied to written forms of the languages? Or were the names really invented as denotations for the newly created written forms? Since our sources are only written ones, it is always hard to know anything about the spoken language. However, there are several reasons to believe that the names in the early period referred mainly to the written forms and were used primarily by a literate elite.

In the first place, as was pointed out earlier, it is hardly probable that ordinary people had any general names for their way of speaking. Second, one can find positive evidence for the nature of language names in the Romance area in contemporary discussions in literary sources, written by highly literate and linguistically sophisticated persons. A recent overview is found in Holtus (1987). The most important texts are from the thirteenth century.

It emerges that still in the thirteenth century the situation depicted is clearly that of a coherent area with dialectal variation. Raimon Vidal writes, in a discussion about proper literary forms: 'per totas las terras de nostre lengage son de maior autoritat li cantar de la lenga lemosina qe de neguna autra parladura' (in his *Razos de trobar*, p. 6: 'throughout all the lands of our "lengage" the songs in "lenga lemosina" are higher esteemed than those in any other idiom'). In the context, the phrase 'nostre lengage' seems to refer to the entire Romance area; at least it includes the whole of modern France. In this area songs in 'la lenga lemosina' are universally admired. This situation seems similar to that in ancient Greece, when texts in the Ionic dialect as well as texts in the Doric one were read and admired in all Greece. It is also similar in that in both areas an author did not necessarily write in his native dialect, but rather in the one that was regarded as appropriate for the *genre*.

The Englishman Roger Bacon (in *Opus Tertium*, p. 90) very explicitly distinguishes between *idiomata* and *linguae*, pointing out that one *lingua* may have several *idiomata*. As examples of *idiomata* he mentions *Picardicum et Gallicum et Provinciale*, 'and all the *idiomata* from Apulia all the way to Spain'. And he continues: 'Nam lingua Latina est in his omnibus una et eadem, secundum substantiam, sed variata secundum idiomata diversa.' ('For the Latin language is one and the same in this whole area, according to its substance, but varied according to the different *idiomata*.') Clearly, the term *idioma* here has a meaning very close to 'dialect'.

Of particular interest is the extraordinary treatise by Dante, *De vulgari eloquentia*. Since it is discussed in another contribution to this volume (Chapter 19), I will be very brief here, and only note in passing that the first book of the work provides much unique information about the linguistic situation and a very professional theoretical analysis. As for the Romance part of Europe, Dante maintains that it obtained the same language, or *ydioma*, after the confusion of Babel, but that through later language change, this *ydioma* is now tripartite, *tripharium*. He characterizes the three divisions in the following way: 'alii *oc*, alii *oïl*, alii *sì* affirmando locuntur, ut puta Yspani, Franci et Latini' (*De vulgari eloquentia* 1.8.6). ('Some use *oc*, some *oïl*, and some *sì* in affirmation, as for example the Spaniards, the French, and the Latins.') This division of the area into three well-defined parts is found in a treatise that has as its main theme the definition of a standard form of *latium vulgare*, which is what we call written Italian. The written forms of French and Occitan were already well established. There can hardly be any doubt that Dante's way of structuring the Romance dialect continuum was heavily influenced by his knowledge of the written forms of language. With three established ways of writing, there should be three main spoken forms too.

This evidence strongly suggests that the prevalent picture among literate people in the thirteenth century was that there existed a coherent area in which the spoken language was similar, but with dialectal variation, and in which there existed one main written form, usually called *lingua Latina* (but named *gramatica* by Dante). Of the dialects, the ones with written forms attract most attention. In the most important text, that by Dante, we see the beginnings of a fixed relation between written forms and large dialect areas.

It is clear that the process of language naming is a long and gradual one, and that there are no indications that the names, or any concepts similar to the ones now associated with the names, appeared before the written forms. On the contrary, it seems credible that the notion of Romance languages common to large regions appeared only in connection with or even after the elaboration of standard written forms.

This brings us back to the reasons for language naming. If the creation of written language forms is intimately connected with naming, then the causes for both may be similar. Now, it is reasonably clear which social factors contributed to the success of the written languages. They were associated with important forces in society, in the beginning notably the feudal nobility, that had reasons and means to assert themselves and their way of life in distinction and sometimes in opposition to the Church with its Latin dominance. From the beginning, the written Romance languages were associated with the secular rulers and courts, as is attested by Dante. He requires (*De vulgari eloquentia* 1.18) that a *vulgare illustre* should be, among other things, *aulicum* and *curiale*, by which he means that it should be linked to a palace and a court, and he sees it as a difficulty that this is not the case in Italy.

Naturally, it is not possible here to follow the further development towards the idea of national languages. What has been said is enough to establish some basic facts about language naming. In the first place, there is no evidence of a clear notional distinction between any Romance language and Latin before the eleventh century. Before that, what existed was the name of Latin and possibly a number of makeshift designations of different dialects. In the second place, the introduction of language names is closely connected with the creation of written language forms. Thirdly, the early history of the names as well as the written forms is linked with powerful and numerically small groups in society rather than with people in general. In sociolinguistic terms, the metalinguistic change is definitely a change from above, not from below.

In sum, we can say that all through the Early Middle Ages, there was only one language name, that of Latin, despite considerable linguistic diversity, for no one needed any other name. Only when there existed significant new entities to talk about, namely the new written standards, did new names appear.

At this point, it seems appropriate to point to a parallel development in another part of the world. It is described in Janson and Tsonope (forthcoming). In southern Africa there is a vast area with a dialect continuum reminiscent of the Romance one, although on the whole the dialectal differences are smaller: people from different regions can usually understand each other well without much training. This is the so-called Sotho-Tswana group of Bantu languages. The area comprises much of northern South Africa and the states of Botswana and Lesotho. The size of the area is comparable to that of France and Spain together, but the population is much smaller.

In this area, there was traditionally a large number of independent states, or tribes, without any central authority. No written language existed until the arrival of European missionaries. It is uncertain whether there existed any name for the language of the whole area: the word *setswana* may possibly have served that purpose. On the other hand, each state had a name, and a language name could always be formed by prefixing *se-* to the stem of that name. Thus, the language of the Kwena state could be called *sekwena*, the language of the Sotho state, *sesotho*, and so on.

Now, when the first English missionaries settled in the western part of the area around 1820, they immediately began to translate the Bible and other religious texts, creating a written language in the process. They called the language Setswana, which seems to have been the name used by the native speakers they met. About twenty years later, French missionaries set up a mission in the southern part of the area, in the Sotho state. They also translated texts, partly the same ones. In the beginning, they considered themselves as translating into Setswana, but after a while, they decided that their written language was really Sesotho. Several decades later, history repeated itself when German missionaries began work in the eastern part of the region, in the Pedi state. Initially, they thought that they translated into Sesotho, but after some time, they found out that they were writing in Sepedi.

Thus, at the beginning of the twentieth century, three different written languages were established. This had comparatively little relevance at the time, since the missionaries were only moderately successful and literacy remained at a low level. However, during the last three decades, the situation has changed drastically. Setswana and Sesotho are now the official languages of the states of Botswana and Lesotho, respectively, and there literacy is almost universal in the young generation. In South Africa, too, all three languages are recognized as separate entities and taught in schools. Thus, the area is now no longer divided into several scores of states, each with a separate language name, but has exactly three written language forms and three language names.

There are some obvious similarities between this rapid development and the much longer one in the Romance area. In the first place, the connections between language naming and the creation of written language forms seem to have been equally strong in both cases. Second, the language names did not spread among the users from some unknown source, as language changes often do. Rather, they were deliberately imposed by small but influential groups. Third, the full significance of the name and the written form did not appear at once. Only the rise of literacy, the introduction of systems for universal education, and the association of state power with ethnicity, gave rise to a situation in which most inhabitants of a region believe that they speak and write one particular named language.

To finish up, I would like to put forward some tentative conclusions that I think are valid for the cases studied here and may have further relevance.

In the first place, language change and language naming have little to do with each other. Even extensive and rapid change may occur without any change in name, and names may be changed without any language change at all. Second, the split of a dialectally diversified area into several named languages is intimately connected with the introduction of different written forms of language. As a matter of fact in both areas studied it seemed that the written languages were created first, while the association between them and the spoken language of a large area became fixed only later on. Generally, it seems that related and contiguous language forms are not given separate names unless there are separate written forms. Possibly it may be the case that the notion of a language as we understand it in western culture implies a written form much more strongly than linguists usually want to believe. Third, language naming may have both political causes and political consequences. A language name, with its written language, may be propagated by some group to further its own interests. On the other hand, the fact that a name and a written form exists may have very important consequences for future political and cultural development. Thus, the naming in itself constitutes a political and cultural change.

BIBLIOGRAPHY

Bacon, Roger (1859) *Opus Tertium*, ed. J.S. Brewer, London.
Dante Alighieri (1957) *De vulgari eloquentia*, ed. A. Marigo, Florence: Le Monnier.
Holm, J. (1989) *Pidgins and Creoles*, vol. 2: *Reference Survey*, Cambridge: Cambridge University Press.
Holtus, G. (1987) 'Zur Sprach- und Wortgeschichte von "latino" und "volgare" in Italien', in W. Dahmen, G. Holtus, J. Kramer, and M. Metzeltin (eds), *Latein und Romanisch: Romanisches Kolloquium I*, Tübingen: Narr, 340–54.
Janson, T. and Tsonope, J. (1991) *Birth of a National Language: the History of Setswana in Botswana*, Gaborone: Macmillan.
Lot, F. (1931) 'A quelle époque a-t-on cessé de parler latin?', *Archivum latinitatis medii aevi* 6: 97–159.
Norberg, D. (1966 [1974]) 'A quelle époque a-t-on cessé de parler latin en Gaule?', *Annales* 21: 346–56, reprinted in D. Norberg (1974) *Au Seuil du moyen âge*, Padua: Antenore.
Smith, A. D. (1986) *The Ethnic Origin of Nations*, Oxford: Blackwell.
Vidal, Raimon (1972) *Razos de trobar*, ed. J.H. Marshall, Oxford: Oxford University Press.
Wright, R. (1982) *Late Latin and Early Romance in Spain and Carolingian France*, Liverpool: Cairns.

4 Spoken and written Latin in the last centuries of the Roman Empire. A contribution to the linguistic history of the western provinces

József Herman

Respectful courtesy, at least, is due to the dead: so let me state at the beginning that if our field of study – that is, research devoted to the diachronic continuum leading from Latin to separate Romance languages – is based on a tremendous wealth of ascertained and well-ordered material, we owe it to the achievements of scholars like Hugo Schuchardt. He worked through an incredible amount of texts never really considered before him, in order to produce his *Vokalismus des Vulgärlateins*, a work upon which our knowledge of the phonetic changes in Late Latin is still ultimately established. Also, if we are able today to envisage the history of Latin from the classical age to Romance as one exceptionally complex but coherent process of linguistic change, with continuous interactions between literary traditions and ambitions on the one side and spoken usage of more or less educated native speakers of Latin on the other, between received grammatical norms and new habits, between old heritage and modified conditions of communication, this we owe to the great Nordic school of Latinists. Foremost among these was Einar Löfstedt, who so aptly concealed – behind an apparent lack of theoretical interest and a non-committal scholarly style – a strong synthetic vision of the history of language.

This has to be said because, along with all this wealth and all these lucid insights, we also inherited a fair amount of confusion, mainly in terminological guise. We are lost in the labyrinth of ill-defined designations and overlapping pseudo-categories like Late Latin, Early Medieval Latin, Literary Latin, Written Latin, Vulgar Latin, Popular Latin, Colloquial Latin, Spoken Latin, Romance, Early Romance, Proto-Romance, Pre-Romance – and the rest. This is so much the case that worthy colleagues seem to spend a lot of their energy in fighting terminological battles.

I definitely do not have the intention of adding a new sheet of paper to this already messy dossier. I simply raise this point in order to put forward another consideration: I think that if, in our field, the terminological trouble is deeper than in some parallel branches of historical linguistics, it is not due to specific intellectual short-comings of our own or of our predecessors, but to substantive features of the field itself. I think that our difficulties in finding adequate and duly delimited concepts and designations to cover the developmental stages and the sociocultural variants in the broad transition process from Latin to Romance stem from the exceptional complexities of these stages and varieties in the sociologically very manifold and immensely widespread Latin speech community. They stem, moreover, from some specific features of what we could call the metalinguistic situation in the transitional age. At that time the knowledge of the speakers about their own language, their linguistic awareness, their feeling of linguistic identity, influenced as they were by the prestige of the written tradition, could not reflect the real situation and the diachronic movements of the language without some necessary simplifications and inadequacies.

There is a point here – theoretical as well as methodological – which I wish to stress very strongly, because its neglect is the origin of many terminological troubles and various failures: there is a fundamental logical necessity to clearly distinguish between the metalinguistic aspects of a diachronic process – that is, the options and views prevailing in the linguistic community as far as the language of the community is concerned – and the linguistic changes themselves. This second aspect – language change – is naturally *par excellence* the object of diachronic research. The metalinguistic side, however important and even informative in its own right, is not language history in itself; it can even happen that it gives a somewhat distorted image of the real linguistic situation. I shall briefly come back to this point in my conclusions.

This being said, I can pass now to the problem indicated in the title of this paper, viewed, at first, under this metalinguistic angle. I begin with a minor remark. The evidence I shall make use of in order to clarify the metalinguistic attitudes of fourth- and fifth-century people consists almost exclusively – apart from some grammatical treatises – of examples and statements taken from Christian, mainly patristic, texts. This apparent bias is easy to justify. The Christian faith was based on the Scriptures, that is, a considerable corpus of written texts, so that to propagate Christian-ity meant, in practice, to make these texts known, to explain them, to bring them close by readings, recitations, comments, and manifold elaborations to people coming from various and, for obvious reasons, mainly lower social and cultural settings. Thus, for Christian writers and especially the most eminent ones, the conditions under which a written text could or could not be understood, was or was not suitable, when read or recited, to persuade and attract a heterogeneous public, represented an ever-present and central issue. Thus, the Christian views on communication and communicability, the metalinguistic stand of Christian authors on the relations between the texts and the uttered and perceived spoken language can be considered as representative of the Latin linguistic situation at large.

At first sight, these relations seemed to have been essentially unproblematic. I have shown in a recent paper[1] that, in the sixth century, the general Christian public, the *populus fidelium*, were presented as completely able to understand biblical texts and commentaries on the Scriptures when they were read aloud to them. It is not astonishing that this was even more naturally the case in the two last centuries of the Empire. One clear proof will be sufficient: in the year 441, the Council of Orange decided (Conc. Araus. 27, *CC* 148, p. 83, l. 75) 'Euangelia deinceps placuit catechumenis legi apud omnem provinciarum nostrarum ecclesiam'; a decision which evidently means that everybody being prepared for baptism was considered in Gaul as able to follow a recitation of the Latin text of the Gospels. Besides, there is clear and partly well-known evidence, in the synodal decisions and elsewhere, which shows that in its everyday life the Church worked, after its complete legalization, not unlike the state, with a written administration which was considered as the documentary registration of corresponding oral acts. Members of the Church, even at low levels, quite naturally were able to read, and the first signs of decline in this respect would appear only in the middle of the sixth century.[2] Written language was considered as being evidently of the same linguistic essence as colloquial, everyday usage; Saint Jerome, born in the Illyricum, and who considered himself, being a native speaker of Latin, as a *homo Romanus* (*Ep.* XV, 3), says in a nicely playful sentence of a letter written in Syria (*Ep.* VII, 2) that the Latin letters he receives are his only partners of conversation in a country of Barbarians.

Still, our authors are very much aware that the real situation was far from being so simple and so favourable.

Even if we disregard the obvious difficulty which arose in some provinces from the ignorance of Latin – or Greek – as a language (see, for instance, the complaint of Saint Augustine, *Ep.* 84, 2, 1), it is often noted that speakers of Latin who had no or only scarce literary and grammatical training were themselves unable to understand or at least to completely follow texts beyond a certain level of linguistic complexity. Saint Jerome notes, for instance (*Ep.* LVIII, 10), that the prose of Saint Hilarius, with its Gallic oratorial style, its Greek rhetorical flowers, and especially its long sentences, 'a lectione simplicium fratrum procul est'. Elsewhere he remarks (*Ep.* LII, 8) that speed and volubility of diction are admired by simple people ('imperitum vulgus'; or, as he says in the same letter, 'vilis plebicula et indocta'), who usually admire what they do not understand.

It can naturally be said that all this is not astonishing, and that these are stylistic limitations every writer or speaker in any age or in any language has to be aware of when writing or speaking to a so-called popular, moderately or minimally schooled public. Let us add that these limitations are very much in line with the Christian stylistic ideal of *simplicitas*, a very practically orientated ideal which adheres to the necessity of communicating the message to everybody and in such a way that it can be understood. 'Being understood' has to be taken, in this age of perpetual doctrinal disputes, in a very strong sense: understood without any possibility of double meaning, of equivocation as to the object and content of faith. From Lactantius to fifth-century synodal decisions, long series of texts could be quoted to illustrate this attitude – but this would lead us far from our subject.[3]

But – here we reach an essential point which brings us near the very core of the problem – some Christian writers clearly had the feeling that the obstacles to overcome in spreading the message among the *indocta plebicula* were not simply of a stylistic nature, whatever the words 'style' and 'stylistic' may mean for us at closer scrutiny; that it was not sufficient, in order to be understood, to avoid oratorial pretensions, rare words, long, complicated periods and to speak – or to read out – slowly and distinctly. They felt that between the oral usage of the *plebicula* and the system of the written tradition, even read out, there were differences which were – even if apparently peripheral – of a systemic nature, as they concerned the functioning of some grammatical rules and certain organizing parameters of the lexicon.

Let us see some examples of this dim but unmistakable metalinguistic knowledge. Augustine, at a certain point in his *Enarrationes in Psalmos* (XXXVI, s. III, 6; *CC* 38, 371), makes a passionate and eloquent sortie against grammarians: 'Quid ad nos quid grammatici velint? Melius in barbarismo nostro nos intelligitis, quam in nostra disertitudine vos deserti eritis.' If we take a closer look at the problem he speaks about, the difficulty seems to be unimportant ('Feneratur quidem latine dicitur et qui dat mutuum et qui accipit: planius hoc autem dicitur si dicamus fenerat').

Besides, as so often, Augustine exaggerates: although *feneratur* was in principle the correct variant, the active *fenerat* never really was considered as a barbarism and was often used even by very good authors. But through this minor problem Augustine takes a more general stand: he accepts as rightful a usage in which verbs with an active construction always have an active form – that is, where deponents as a category do not exist – and besides, he takes advantage of this issue to establish the merits of barbarisms, if helpful in spreading the message. There is another text by Augustine, better known and often cited, but never – as it should be – extensively.[4] The logical structure of the passage is similar to the previous one: there is one concrete issue (vindication of the right to use the analogical *ossum* for *ŏs*, *ōs* retaining the declension *ōris*, etc., as this analogy prevents the confusion of *ŏs* and *ōs* in a usage where the phonological opposition of short and long vowels does not exist any more). Unlike the previous one, this example is in itself linguistically significant, as it establishes the necessity – which certainly was already clearly felt in 'popular' speech – to accept the structural rearrangements in inflectional and derivational morphology which inevitably followed from the loss of quantitative vowel-distinctions. Moreover, the concrete case gives Augustine a splendid opportunity to oppose the way of speaking which was *latinum* to *vulgi more sic dicitur* and to recommend the latter if clear intelligibility cannot be obtained in conformity with established grammatical norms. There is a similar instance in Saint Jerome's writings (*Hiez.* XII, 40, 5–13 and XIV, 46, 1–5, *CC.* 75, 561, 712). Closer to his grammar and to scholarly tradition, Jerome does not really identify himself with the barbarism he feels necessary to adopt (neglect of gender difference between *cubitus* and *cubitum*, where the special meaning of 'ell' is tied in principle to neuter), but he explains this apparent weakness as a virtue: he does it 'propter simplices quoque et indoctos quorum in congregatione ecclesiae maior est numerus' (*CC* 75, 712).

Besides, a man like Jerome knows very well that the usage of the *imperitum vulgus* does have a vocabulary which is to a certain extent specific, with elements which normally do not appear at the level of the texts, not even in those which adhere to the stylistic ideal of simplicity. Some of these emerge in the texts in a particular way: Jerome, as he says in *Ep.* LXIV, 112, wishes 'pro facilitate abuti sermone vulgato' and translates some rare or difficult expressions of the biblical text with a word which 'vulgo dicitur' (in *Is.* V, 28, 23, these words introduced *flagellum* in the sense of French *fléau*, that is, 'scourge'), or which is a 'consuetum verbum' (like *coxale* 'a sort of belt' in *Zach.* III, 11, 14), and similarly a fair number of others. In a remarkable way, all these elements presented as being in general use, are in fact *hapax legomena*, or almost, at the level of the texts, and we would not have met them without Jerome's helpful commentary. We know very well from the 'hypothetical' forms reconstructed from Romance that hundreds of words and expressions, kept in the background by more distinguished and usually less specific written synonyms, lived in the language of the *vulgus*. What interests us here, is the metalinguistic aspect of the problem: Jerome and a great number, certainly, of others were completely aware of the fact that there was a sort of 'parallel' vocabulary understood by all, while many elements of the seemingly current traditional vocabulary were restricted to written usage, or to its direct oral expression.

We shall have a rapid look at pronunciation, at phonetics, when we turn to the 'linguistic awareness' of the grammarians. For the time being, there is only one point to be stressed: the Fathers seemed to consider that their way of pronouncing Latin – that is, the pronunciation of the *eruditi* – was not identical to the way of speaking of their popular public, or at least a good part of it. We have in this respect some clear testimonies. Ambrose says, for instance (*de officiis ministrorum* 23, 104, Migne *PL* 16, 59), 'sit (vox) sane distincta pronuntiationis modo, et plena succi virilis: ut agrestem et subrusticum fugiat sonum'. Jerome, as usual, is more specific (*Ep.* CVII, 4): 'Ipse elementorum sonus et prima institutio praeceptorum aliter de erudito, aliter de rustico ore profertur. Unde et tibi est providendum, ne ineptis blanditiis feminarum dimidiata dicere verba filia consuescat.' The interpretation of the terms *rustici*, *subrustici*, *agrestes* for our period is problematic. As they are opposed to the *eruditi* in the text of Jerome (who, among other things, do not swallow a portion of the word, that is, probably, the final syllable with its flectional function), these pejorative terms could probably be simply interpreted as 'without schooling'. It should be added that Augustine opposed his own pronunciation to the general African one by stressing that he himself was able to distinguish *manifesto sensu* short and long vowels – a feature whose importance seemed exceptional.[5]

Generally speaking – and going on this point beyond the problem of pronunciation – there seems to have been a clear feeling among people of a more or less standard schooling and literary training that they had to take special care if they wanted to enter into satisfactory and successful verbal communication with the *indocti* and the *rustici*. We read in an interesting text of the second half of the fifth century (about 475):

> viduae vel sanctimoniales quae ad ministerium baptizandarum mulierum eliguntur, tam instructae sint ad id officium, ut possint aperto et sano sermone docere imperitas et rusticanas mulieres, tempore quo baptizandae sunt, qualiter baptizatoris ad interrogata respondeant et qualiter accepto baptismate vivant.
>
> (*Statuta eccl. antiquae*, 100, a. circ. 475, *CC* 148, p. 184, l. 268)

Here again, it is not quite clear what *aperto et sano sermone* means; but as the use of this kind of *sermo* is, for the women instructors concerned, the result of a special training, at least of a set of pieces of advice or a certain exercise, it must be a speaking habit appreciably, if not essentially, different from their current usage.

Before trying to see if and how far all these metalinguistic views were coherent with linguistic reality, we briefly examine some aspects of contemporary grammatical treatises. For obvious reasons, the metalinguistic attitudes of grammarians seem to be simple: their aim being to help their students and readers in the understanding of classical texts and in reading, writing, and speaking in conformity with classical norms (or norms considered as such), they have a normative view of a more or less homogeneous Latin linguistic universe, based on rules whose neglect leads to definite – although somewhat clumsily defined – categories of errors, mainly barbarisms and solecisms. A barbarism is not only and necessarily what we (or even the Fathers of the Church) would call a vulgar speaking habit, but even occasional slips of the tongue and practically all kinds of unprecedented innovations are covered by this term. Consequently, the grammarians cannot be expected to give a coherent and systematic view of linguistic varieties outside what they consider the norm; nor can we hope to find in their books any clear statement on the existence or non-existence of such varieties. All we have are sometimes precious, but always isolated and occasional glimpses, mainly among the *vitia*, on spoken habits.

Even these pieces of information are rather difficult to use, because they are chronologically very much garbled. For seven centuries or more, from Varro to Cassiodor(i)us, grammarians copy each other, take over arguments, definitions and examples, conceal their own findings in unending enumerations of transmitted material.[6] So even the image they give about the pronunciation of their own age is rather confused. The best observers among them, like the excellent Consentius, or the somewhat loquacious, but often original, Pompeius, quote features of contemporary pronunciation as being in agreement with received norms. So, about two centuries after the fact, the assibilation of *t* before *yod* (from the second to the third centuries, according to inscriptional evidence), is mentioned by Servius (K. IV. 445); Papirianus (ap. Cassiodorum, K. VIII, 216) and Pompeius (K. V, 286) recognize it as a received pronunciation. A number of grammarians of these centuries note in often quoted remarks (add Sturtevant 1940: 107–19 to the source-books cited by Wright 1982: 54) the differences of vowel quality between long and short *e*, *i*, and *o*, *u* respectively. But in other cases, they recommend evidently obsolete pronunciations, concerning, for instance, the use of *h* (Consentius, K. V, 392 or Sacerdos, K. VI, 451). They are very far from being permissive towards contemporary current pronunciation or from simply reflecting some imaginary 'vernacular', as is shown in the long lists of errors given in several treatises. Just for the sake of example, let us quote some 'condemnations' by Consentius (K. V, 391ff.): singled out as 'barbarisms', among others, are *piper* with long *i* instead of short; *triginta* with the accent on the first syllable; *vilam* or *mile* for *villa*, *mille*; the syncopated form *socrum* instead of *socerum*; *orator* with short *o* in the first syllable; *onorem* instead of *honorem*; *bobis* for *vobis*; and so forth.

From all these more or less scattered and, for us, very unsystematic remarks and interdictions, one basic fact seems, however, to emerge: if the grammarians are more or less permissive with regard to some minor changes, they always condemn the tendencies which could endanger the syllabic structure of the word; confusion of simple and double consonants, metatheses, and syncopes are always noted with disapproval, and all the grammarians are completely adamant about the necessary distinction of long and short vowels, and very much aware of current 'mistakes'. This is naturally the case with Pompeius too; if we go back to his text instead of one isolated quotation, it becomes clear that he perfectly well knew what this distinction was about, and when he said long and short, he meant 'long' and 'short', and did not, as Wright so nicely puts it, use *longa* and *brevis* as 'technical terms unconnected with' duration (Wright 1982: 58).[7] The reasons which compelled the grammarians, in what seems to us now a desperate rearguard fight, to condemn systematically the neglect of the 'classical' vowel-duration system were obviously twofold: on the one hand, the whole tradition of metric poetry was inseparably tied to this system and so were the rhythmic patterns of oratorial prose; on the other, the grammarians constructed some rules of inflectional morphology – and they did very rightly so – on the inherited distinction of long and short vowels (so, for instance – but there would be many more ancient examples – Pompeius, to remain with him, speaks at length about the relationships of long and short -*e* ablatives and the declension types, K. V., 189–90). They were consequently more or less clearly aware of the fact that, letting the duration system disappear, they would let go with it a substantial part of their own teaching.

We are now in a position, I think, to trace the main lines of the metalinguistic views which prevailed in the literate, grammatically trained milieus of the fourth and fifth centuries, concerning the situation in Latin and especially the relation between written tradition and spoken usage. We have to stress beforehand that these views represent a one-way approach to reality. They are inevitably, so to speak, lopsided: they reflect the viewpoint of thoroughly schooled people who produce written works – or try to teach how to produce them – and who are interested in only one side of the relation between the written universe and spoken language: they try to state how far and under what conditions, with what kind of practical limitations, written texts (or sermons, recitations, public talks conforming to written norms) can penetrate the public, how far they are readily understood. They are definitely not interested in the other side of the problem: the questions raised by the written recording, if any, of everyday spoken language.

Seen with this bias, the linguistic situation seemed to them essentially favourable. Written texts, when read or listened to, were considered to be normally and usually understood by large popular publics, even unschooled or totally illiterate, on condition that authors and orators conformed to some seemingly obvious limita-tions: the texts had to be 'simple', without long and complicated periods, without neologisms or new foreign words, and, when said or read aloud, this had to be done without undue speed, with clear and distinct pronunciation. This means that the essential unity of Latin as a language was not questioned; it did not even seem to be a problem to be dealt with: lack of schooling and of trained intelligence – essentially sociocultural factors, normally present in every society, or problems to be taken care of by schoolmasters and grammarians – were the only obstacles which could prevent people from understanding the texts which conformed to written tradition. The idea of territorial differences as obstacles to understanding did not and could not occur.

Nevertheless, there was a flaw in this wholly optimistic view. First of all, there was a feeling among the best and most language-conscious authors that some of the grammatical rules normally adhered to in written language could in themselves hinder communication with simpler people, or even with people at large. This concerned apparently secondary morphological details, but the feeling was strong enough to compel some of the Fathers to vindicate a sort of right, for Christian writers, to so-called 'barbarisms'. The grammarians, on their side, did not and could not arrive at such conclusions, but some of their scattered remarks show that in their eyes, too, finer grammatical distinctions were endangered among their readers and clients. Moreover, there seemed to be a distinct feeling that there were differences of pronunciation between *docti* and *indocti*, between *rustici* and – though the word is not used – *urbani*. This surely does not mean that some fundamental features of the contemporary pronunciation of Latin – even some considered by outdated manuals as 'vulgar' – were not common to all, and Wright (1982), in his thought-provoking book, is completely right to stress this point again and again. But inside this unity there were differences, and it seems significant that, in accordance with Augustine, some grammarians felt a danger which could destroy the system of morphophonological rules of the language.

Still, we repeat, the dominant feeling was that of unity: the Romani, from Rome and elsewhere, were sure to speak and to write Latin to each other – with some shifts, differences and fine breaks along sociocultural parameters. The trouble which led Augustine, in a remarkable phrase, to oppose that which was *Latinum* to the speaking habits of the *vulgus* was perhaps clearly felt by some, but too new to be clearly expressed and become part of widespread metalinguistic opinions and attitudes.

We come now to our last question, the most essential perhaps: we shall treat it very briefly. It concerns the congruence between this metalinguistic attitude, these views, on the one side, and the real linguistic situation on the other.

We saw that the learned, the *eruditi*, considered the public, the *vulgus*, only as potential receivers of their message, but not as a source of messages, and so the idea of considering systematically the speaking habits of the *indocti*, as these habits really were, did not even occur to them. So the main source, as is well known, which helps us to approach the usage of the *vulgus* is to be found in the documents which reflect indirectly, but in a written form ready to be analysed, systematic features of the everyday spoken language, that is, documents written, dictated, or more or less formulated, by the *indocti* themselves.

It has to be stated first that the *indocti*, as far as *their* metalinguistic attitudes are concerned, certainly did not feel or consider themselves as a linguistic group apart. Not only did they understand – sometimes with difficulty, due mainly to problems of content – what the *docti* said and wrote, but, when they wrote themselves or, being illiterate, dictated a text to be written – which did not happen to them very often in their lives – they tried to follow the orthographic habits generally established and, as far as they could manage it, they used the morphemic elements they found in the common corpus of written Latin. In some cases, the result of this effort of adaptation was excellent. So, for instance, on the beautiful tombstone of Iulia (*ICVR NS* 11927) from the first half, so it seems to me, of the fifth century: 'fuit mihi natibitas romana nomen si quaeres | Iulia bocata so; que vixi munda [corr. ex muda] cum byro meo | Florentio, cui demisi tres filios superstetes'. If we do not consider some syntactico-stylistic clumsiness, it could be argued that the 'vulgarisms' are mainly or exclusively orthographic.[8]

Nevertheless, in Rome itself, we find many hundreds and even thousands of Christian inscriptions, more or less rough engravings, from the second half of the fourth or from the fifth century – that is from the very age of Jerome, Augustine, Ambrose, or Consentius – in which the adaptive effort so evident in Iulia's case is not present or not successful, and which clearly reflect grammatical structures essentially different from those qualified as *latinum* in Augustine's text (quoted above, p. 33).

I choose some – by no means all – of these specific structural properties and illustrate them at random, noting that hundreds of further examples could be adduced from the inscriptions of Rome and recalling that these features have already been dealt with, more or less often, by others and by myself in the enormous secondary literature on Late and so-called Vulgar Latin.

So it seems that roughly at the time when popular publics were able to understand, with some difficulty sometimes, the sermons of Saint Ambrose and of Saint Augustine, when they were able to follow biblical texts read before them (or, exceptionally, by them), the same people spoke a language which had, among other things, the following particularities:

1 The system of oblique cases, in the declensions, did not correspond any more to distinct syntactic functions; the ablative–accusative opposition did not work any more, not even in the subsystems where the formal differences were not blurred by current phonetic change. We illustrate the point with 'errors' in prepositional phrases:

ICVR NS

9409 'Genuarus placuid se uniter poni cum amicum suum Sibirinu'[9]
11798 'cesque in pace cum sanctis cum quos mereris' (= cum sanctis quibuscum [sepeliri] meruisti)
12566 'vale michi kara im pace cum spirita xanta vale' (= cum fidelibus quibuscum sepulta iaces?)
9521 'in mente habeas in horationes Aureliu Repentinu'

The same point can be illustrated with the total incomprehension of the traditional phrases *se vivo* or *se vivis*, and the complicated declensional errors which follow from it:

11166 'hunc locum me vivum paravi'
11512 'se vivum emit sibi'
10924 'Largianus et Crescentia fecerunt se bibus'
12351 'se vibos'
12293 'Felex et Felecessema se bibi fecerunt'
12258 'Pri[mus]se bibus [f]ecet sibi cum suis'

2 Through an eventually abortive, but highly interesting development, the partial loss of the traditional declensions was compensated for by the tentative building up of a special declension for personal names, out of bits and pieces and analogical copies of certain Greek declension types:[10]

11863 'Clus(iae) Aelianeti Clus(ius) A(e)lianus pater'
12310 'Locus Leopardi et Mercurianetis'
12293 'Dep. Genialinis'
12270 'Locus Aselles'

3 Formal differences between essential elements of the present and the future, and of the future and the perfect paradigms, as well as

between some parts of the -*ĕre* and –*ēre* verbal paradigms, were
hopelessly blurred. For the simple form *quiescit* or *requiescit*, we
find about twenty graphic variants, from *quesquaet* (10964) to
requisqi (11362); for the future-perfect confusion, see 11133
'pr(idie)i[d]. iun. pausabet Praetiosa'.

We can stop here. It is fairly clear, I think, that the language of
the *Sermones* of Saint Augustine or of the *Vetus Latina*, even read
aloud in conformity with the most 'Proto-Romance' pronunciation
we can postulate for these centuries, and the language of the
plebicula of Rome as reflected in these inscriptions, are two distinct
and distinguishable varieties. This means, I think, that the
metalinguistic view concerning the essential unity of Latin was, in
part, a delusion. Inside of the Latin linguistic community, in spite of
many common features in the pronunciation of the prestige groups
and of the popular speakers, in spite of a renewed effort of certain
authors towards a greater syntactic and lexical flexibility, the spoken
language of the non-schooled people, that is of the majority of the
population, slowly drifted away, about the time of the fall of the
Western Empire, from the Latin represented in written texts and in
the careful oral usage of the *eruditi*. This centrifugal tendency had
not gone yet, in the fifth century, far enough to disrupt the
communicative unity of the Latin-speaking community: everybody,
with some care, understood everybody, every literate person could
read everybody's letters or books and could write in Latin to
anybody he wanted to. The delusion of unity reflected the everyday
functioning of communicative practice, but not more; linguistically,
it remained a delusion.

What is the bearing of all this on our research, on our concepts
and – let us not avoid this tedious question – on our terminology? Is
the language variety of the non-schooled already Romance or Proto-
Romance? This would be too simple a solution. I think that, in the
middle of the first millennium, we are faced with a Latin language,
but a Latin language in at least a twofold crisis. First, because a
sociocultural process of differentiation produced an ever deepening
gap between an essentially conservative, slowly changing prestige
variety, bound chiefly to written expression, and a spoken,
everyday, 'popular' variety in relatively rapid, even accelerated
evolution, not to speak of the certainly growing linguistic divergences among different Latin-speaking territories. Second, because,
on the metalinguistic level, neither the learned nor the non-schooled
had nor could have had an even approximately adequate image of

the linguistic situation, and consequently they continued their everyday practice and even their grammatical work as if the unity and the identity of Latin were fundamentally unshaken. As collective illusions often do, this one had its usefulness for at least another century or more, but it produced a complicated and contradictory overall situation – for them and for us. I think that the main bulk of our work should be to follow in every aspect and in every trend this complex crisis of Latin, not looking for Romance and Proto-Romance in every corner, knowing simply that, in this manifold bundle of linguistic change, there are privileged, deeply anchored trends – the abstract image of which, identified mainly through comparative methods, can be termed Proto-Romance, if we wish – which will constitute, not only in the structural reality but even in the linguistic awareness of those concerned, a set of new languages. But this is another story.

ABBREVIATIONS

CC   *Corpus Christianorum.*
ICVR NS   *Inscriptiones Christianae Urbis Romae, Nova Series.*
K   H. Keil, Grammatici Latini, I–VII, Leipzig: Teubner, 1855–80.
PL   J.P. Migne (1844–64) *Patrologiae cursus completus. Series latina*, Paris: Teubner.

NOTES

1 Herman (1988: 60–2); the evidence concerns Italy and southern Gaul. It is possible that, in the sixth century, this was no longer true for some other regions, especially the north of Gaul.

2 In 533, the Concilium Aurelianense (*CC* 148, 101) prescribes 'Presbiter uel diaconus sine literis uel si baptizandi ordinem nesciret nullatenus ordinetur'; in 589, at the Concilium Narbonense, (*CC* 148, 256) the same interdiction has to be repeated.

3 For instance Lact. *diu. inst.* 6, 21, 5; ibid. 5, 1, 15; S. Hieron. *Ep.* XXXVI, 14, and many others. This highly 'content-orientated' stylistic ideal corresponds not only to the sociocultural conditions in which Christian doctrine had to be propagated but, 'simplicitas' being a characteristic of the basic biblical texts themselves, especially in the so-called *Vetus Latina* versions, it was sometimes given a specific, almost mystical, value.

4 Here is the text, still somewhat abridged: *de doctr. Christ.* IV, x (*CC* 32, 132–3):

Quamuis bonis doctoribus tanta docendi cura sit uel esse debeat, ut uerbum, quod, nisi obscurum sit uel ambiguum, latinum esse non potest, uulgi autem more sic dicitur ut ambiguitas obscuritasque uitetur, non sic dicatur, ut a doctis, sed potius ut ab indoctis dici solet. . . . Cur pietatis doctorem pigeat imperitis loquentem, *ossum* potius quam *os* dicere ne ista syllaba non ab eo, quod sunt *ossa*, sed ab eo, quod sunt *ora*, intellegatur, ubi Afrae aures de correptione uocalium et productione non iudicant.

5 See some indications about this in Herman (1982: 288–9).

6 Wright's excellent and intelligent book is unhappily somewhat hasty in its quotations and consequently in some of its arguments; for instance, the most important of the examples he quotes from Cassiodorus are copied by the latter from Annaeus Cornutus, a grammarian of the Neronian period (see Wright 1982: 78ff.).

7 Some evidence for this is as follows: Pompeius speaks not only about the duration of *o* and *e*, but also of *a* (K. V, 106–7), where there was probably no qualitative difference, at least no perceptible one, between long and short variants; in another passage (ibid. 112–13), speaking about long and short syllables, he explains tolerably well the difference of duration between long and short vowels, including the 'critical' items *e* and *o*.

8 I think, however, that the educated made some systematic effort to keep the consonant *b* as a pure stop, and hence to maintain [b] and [v] or [w] apart. It is practically certain that they did not pronounce, at the end of a sentence or a clause [so] for *sum*, but that a nasal was produced in this position, as monosyllabic words are usually conservative in this respect. I am convinced – but this is not at issue here – that the pronunciation of this text was not of the sort Jerome or Ambrose would have approved, not to mention Consentius.

9 All the inscriptions quoted are taken from *ICVR NS*.

10 See for this problem Leumann (1977: 459–60). A more extensive and deeper analysis would be useful and probably rewarding.

BIBLIOGRAPHY

Herman, J. (1982) 'Un Vieux Dossier réouvert: les transformations du système latin des quantités vocaliques', *Bulletin de la Société Linguistique de Paris* 77: 285–302.

—— (1988) 'La Situation linguistique en Italie au VIe siècle', *Revue de Linguistique Romane* 52: 55–67.

Leumann, M. (1977) *Lateinische Laut- und Formenlehre*, Munich: C.H. Beck.

Sturtevant, E. H. (1940) *The Pronunciation of Greek and Latin*, 2nd edn, Philadelphia: William D. Whitney Linguistic Series.

Wright, R. (1982) *Late Latin and Early Romance in Spain and Carolingian France*, Liverpool: Cairns.

5 Latin and Romance: fragmentation or restructuring?

Alberto Varvaro

In a recent issue of *Revue de Linguistique Romane* József Herman, with his usual clarity, learning, and caution, described the linguistic situation in sixth-century Italy as follows:

> Ce latin n'est pas, pour les contemporains, un latin d'Italie, une langue locale: son unité par-delà des limites de la Péninsule n'est jamais mise en doute. L'idée d'une diversité territoriale affectant l'usage commun et l'intercompréhension entre régions de la Romania n'effleurait personne . . . Tout ceci ne veut naturellement pas dire qu'il n'y ait pas eu de différences territoriales dans le latin parlé de l'époque, entre anciennes provinces et même à l'intérieur des provinces. Ce qui est certain, pourtant, c'est que ces différences n'entamaient pas, pour les contemporains, l'unité fondamentale du latin . . . si le sentiment de l'homogenéité territoriale du latin était une illusion, cette illusion se fondait sur l'expérience continue de l'intercommunication et l'intercompréhension sans obstacle entre latinophones appartenant à des régions diverses.
>
> (Herman 1988: 65–6)

There is an element of paradox in these conclusions, of which Herman shows himself to be well aware when he talks of a 'curieuse contradiction' and of 'la leçon la plus inquiétante' (ibid., p. 66).

We can safely forget about the conflict between the views expressed here and the arguments, based on relative phonetic chronology, which led scholars to conclude in favour of an early date for the fragmentation of the Latin linguistic territory. Indeed, it would not be completely wrong to claim that logical rigour and the 'esprit de système' will not serve to resolve such a difficult historical problem. However, the later we place the break-up of the unity of Latin, in both a geographical and a social sense, the more the formation of the Romance languages, for which the earliest texts give us precise *termini ante quos*, becomes a phenomenon which is concentrated in a short period, and thus a 'catastrophe' for which valid internal and external reasons have to be found. Yet by the end of the sixth century the collapse of the Western Empire had been over for some time and only the Italian peninsula had recently suffered its worst trauma: the Lombard invasion. In the other areas – Germania, Britannia, Gallia, Hispania, Africa – the main political and social catastrophes were already well in the past, with the sole exception of the Moslem invasion (but in any case by 711 the Romance of Moslem Spain must already have had many of the characteristics of Mozarabic which are only documented at a later date). What then are we to conclude?

József Herman is careful to say that the documentary evidence only tells us what contemporaries thought, not what the situation really was. He none the less expresses the view that a belief such as he describes must have received regular confirmation in the course of day-to-day language use and successful communication:

> Les contemporains avaient . . . le sentiment que les textes écrits faisaient normalement et régulièrement partie de l'univers langagier de la population entière et que, d'autre part, le parler spontané avait, dans l'écrit, une contropartie adéquate qui n'était pas linguistiquement inaccessible aux locuteurs . . . ce sentiment reposait sur l'expérience de la réussite courante, normale, quotidienne de la communication au niveau de la communauté entière, et avait par conséquent un fondement solide dans un réalité vécue, donc transitoire.
>
> (Herman 1988: 64)

If we wish to resolve this paradox, which is in the end none other than the old paradox of the origins of Romance, we must find an explanation which reconciles facts which seem irreconcilable.

Before I attempt to put forward a hypothesis, I think it may be helpful to bear in mind one further fact, which has long been known but which does not seem to me to have been correctly interpreted. The majority of Romance phenomena, with few – even if important – exceptions, are already documented in Latin texts. By putting together this vast collection of data, scholars have even constructed a linguistic variety, to which the name 'Vulgar Latin' has been given. Some have gone so far as to think of a 'Vulgar Latin' system which can be represented by means of a grammar. Some indeed have postulated a situation of Classical vs Vulgar Latin diglossia.

Such constructs are a mirage. From the chronological point of view this 'vulgar' documentation is spread over a period of several centuries, from archaic Latin right through to the High Middle Ages. From the social point of view it is towards the 'low' end of the scale, but the stratification is complex. But even more significant is the fact that from a geographical point of view the documentation of Romance phenomena in Latin texts does not coincide at all with the Romance distribution of the corresponding phenomena.

Some years ago I looked briefly at the voicing of intervocalic voiceless consonants, and concluded: 'The examples of voicing are relatively few, but they surface a little everywhere (therefore characterising no province in particular) and obey different conditions from those that we find in the Romance languages' (Varvaro 1982–3: 71). The picture that emerges from an examination of the documentation relating to final -*s* is no different. This important morphological element seems liable to be lost from quite an early date (first century AD), even in texts which are not particularly 'vulgar', but only ever in a limited number of instances. Moreover, and most importantly, evidence of this loss is sporadically to be found throughout the Empire and not just in those regions where the Romance vernaculars do not subsequently exhibit any trace of final -*s*. It is quite clear, *en passant*, that in this way Walther von Wartburg's theory is seriously undermined (see also Varvaro 1980). Similar remarks can be made in connection with other phenomena.

We find ourselves therefore faced with the following picture:

1 The documentation of the phenomena that we now call pre-Romance is more or less ancient, more or less sporadic, but is never – or only to a limited degree – characterized geographically.

2 Such documentation has to be isolated from a vast mass of other phenomena which fall outside the norm of Latin, but which had none the less no consequences in the subsequent linguistic evolution of Romance (copious exemplification is already to be found in Schuchardt 1866–8).

3 The clues, however inconclusive, that we can derive from the comparison of the Romance languages also argue in favour of the relative antiquity even of phenomena which are not directly attested (I am thinking, for example, of the appearance of the category of the article and of its realization by means of the same forms in most of the languages; of the largely uniform restructuring of the verb system; etc.).

4 The written language begins to exhibit regionally marked features only from the fifth century onwards (Herman 1967: 119).

5 The awareness of the linguistic unity of western society remains alive in the sixth century.

6 By contrast, immediately after the year 800 there appears a clear realization of the unbridgeable rift between Latin and Romance and – a point which is often undervalued – there is early evidence of reliably identified and differentiated social entities which are not unrelated to linguistic identities (see Lusignan 1986; Varvaro, 1989).

We consider as unjustified the old hypothesis that there coexisted within Latin from an early date two linguistic strata, one truly 'Latin' and one 'Vulgar Latin'. We also consider as undemonstrable, and indeed improbable, the existence even at a later period of a state of diglossia. Further and with even more justification we reject as no more than an intellectual construct the idea of 'Proto-Romance', which is, to use a term drawn from the theory of perspective, the vanishing point of the geographical spread of Romance. Finally we find ingenious but unsatisfactory the hypo-thesis which would replace a postulated situation of true diglossia with one of apparent diglossia produced by the conservatism of the written language, a conservatism which masks, and at the same time by virtue of its increasingly ideographic character authorizes, the centrifugal tendencies of the spoken language. What then remains by way of explanation?

In Imperial times the linguistic world of Latin had several important properties: a minority endowed with enormous political, social, economic, and cultural prestige was absorbing a large majority who were less and less convinced of their own original and diverse identities. Where Latin had a rival with the force of Greek this phenomenon did not take place. But in the west, at the end of the Empire, the non-Latinized peoples were mere recessive pockets, always peasants or highlanders, who, moreover, still remained exposed to the linguistic consequences of ongoing Christianization. In fact, only Basques and Bretons were able to avoid Latinization; even the Germans, despite the fact that they now held power, gave way to this trend in all the areas where they were not in a majority.

Yet, if we go back to the centuries of the Empire, the Latin spoken by these recently Latinized masses undoubtedly tolerated infringements of the norm. I have no wish to exhume and give credit to the substratum hypothesis (which is in my view a limited and largely lexical phenomenon), nor do I deny the extreme power of the Latin norm, which was sustained by a political and military class which was for the most part homogeneous and capable of absorbing without great difficulty new elements from outside. I would say only that a vast process of Latinization, which involved at the same time acculturation, could not prevent the proliferation of those phenomena which we now call 'vulgar' and which can be documented here and there when they reach the written texts (and when the relevant written texts reach us). Like all non-standard phenomena in all languages, some were widely tolerated and some less so, and some were repressed as being too popular (socially and/or geographically). It is likely that we shall find the first type widely documented (think, for example, of the loss of final -*m*), the second less so, and the third hardly at all, as a result of the differing degrees of self-censorship of the writers.

The linguistic universe of Latin must have seemed like a large, solid space under a solid but elastic dome (the norm), beneath which there operated ungovernable forces of innovation, of deviation, and, in the ultimate analysis, of expression. There is no doubt that some of these centrifugal forces must have been locally specified, especially in regard to pronunciation and lexis, but those which we can best document appear to be similar, if not indeed identical, everywhere. This explains the widespread feeling that the Roman world was linguistically homogeneous. In reality it was, in the sense that the norm was in the main unitary and variation was everywhere similar and always held strictly in check by the norm.

In a certain sense, I would hazard the view that the origin of the Romance languages was nothing more than the shifting, if not indeed the collapse, of the dome and thus the loss of the centripetal orientation of the variation. For me the decisive moment remains (after the crisis of the third century) the collapse of the Empire: not that precise date, AD 476, or any other; but that is the moment in which in each area people lose, or more precisely feel they have lost, the consciousness of belonging to a whole and acquire instead a sense of local identity. Of course, the 'universalistic' awareness does not disappear altogether, and it explains the continuing vitality of Latin. However, it is by now a peculiar characteristic of the more learned clergy and the literate, two groups which tend in any case to become one. For the rest of society, the reality is different: the name may well remain, but *romanus* (and its various vernacular forms) becomes synonymous with 'native of each region'.

When this happens, the Latin norm continues to have meaning for those who maintain the 'universalistic' awareness of the Roman world. For the others the norm is represented by the speech habits of the people who hold power and give the orders. But the ruling class is now for the most part made up of people of little learning, often Germanic in origin, who – when they are not speakers of other languages – have only a recent and uncertain grasp of Latin. Variation, which was at one time held in check by the norm, is constrained only by the practicalities of communication, which now, however, takes place only in limited and local contexts. In each area one of the early variants becomes the norm; each group makes its own choice, bearing in mind only its own needs and those of the neighbouring groups with which it communicates. The diastratic variation changes and crystallizes into diatopic variation.

If this was indeed what happened, we can explain why a large part of the innovations of the Romance languages are already documentable in Latin times, as exceptions to the norm, and why others, although not actually documented, must still be considered of similar antiquity. It remains for us to explain why this new state of affairs was only registered after a certain period of time had elapsed. I would state first that the phenomenon certainly took place at different times in different parts of the Empire in virtue of the different conditions that obtained in each place. Nor do I see a lack of continuity between the grand process of Latinization and the break-up of Latin homogeneity into the multiplicity of the Romance vernaculars.

A parallel case seems to me to be discernible in the process which has been in progress in Italy for the last hundred or so years. We are witnessing a wider and wider diffusion of standard Italian, which is being adopted by dialect speakers and, in a number of cases, even by speakers of other languages (although from a practical point of view the distinction is irrelevant in so far as for many dialect speakers Italian is as incomprehensible as it is for speakers of Greek or Slovene). Now that the diglossic stage has been passed, there exists today a vast amount of variation, all firmly held in check by the norm of a standard language which is relatively stable, even if not totally immobile. Granted, pronunciation and some lexical phenomena enable one to identify the origin of almost every speaker, but this does not prevent us finding similar deviations from the norm in every region. It is this state of affairs which has given birth to the somewhat mythical concept of a unitary popular Italian. Standard Italian, admittedly in its various regional but none the less mutually comprehensible forms, is now understood by (almost) everybody, even by those who almost never use it themselves. No political party or church would think of using any other language to attract adherents and to keep them united: the cases of the official use of other varieties have ideological and not practical origins. Here too we have a solid, if elastic, dome which covers and keeps in check a seething mass of variants, some of which will disappear, others will become part of the norm, and yet others will remain as variants; some are tolerated, some less so, some are repressed (the documentation is inversely proportional to the degree of repression).

What would happen if the centripetal forces disappeared? What if a political, social, or demographic upheaval were to blunt the sense of Italian identity, so recently formed and whose prestige is still so precarious? Power would undoubtedly go to the regional or local varieties of Italian. The latter admit a considerable degree of variation, within which processes of selection would operate to create new local norms, which would in turn gradually become available as alternatives to the original norm. I do not doubt that there would be a period in which some social groups would continue to use the unitary norm, especially in writing. And everyone else would continue for some time to think that nothing had changed, that they were still all Italians, that everyone spoke Italian, that there was no need for any other means of communication.

What is it, in fact, that has changed, both in our fictitious example and in Late Latin? In the extreme case no new phenomenon need, in the first instance, have come into being. All that has changed are the relations and the values: fragmentation is nothing other than the delayed consequence of a profound restructuring of the sociolinguistic system of the community. But everyone can continue to believe that this system is unchanged until lack of understanding, the acid test of linguistic functionality, shows that it is not so.[1]

NOTE

1 The English version of this paper was jointly prepared by Nigel Vincent and Roger Wright.

BIBLIOGRAPHY

Herman, J. (1967) *Le Latin vulgaire*, Paris: Presses Universitaires de France.
—— (1988) 'La Situation linguistique en Italie au VIᵉ siècle', *Revue de Linguistique Romane* 52: 55–67.
Lusignan, S. (1986) *Parler vulgairement. Les intellectuels et la langue française aux XIIIᵉ et XIVᵉ siècles*, Paris and Montreal: Vrin and Presses

de l'Université de Montréal.

Schuchardt, H. (1866–8) *Der Vokalismus des Vulgärlateins*, Leipzig: Teubner.

Varvaro, A. (1980). Introduction to W. von Wartburg, *La frammentazione linguistica della Romania*, Rome: Salerno, 7–44.

—— (1982–3) 'Omogeneità del latino e frammentazione della Romània', *Annali della Facoltà di Lettere e Filosofia dell'Università di Napoli* 25: 65–78.

—— (1989) 'La tendenza all'unificazione dalle origini alla formazione di un italiano standard', *L'italiano tra le lingue romanze. Atti del XX Congresso Internazionale della Società di Linguistica Italiana (Bologna 1986)*. Rome: Bulzoni, 27–42.

6 Phonology, phonetics, and orthography in Late Latin and Romance: the evidence for early intervocalic sonorization

Thomas D. Cravens

Consider the following statement:

> Romance scholars have reached the point in their study of Romance dialects where the individual facts of phonological development from late Latin to Romance are about as well known as they are likely to be, barring the discovery of new manuscripts and inscriptions that will give us data of an unexpected kind.
>
> (Barbarino 1981: 1)

At the time of its publication, this might have represented the thinking of many Romanists, and there is little in print to suggest that Latinists did not share this view, adjusted to an earlier *terminus ad quem* (Adams 1977 is a shining exception; the lack of discussion of intervocalic consonantism in Porzio Gernia 1976–7 seems symptomatic). At first glance, this assertion may seem quite reasonable, and it is, if the notion of 'fact' is taken literally as something approaching secure knowledge: unambiguous data or first-hand phonological description (first-order knowledge; see Lass 1980: 59) are surely as close as we can come to real facts in examining a language no longer spoken, and until we have more of either, our supply of secure knowledge will not grow.

The author appears to use the term 'fact' loosely, however, in the sense of general understanding. Taken to its extreme, this would imply that there is little hope for progress in understanding of problematical data through application of improved methods of interpretation. Pursuing the extreme reading, denial of the value of theoretical investigation implies in turn that understanding achieved by means of principled inference (second-order knowledge; Lass again) is either impossible or without value. Surely no historian – linguistic or other – would accept this strong claim, yet in many investigations of the origins of voicing in Western Romance, its tacit, perhaps unconscious, acceptance seems to have been widespread until the appearance of Wright's *Late Latin and Early Romance in Spanish and Carolingian France* (1982; noting here the exceptions of Figge 1966 and Politzer 1955).

In his contribution to the seventh ICHL, Wright pointed out that Romance scholars sometimes 'work with assumptions that seem absurd to a general historical linguist' (Wright 1987: 619). An example he cited was the once fairly common assumption that the spelling of Late Latin texts represents something in the realm of direct transcription of speech. Wright's 1982 book made it clear that the presupposition of one-to-one letter-to-sound correspondence is untenable for confidently positing phonetics or even phonology from a direct interpretation of Late Latin spelling. We are now both challenged and encouraged to reassess long-standing canons with more subtle methodology, employing independently motivated principles established in other realms of linguistic enquiry.

I hope to show here that consideration of just a few common observations regarding orthography and phonological change permit a coherent interpretation of otherwise intractable facts which are essential to understanding the origin of voicing of intervocalic /p t k/ in Romance (see Naro 1972a, 1972b, Wanner 1977, Cravens 1988 n. 3, 1989 n. 2 for discussion of substratum, which will not be pursued here).

THE PROBLEM

There are three major questions of interest in connection with the history of intervocalic voicing in Western Romance, none of which has ever been answered satisfactorily. Two of these refer to the real-time chronology of the changes: (1) when did voicing begin? and (2) when was voicing accepted as a restructuring? The third refers to the linguistic character of the second: (3) how (if possible, why) did restructuring come about? The present brief study addresses the first question, which, though at first glance of less linguistic interest than the other two, has in its fuller projection consequences of considerable import regarding the solution of other problems of both a typological and a purely linguistic nature.

At chronological poles, the basic facts seem clear. It is commonly assumed that Latin had a voiceless series /p t k/ realized as [p t k], at least before non-front vowels, and the modern Western Romance speech types show that through time these segments have developed in the most conservative case as /b d g/ realized [b d g] (Brazilian Portuguese), in the most innovative as null, reflecting loss at the underlying level (original /t/ and /k/ in French).

Latin	French	Portuguese	Spanish
CAPILLU	*cheveu*	*ca*[b]*elo*	*ca*[β]*ello*
VITA	*vie*	*vi*[d]*a*	*vi*[ð]*a*
AMICA	*amie*	*ami*[g]*a*	*ami*[ɣ]*a*

Primary data such as these form the starting point of any study of the history of Western Romance voicing. However, there is reason to question the most basic relevant assumption regarding Latin phonetics: how secure is it that /p t k/ were consistently realized as [p t k]?

Even the most cursory glance at modern data suggests that something may be amiss. This is especially clear in evidence from the typically non-voicing dialects of central and southern Italy. This large area has a small minority of words with historically restructured intervocalic voicing (roughly 8–10 per cent of the lexicon; Izzo 1980), which can be categorized in two groups by areal arrangement: words with restructuring confined to one zone or a few scattered zones (*ago* type), and those with restructured voicing throughout central and southern Italy, with only minor pockets of exceptions (*pagare* type). The third type, which can be represented by *pecora*, has undergone restructuring only in the regularly voicing and degeminating dialects of the north, motivating the well-known La Spezia–Rimini line (see Figure 6.1).

Politzer suggested that the voicings are 'retentions of an ancient lenition' (1955: 72–3), indeed, 'that practically all of Italian consonantism shows in varying degrees remnants of the early Latin lenition' (75), where lenition is presumably to be understood as phonetic weakening without restructuring, i.e. a classic allophonic rule (see also Pei 1943 for objections to von Wartburg's east–west typology). This view has since been seconded by a few (directly by, e.g., Figge 1966, Giannelli and Savoia 1979–80; indirectly by Campanile 1961, Wanner and Cravens 1980), but seems to have received little consideration in most quarters, much less acceptance.

A second clue that something might be wrong with the assumption of homogeneous [p t k] for Latin /p t k/ is found in Latin inscriptions, papyri, and ostraca scattered throughout the Empire. The examples are few, but they are consistent: /p/ is found spelled as <B>, /t/ is rendered <D>, and /k/ is represented as <G>. To cite a few in addition to well-known <PAGATUS>, <TRIDICUM> in

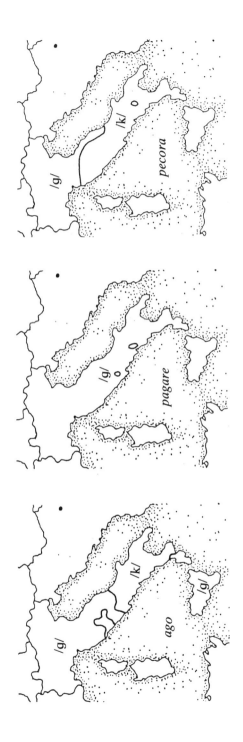

Figure 6.1 Historical outcomes of /k/ in *ago* 'needle' (*AIS* 8.1539), *pagare* 'pay' (*AIS* 8.1589), *pecora* 'sheep' (*AIS* 6.1068)

graffiti at Pompeii, <PECCADIS>, <PECADO> (*CPL* 45b, 1; 45a, 7
– Karanis, before AD 115), <AUDEM> for AUTEM (*CPL* 237II, 5 –
Fayoum, Neronian period), <DEBULSORI> (*CIL* 3.5460 – Noricum,
c. AD 234), <DUBLICES> (*CPL* 292, Tell Edfou (Egypt), first
century) (see Odenkirchen 1952, Tovar 1948, 1951 for more
complete lists; Campanile 1961, Adams 1977 for examples from
papyri). There are also cases of reversal, which we may presume to
be hypercorrection, e.g. <DETUCI> for DEDUCI (*CPL* 103, 22 –
Fayoum, 40–37 BC), <CANDITATUS> (*CIL* 6.32420). From these
and other examples, Campanile (1961: 59–60) infers that

> Tale materiale ci permette di concludere, al di là da ogni
> ragionevole dubbio, che la sonorizzazione delle sorde intervoca-
> liche ha inizio nel sec. I dell'era volgare. Si tratta, naturalmente,
> solo di un'incipiente tendenza, destinata a rinforzarsi e a
> generalizzarsi nei secoli successivi in una vasta parte del dominio
> latino.

Refining somewhat the notion of incipient tendency, the two types
of spelling error can be viewed as circumstantial evidence of a rule
voicing /p t k/ without systematic restructuring, as proposed by
Figge (1966: 450ff.). Allophonic voicing would have brought the
realizations of /p t k/ and /b d g/ to real or perceived surface merger,
inducing reduced transparency of phonological form.

There are two major objections to this scenario. First, as just
mentioned, spellings of <B>/<V>, <D>, <G> for Latin /p/, /t/, /k/
are rare; too sporadic, according to some (e.g. Weinrich 1960) to
stand as even faint circumstantial evidence of voicing. Second, the
modern dialects of central and southern Italy have had only
statistically minor, unsystematic restructuring of the type /p/ >
/b/–/v/, /t/ > /d/, /k/ > /g/ as found in Western Romance (arguably
the ultimate outcome of allophonic voicing in the word), while
Rumanian is lacking even these presumably random cases; moreover, within Western Romance, dialects straddling the west-central
Pyrenees appear never to have had systematic restructured voicing
(Elcock 1938; for an attempted interpretation Cravens 1988). These
objections must be met.

SPORADIC MIS-SPELLING

Barbarino's *Latin and Romance Intervocalic Stops: a Quantitative
and Comparative Study* is the most recent detailed study to illustrate
the infelicitous conclusions which can be reached if sporadic

systematic mis-spelling is dismissed as insignificant. With Christian inscriptions through the seventh century as a data base, the author counted occurrences of <B>/<V>, <D>, and <G> where <P>, <T>, and <C> would be expected, in order to decide, on the basis of percentage figures of deviations, when the restructurings /p t k/ > /b d g/ of Western Romance first show indications of appearing. Since even the most frequent mis-spelling – <B> for <P> in Gallia Lugdunensis – is found in only 5.2 per cent of possible occurrences, he concludes that 'the earliest conclusive evidence of a general sonorization of Latin intervocalic /p, t, k/ is later than the time of our inscriptions, i.e. later than the seventh century, in all parts of the Western Romance dialect area where this phenomenon later occurred' (Barbarino 1981: 134).

Yet, if the text of the Strasbourg Oaths is genuine, we find in the earliest Romance document known to be designed specifically to reflect vernacular phonology accurately that by the year 842, every possible intervocalic voicing is represented as such in a register characterized by Muret as '*aulicum et curiale vulgare*' (a view seconded by Ewert; Elcock 1960: 339), for the entire voiceless series, including /t/ and /k/ before /r/: *poblo, savir, podir, fradre, fradra, fradre, sagrament*. In contrast, the Latin text which introduces and frames the representation of Romance speech shows no relevant mis-spellings, but maintains *populus, fratrem* vs the Romance *poblo, fradre*. The Strasbourg Oaths must be taken to show that voicing was regular at least by the mid-800s, quite likely throughout the lexicon if we can take the words found in the Oaths as representative. Furthermore, though it could be argued that since the text is intended as a pronunciation guide, the transcription might be essentially phonetic, thereby reflecting allophonic voicing rather than completed restructuring, it must be considered that failure to observe allophonic voicing would not only cause no confusion for a native audience (Tuscans understand [lakaːsa] for *la casa* as well as they do [lahaːsa]; the foreigner's [vida] for *vida* is perfectly clear to a Spaniard), but that it could even be helpful (cf. a deliberate abeyance of AmE 'flapping' in e.g. *wri*[tʰ]*er*, to avoid confusion with *rider*). Barbarino's conclusion thus entails positing not just that *surface realizations* would have passed from consistently voiceless to consistently voiced in less than two centuries, but that *system-wide restructuring* from /p t k/ to /b–v d g/ would have come about in that period. This is not an impossible prospect, perhaps, but it is one which raises legitimate doubts regarding the reliability of the method employed.

Used with appropriate caution, the count method can work well for discovering features of lexicon or syntax, but it is ill-suited for examination of orthographic deviation, for a number of reasons. First, there is no principled way to decide what percentage of deviations might constitute grounds for declaring that a change has taken place. We may all agree that, say, a 76 per cent occurrence of <D> for <T> scattered randomly through the lexicon would be an indication that a change has occurred. But what of 26 per cent, or 16 per cent, or 6 per cent? Any threshold is arbitrary. Second, and more crucially, complete lack of mis-spelling cannot stand as secure evidence that no change has developed. As Wright and others have already pointed out more than once, correct spelling may just as well mean that the scribe or stonecarver knew how to spell and/or copy. The result of a statistical count, applied in the situation of an archaizing conventional writing system, is essentially an index of literacy. Errors can, indeed, offer clues to sound change, but nothing more than mastery of spelling at the source can be adduced from texts in which no errors are found. In Barbarino's approach, there would be reason to suspect voicing only if a relatively large incidence, or large increase in incidence of deviant spellings should appear at a certain time, or in a certain region. He found no such large incidence or increase, thus his conclusion that voicing was non-existent through the seventh century.

There is another possible conclusion from this study, however. From the two factors just mentioned follows the third and most essential weakness in blunt application of this method: though the counts and resulting percentages are primary as the first step in discovery procedure, in themselves they are of little significance without externally motivated principles of interpretation. The major obstacle to achieving a more meaningful result in the present instance is that, though the author is aware that Latin spelling as a possible representation of Romance speech is essentially archaic convention rather than phonetic or phonemic transcription (Barbarino 1981: 13), no principled methodology is introduced for analysing the data in light of this, other than a watchful eye for high percentages of systematic mis-spelling. This leaves the 5 per cent occurrence of <B> for <P>, for example, to be dismissed as inconsequential with regard to determining when voicing came about (either phonetically or as a restructuring). Such spellings are left as an essentially unmotivated phenomenon with no explanation, other than perhaps that offered earlier by Bassols de Climent: 'Generalmente se trata de errores del lapicida; recuérdese que sólo un trazo distingue la *P* y *C* de la *B* y *G'* (1962: 171). In contrast to this, the case of Modern American English confusion of <t> and <d> demonstrates that very sporadic systematic mis-spelling can be motivated by concrete phonological factors.

Mis-spellings of the type found in Late Latin texts for /p t k/ are found in American English for /t/, and like the Latin cases, their statistical occurrence is minuscule, so that one can search hundreds of pages of American text without encountering a single example. Still, their appearance is not uncommon in sources with few literary pretensions, and their character is constant: the deviations are found for <d> and <t>, not for <b> and <p> or <g> and <c>/<k>, and they occur in the word to represent full occlusives in speech, in any intervocalic position except immediately preceding a stressed vowel, thus <potado> for *potato* as a possible spelling error, but not *<podado> or *<podato>.

Students of mine have produced <equidable> for *equitable* and <heredical> for *heretical*, as well as reversals such as <parametic> for *paramedic* and <commotities> for *commodities*. A recent advertisement in the *Wisconsin State Journal* described a house for sale in <Partyville>, found on maps as *Pardeeville* (stress on /a/). Though this example may have been produced in a playful spirit, phonetic similarity enables it. Not long ago, the American magazine *Homeowner* published a one-page article in which the word *sporadic* appeared twice, once spelled with a <d>, once with a <t>. In a 1976 article, Peter Maher pointed out a case in which this confusion may have been costly: in 1970 a finalist was eliminated from competition in the forty-third US National Spelling Bee – the winner of which receives a substantial cash prize – by spelling *heretical* with a *d*, just like my own student. Maher also reported an extreme example of the same phenomenon from speech, rather than spelling. He once overheard one of his young sons say 'I don't like Joey; he *buds*.' When asked what he meant, the boy replied 'He's always *budding* in' (Maher 1976: 15–16).

Surely, few linguists of any persuasion would doubt that these anecdotal examples reflect confusion as a result of the rule of so-called *t*-flapping, which produces surface merger of /t/ and /d/ between vowels if stress does not follow immediately. In the case of *bud*, the child's analysis had apparently gone beyond confusion, to – from the historical point of view – a restructuring of *butt* motivated by his analysis of the surface form of *butting*.

It must be considered that Latin spelling deviations might derive from essentially the same situation, i.e. surface merger (or realizations near enough to merger to cause uncertainty) of underlying voiced and voiceless stops intervocalically as the result of a low-level rule of allophonic weakening, in this case, not sensitive to stress. A scribe or stonecutter might produce <EXTRICADO> for EXTRICATO (*CIL* 3.3620; Pannonia Inferior c. AD 217) just as the present-day speaker of American English might write <equidable> for *equitable*; the realizations in speech are, or are perceived as, equivalent. Similarly, the writer of Latin who generated <CANDITATUS> for CANDIDATUS would again be demonstrating the same hypercorrect misinterpretation as today's American student who writes <parametic> for *paramedic*: the writer is aware that the fast-speech [d] is often represented by <t> in writing. Many Romanists, when confronted with Latin spellings of the same type of deviation, either ignore the possible ramifications of their existence, or argue that their sporadic occurrence in texts militates against the possibility of Latin having had a low level rule of allophonic weakening by which phonemically voiceless stops could, for some speakers at least, be interpreted from the evidence of normal speech as phonemically voiced.

Sporadic testimony of allophony through the appearance of spelling deviations is to be expected, however. In addition to the fact that Western writing systems in general are phonemically based rather than phonetically based, and thus simple allophony is not indicated in conventional orthography, a number of variables conspire to keep evidence of subphonemic wandering to a minimum. It is often repeated in studies of this kind that writing is a conscious act subject to various degrees of standardizing control; that is, that motivated insecurities can be reduced by education. In an alphabetic orthographic system, the character and the intensity of the learning process are, presumably, determined by relative consistency in mapping of grapheme to phoneme and by the type of mapping employed. The near-perfect morphophonemic spelling of Finnish, for example, reduces the effort of writing to something very near that of phonemic transcription. Mis-spellings of native or orthographically nativized words (leaving aside, e.g., <vichy> [vis:y] 'mineral water') may arise due to mismatches between local dialect and the Helsinki-based standard, but given the pronunciation of a word, a Finn in control of the alphabet can spell it. At the opposite pole is the lexical iconicity of French, whose orthographic conventions typically supply more than one graphemic representation of a single phonological unit. It must be accepted that <o>, <ô>, <eau>, and <au> represent [o], for example, and through repetition one must develop an eye for the spelling of *mot, dôme, eau,* and *gauche.* Anglophones can surely sympathize; even some who hold a Ph.D. in linguistics will confess that from time to time they write a word more than once to see which version looks right.

Another point to acknowledge is that many lexical roots appear in inflectional or derivational configurations which enable recovery of the underlying form. The American who writes <equidable> would, presumably, be far less likely to write <lader> for *later,* since, whereas the derivational relation of *equitable* and *equate* may well be opaque for many speakers, the final consonant of *late* reinforces the integrity of /t/ in *later* in such a derivationally transparent pair. This is not a guarantee that mis-spellings will not occur, as is shown by <tudor> 'tutor' when *tu*[th]*orial* is available for testing, or, for an example of a vowel reduced to schwa, <luxery>, testable with *lux*[ʊ]*rious,* but it can be assumed that the more common the pair, the more likely it is that spelling errors will be avoided, working in tandem with the word-specific test of deliberate slow-speech pronunciation.

In sum, just as conscious awareness of possible confusion in writing a language with allophonic (near-) convergence can lead to hypercorrection, the same circumstance may engender special care and constant control against misinterpretation, prompting correct guesses of standard orthography or especially studied knowledge.

Sparse and irregular manifestation of spelling confusion is thus no argument against the possibility of principled interpretation of those few occurrences of apparent uncertainty which are found. The linguist of a millennium hence, if presented with no more data than those found in a few scattered twentieth-century American texts, would be correct if he or she were to posit from the instance of <sporatic> and <sporadic> in *Homeowner* magazine that American English of the 1980s had a phonological rule whereby, for at least some speakers, intervocalic /t/ and /d/ had realizations sufficiently similar to cause uncertainty in spelling. The more such attestations he or she might find, the more justified the deduction would be, the recurrence of the phenomenon in a number of lexical items in the production of a number of writers serving to reduce the possibility that the first few instances discovered were personal quirks, or lapses following no coherent principle. Importantly, however – repeating from above – *the lack of confused orthography in any number of texts would be no counter-argument to the hypothesis.* The conclusion that texts without <t>/<d> mis-spellings necessarily were written by twentieth-century Americans lacking convergence of /t/ and /d/ in their normal speech would be false, and the present article is a case in point. In this paragraph (in the original text at least), the words *possibility*, *scattered*, *items*, *writers*, *repeating*, *product*, and *according* are spelled according to standard conventions. Consistent standard spelling with <t> or <d> in this text does not reflect a lack of surface merger, but rather, as a result of schooling, secure underlying forms strongly influenced by practised knowledge of English spelling. As I pronounce them, the surface realizations of the relevant /t/ and /d/ are (or appear to me to be) identical.

RUMANIAN AND THE DIALECTS OF THE WEST-CENTRAL PYRENEES

The fact that restructured voicing of /p t k/ did not occur in Rumanian dialects, and at least not regularly in the dialects of central Italy, southern Italy, and parts of Sardinia, nor in the ultraconservative speech of the Elcock Zone straddling the Pyrenees (Elcock 1938), precludes positing a date as early as the first or second century for *phonemicized* voicing, but not necessarily for *phonetic* voicing.

There is no more reason to assume absolute homogeneity among, or within, varieties of Latin than there is in any closely knit group of speech types today. In fact, St Jerome (c. 340–420) tells us outright that Latin varied regionally: 'cum . . . et ipsa latinitas e regionibus quotidie mutetur et tempore' (quoted from Mihăescu 1978: 51, n. 6). Sociolinguistic studies of the past two decades suggest that variation is normal, in the community as well as in the speech of any given person. Examples from Modern Tuscan serve to illustrate.

In a detailed study of intervocalic /k t p/ based on extensive field work, Giannelli and Savoia (1978, 1979–80) found considerable variation throughout the region. To the south-west of Florence in the area of Orbetello, the realizations [k], [t], [p] coexist with [ɣ], [ð], [β]. To the north-west, near the coast of the Versiglia, variation is more subtle: /la#kasa/, for example, may be [lakaːsa], [laka̠ːsa] (lax, unvoiced), [laxaːsa], [lahaːsa], or [laaːsa], with analogous series for /p/ and /t/, but without the possibility of complete disappearance.

Preliminary data from a sociolinguistic study in progress of the consonantism in Bibbiena, beyond the Pratomagno to the east of Florence in the Casentino, show more precisely the array in Table 6.1 for three speakers' renditions of intervocalic /k/ in two contexts, reading aloud and in free conversation.

Table 6.1 Intervocalic /k/ in Bibbiena for three speakers

	Reading	*Conversation*
(a) F, 15–24, white collar		
[k]	15/32 = 46.88%	55/140 = 39.29%
[h]	12/32 = 37.5%	54/140 = 38.57%
[x]	4/32 = 12.5%	21/140 = 15.0%
[k̭]	1/32 = 3.13%	9/140 = 6.43%
[∅]	0	1/140 = 0.71%
(b) F, 35–50, blue collar		
[k]	34/52 = 65.38%	96/189 = 50.79%
[h]	17/52 = 32.69%	55/189 = 29.1%
[x]	1/52 = 1.92%	29/189 = 15.34%
[k̭]	0	8/189 = 4.23%
[∅]	0	0
(c) M, 15–24, blue collar		
[k]	10/27 = 37.04%	16/60 = 26.67%
[h]	11/27 = 40.74%	19/60 = 31.67%
[x]	4/27 = 14.8%	3/60 = 5.0%
[k̭]	2/27 = 7.41%	12/60 = 20.0%
[∅]	0	0
[ɣ]	0	7/60 = 11.67%
[x̣]	0	2/60 = 3.33%

Source: Luciano Giannelli and Thomas D. Cravens (work in progress).

A number of points are relevant here: (a) any phonological rule describing the manifestations of /k/ in these dialects must be variable; (b) calculations for Bibbiena show that, if the results for these three speakers are typical, variability in Bibbienese is such that it is not possible to identify one realization as the norm; (c) no two speakers have exactly the same array of realizations in actual speech.

The figures for [k] while reading, and independent observation on site, indicate that full voiceless occlusion is the preferred variant of the most careful register and of overt prestige in Bibbiena. It is the one given in answer to direct queries about local pronunciation, and some informants reported that the realization [laha:sa] for *la casa* did not exist in the town, though none failed to have spirantization in their speech. A middle-aged shopkeeper, asked at the end of the interview if he ever employed a pronunciation such as [laha:sa], replied emphatically 'Non lo di[h]o mai!' ('I never say it!').

The immediate conclusion to be drawn is common knowledge to all linguists, yet often overlooked in discussions of Latin: variation is normal, citation forms do not necessarily constitute a true reflection of real speech, and native speakers often perceive their linguistic behaviour as being other than what it is. There is no reason to believe that these observations would not have been as true in areas of Roman conquest in the second or third century AD as they are now in Tuscany, or in any other place and time. Positing variation in surface forms of Latin intervocalic /p t k/ does not automatically supply a convincing account for the lack of even sporadic voicing in Rumanian, but the consideration of variation as normal does allow a plausible working hypothesis. The simplest scenario is rule regression, the classic example being vowel epenthesis before word-initial sibilant clusters in Romance. Once apparently obligatory throughout *Romania continua*, it is now:

in Rumanian: extinct – if ever it was present (Mihăescu 1978: 193) (e.g. *sta*);
in French: digested and forgotten (*être*);
in Italian: moribund (*stare*; disappearing after /n/: *in Svizzera* gaining ground over *in iSvizzera*; fossilized after /r/ in *italiano sostenuto: per iscritto*, vs normal speech *per scrivere*);
but in Spanish: unrelenting (*'¡Radio Barcelona! ¡Música non-estop!'*), to the point of being required for nativized spelling of borrowings (*estándar*).

Both ancient and modern circumstantial evidence for pan-Romance allophonic voicing suggests that a similar scenario is not implausible.

	Rumanian	*Italian*	*Spanish*	*French*
SAPONE	săpun	sapone	jabón	savon
ROTA	roată	ruota	rueda	roue
URTICA	urzică	ortica	ortiga	ortie

The alternation restructured in the word in Spanish, restructured and suffered loss except for reflexes of /p/ in French, left fossilizations of its demise in Central Italian (LOCU > *luogo*, FICATU >*fegato*, SPATA > *spada*, alongside FOCU > *fuoco*, AMICA > *amica*, LATU > *lato*), and regressed completely in Rumanian. (For specially conditioned devoicing see Fanciullo 1976; also Repetti and Tuttle 1987: 93–6, for Sicilianization of Gallo-Italian dialects.)

The situation in the Pyrenees may be far less troublesome. Simple loss of allophonic voicing is a distinct possibility, and it may be no accident that both Rumanian and the conservative Pyrenean dialects suffered collapse of original voiceless geminates with the homorganic single stops. However, in response to Cravens (1988), where it was posited simply that Belsetán, for example, might never have had voicing, Edward F. Tuttle has pointed out (personal communication) that there are indications of possible devoicing induced by apocope, along the lines of neighbouring Catalan. There are numerous exceptions to preservation, and these are often in words with constantly intervocalic consonants, either feminines (e.g. *aneda* 'wild duck') or those which otherwise provide structural protection from a possible apocopating position (*bodillo* 'intestine'). What appears today to be simple lack of voicing could derive either straightforwardly from reinterpretation of apocopated forms, the masculine of the posited alternation *cremat/*cremada* 'burnt' giving rise to *cremata*, for example, or in cases not allowing apocope, from a more tendential selection of, e.g., /t/ to replace /d/, doubly pressured by apocope-induced restructuring elsewhere in the lexicon and by hypercorrection *vis-à-vis* more prestigious Castilian. Not to be discounted is Tuttle's further suggestion that the masculine form may be taken as basic (unmarked with regard to the feminine), thus a motivated source for reinterpretation. Belsetán *almut*, pl. *almudes* 'almud (measure of grain)', deriving from Arabic *mudd*, reinforces the argument (see Elcock 1938 and Badía Margarit 1950 for examples).

Both of these postulations are speculative, though not equally so. On the scale of plausibility described by Sarah Thomason in her plenary address to the ninth ICHL, the account of devoicing in Pyrenean Romance would seem to fit close to the pole of 'respectable hypothesis'. The argument for regression of allophonic voicing in Rumanian is certainly situated further in the direction of 'idle speculation', though just how close it comes to deserving that opprobrium fully cannot be decided objectively. Regression could, in fact, be an illusion in at least two distinct senses. Most obviously, voicing might never have been present in Latin during the period of Roman conquest and occupation of the Eastern provinces in the first place (Bichakjian 1977), in which case the entire argument presented here is vitiated. Or more subtly, allophonic voicing may have been present in the speech of those from Italy, though never truly absorbed by the native population, not a true case of language-specific substratum causation, but a more general effect involving faulty acquisition and generational transmission of phonetic detail (for indirect corroboration of the possibility, see Elman *et al.* 1977).

CONCLUSION

The complete lack of indication of voicing at any level in Rumanian precludes positing Latin allophonic voicing with the vigour of Campanile's statement quoted on page 56. Yet all other evidence appears to be consonant with this hypothesis, and the case of today's American English shows that the existence of such a rule can motivate highly sporadic, but systematic mis-spellings such as those found in Latin sources.

Ignoring the thorny question of Rumanian development for the nonce, the spelling deviations in inscriptions, papyri, and ostraca are amenable to principled interpretation. Keeping the American English spellings in mind as possible parallel phenomena, Latin <B>, <D>, and with some reservations <G>, where <P>, <T>, or <C> would be expected, provide circumstantial evidence of the possibility that, perhaps as early as the first century, and throughout the area of Roman domination, at least some registers of Latin had a rule of allophonic intervocalic voicing which provided the historical opportunity for subsequent restructuring of two basic types, determined by local conditions whose exploration is beyond the scope of this chapter.

The alternative position, that Latin had no such voicing, leaves the Latin mis-spellings unaccounted for, reduces irregular Italian voicing to either *ad hoc* categorization as northern borrowing or a simple mystery, and deprives the restructured voicing which eventually emerged in Western Romance of a coherently interpretable, (circumstantially) documented historical source. The view of language as constant becoming, of – to paraphrase Clark in a different context (1987: 283) – developments occurring in a space determined by pre-existing conditions, is lost. The cost of not entertaining the possibility of allophonic voicing in Latin is thus high, whereas the gain in understanding to be derived from adopting it as a working hypothesis is potentially great. The arguments of Campanile, Politzer, Figge, and others are not ill-founded, and it is in our interest to explore them and their consequences further. As the response to Wright (1982) has shown, the results of reassessing our most basic assumptions can be remarkably invigorating.

BIBLIOGRAPHY

Adams, J. N. (1977) *The Vulgar Latin of the Letters of Claudius Terentianus*, Manchester: Manchester University Press.

AIS = Jaberg, Karl and Jud, Jakob (1928–40) *Sprach- und Sachatlas Italiens und der Südschweiz*, 8 vols, Zofingen: Ringier.

Badía Margarit, Antonio (1950) *El habla del Valle de Bielsa (Pirineo Aragonés)*, Barcelona: Instituto de Estudios Pirenaicos.

Barbarino, Joseph Louis (1981) *Latin and Romance Intervocalic Stops: a Quantitative and Comparative Study*, Madrid: José Porrúa Turanzas.

Bassols de Climent, Mariano (1962) *Fonética latina*, Madrid: Consejo Superior de Investigaciones Científicas.

Bichakjian, Bernard H. (1977) 'Romance lenition: thoughts on the fragmentary-sound-shift and the diffusion hypotheses', *Romance Philology* 31: 196–203.

Campanile, Enrico (1961) 'Due studi sul latino volgare', *L'Italia dialettale* 34: 1–64.

CIL = (1863–) *Corpus Inscriptionum Latinarum*, Berlin: Reimer.

Clark, Andy (1987) 'The kludge in the machine', *Mind and Language* 2: 277–300.

CPL = Cavenaile, Robert (1958) *Corpus Papyrorum Latinarum*, Wiesbaden: Harrassowitz.

Cravens, Thomas D. (1988) 'Consonant strength in the Romance dialects of the Pyrenees', in Jean-Pierre Montreuil and David P. Birdsong (eds), *Advances in Romance Linguistics*, Dordrecht: Foris, 67–88.

—— (1989) Review of *Quaderni dell'Atlante Lessicale Toscano*, 2/3, *Romance Philology* 42: 333–7.

Elcock, William D. (1938) *De quelques affinités phonétiques entre le béarnais et l'aragonais*, Paris: Droz.

—— (1960) *The Romance Languages*, London: Faber & Faber.

Elman, J. L., Diehl, R. L., and Buchwald, S. E. (1977) 'Perceptual switching in bilinguals', *Journal of the Acoustical Society of America* 62: 971–4.

Fanciullo, Franco (1976) 'Il trattamento delle occlusive sonore latine nei dialetti salentini', *L'Italia dialettale* 39: 1–82.

Figge, Udo L. (1966) *Die romanische Anlautsonorisation*, Bonn: Romanische Seminar der Universität Bonn.

Giannelli, Luciano and Savoia, Leonardo M. (1978) 'L'indebolimento consonantico in Toscana (I)', *Rivista italiana di dialettologia* 2: 23–58.

—— (1979–80) 'L'indebolimento consonantico in Toscana (II)', *Rivista italiana di dialettologia* 3–4: 38–101.

Izzo, Herbert J. (1980) 'On the voicing of Latin intervocalic /p, t, k/ in Italian', in Herbert J. Izzo (ed.), *Italic and Romance: Linguistic Studies in Honor of Ernst Pulgram*, Amsterdam: Benjamins, 131–55.

Lass, Roger (1980) *On Explaining Language Change*, Cambridge: Cambridge University Press.

Maher, J. Peter (1976) 'Syn-, dia-, and anachronistic linguistics: evidence against "recapitulation"', *Language Sciences* 43: 14–16.

Mihăescu, Haralambie (1978) *La Langue latine dans le sud-est de l'Europe*, trans. Radu Crețeanu, Paris: Les Belles Lettres.

Naro, Anthony J. (1972a) 'On f > h in Castilian and Western Romance', *Zeitschrift für romanische Philologie* 88: 435–47.

—— (1972b) 'A reply', *Zeitschrift für romanische Philologie* 88: 459–62.

Odenkirchen, Carl Joseph (1952) 'The consonantism of later Latin inscriptions: a contribution to the "Vulgar Latin" question', unpublished Ph.D. dissertation, University of North Carolina.

Pei, Mario A. (1943) 'Intervocalic occlusives in "East" and "West" Romance', *Romanic Review* 34: 235–47.

Politzer, Robert L. (1955) 'Latin lenition and Italian consonants', *General Linguistics* 1: 70–8.

Porzio Gernia, Maria Luisa (1976–7) 'Lo stato attuale degli studi di fonologia latina', *Incontri linguistici* 3: 137–52.

Repetti, Lori and Tuttle, Edward F. (1987) 'The evolution of Latin PL, BL, and CL, GL in Western Romance', *Studi mediolatini e volgari* 33: 53–115.

Tovar, Antonio (1948) 'La sonorización y caída de las intervocálicas, y los estratos indoeuropeos en Hispania', *Boletín de la Real Academia Española* 28: 265–80.

—— (1951) 'La sonorisation et la chute des intervocaliques, phénomène latin occidental', *Revue des études latines* 29: 102–20.

Wanner, Dieter (1977) 'The heuristics of substratum', in M. P. Hagiwara (ed.), *Studies in Romance Linguistics*, Rowley, MA: Newbury House, 1–13.

Wanner, Dieter and Cravens, Thomas D. (1980) 'Early intervocalic voicing in Tuscan', in Elizabeth Traugott and Susan Shepherd (eds), *Papers from the Fourth International Conference on Historical Linguistics*, Amsterdam: Benjamins, 339–47.

Weinrich, Harald (1960) 'Sonorisierung in der Kaiserzeit?' *Zeitschrift für romanische Philologie* 76: 205–18.

Wright, Roger (1982) *Late Latin and Early Romance in Spain and Carolingian France*, Liverpool: Cairns.

—— (1987) 'The study of semantic change in Early Romance (Late Latin)', in Anna Giacalone Ramat, Onofrio Carruba, and Giuliano Bernini (eds), *Papers from the Seventh International Conference on Historical Linguistics*, Amsterdam: Benjamins, 619–28.

7 Evidence for SVO in Latin?

Harm Pinkster

The main claim of this chapter is that our knowledge of Classical Latin word order is limited to such an extent that conclusions with respect to the date and the evolution of Romance word order are premature.

WORD ORDER IN CLASSICAL LATIN

Evidence for a syntactic order SOV in Classical Latin

The standard view in Latin linguistics is that Latin essentially had a S(ubject) O(bject) (finite) V(erb) word order. This view can be found in the grammars of Kühner-Stegmann (1912) and Hofmann-Szantyr (1965), but also in Marouzeau (1949) and in recent studies like those of Oniga (1988) and Ostafin (1986). However, as my use of the word 'essentially' suggests, many deviations from the basic SOV word order are recognized. These deviations are of various types. In the first place it is common knowledge that in imperative sentences (in which subject constituents as a rule do not occur) the verb is frequently found in initial position. Furthermore, it has been observed that in subordinate clauses finite verb forms occur in final position with higher frequency than they do in main clauses. (Incidentally, one would not expect otherwise: in subordinate clauses the initial position is reserved for subordinating devices; also subordinate clauses, being 'heavy material', tend to come late in the sentence, while usually not containing 'heavy material' themselves.) We see, then, that sentence type and clause type are responsible for deviations from the assumed basic order. A second type of deviation has to do with the internal structure of constituents. The tendency of 'heavy material to the right' has been mentioned already. Related to this is the opposite tendency of placing 'light' constituents in the first possible position of the sentence. This tendency holds for anaphoric elements as well as for so-called clitical elements (recent discussion in Wanner 1987). Parallels can be found in a wide range of languages. I only refer to the LIPOC rule in Dik's (1989) functional grammar and to Hawkins (1988).

Both types discussed so far have in common that they are of a formal nature. In this formal respect they differ from a third commonly acknowledged type of deviation, which I will discuss now. The initial position, which is claimed to be, in principle, reserved for the subject of the sentence, may be occupied by another constituent for the purpose of 'emphasis', for example in the case of contrast between a constituent in a sentence B and a constituent in the preceding sentence A (excellent illustrations in Schneider 1912). Conversely, the verb may be moved away from its final position by other constituents that convey new or important information. The formulation of the phenomena given here looks like descriptions of fronting phenomena in fixed-word-order languages such as English: deviation from a basic syntactically defined word order for pragmatic purposes. In fact, this is almost a paraphrase of the conclusions of a recent transformational account of Latin word order (Ostafin 1986).

What evidence is there for assuming a basic SOV order in Latin? Not much. In fact, no major grammar, like the ones mentioned, is based on research about the relative order of the S, O, and V. Until recently, we possessed numerical data about a number of authors as far as the position of the verb is concerned (Linde 1923, especially). And we have a witness (in the person of Quintilian) who says

verbo sensum cludere multo si compositio patiatur optimum est. in verbis enim sermonis vis est. si id asperum erit, cedet haec ratio numeris, ut fit apud summos Graecos Latinosque oratores frequentissime.

('If the demands of artistic structure permit, it is far best to end the sentence with a verb: for it is in verbs that the real strength of language resides. But if it results in harshness of sound, this principle must give way before the demands of rhythm, as is frequently the case in the best authors of Greece and Rome.')

(Quint. *Inst.* 9.4.26)

However, Quintilian's statement in all probability is a normative one meant for oratorical (written) prose, not based on observation of actual speech. Linde, as I have stated already, gives percentages of the occurrences of finite verb forms in final position (also on first and intermediate position). I give some of his figures about main clauses: (a) first century BC: Caesar 84 per cent; Cicero 33–54 per cent, depending on the work chosen; Sallust 76 per cent; Varro 33 per cent; (b) Late Latin: Augustine (AD 354–430) 42 per cent (see Muldowney 1937); *Peregrinatio ad loca sancta* (late fourth century AD) 25 per cent; Victor Vitensis (late fifth century AD) 37 per cent. What is most striking in these data is the enormous variation not only between authors, but even in one and the same author: in Cicero's philosophical dialogue *De republica* only 33 per cent of the finite verbs are in final position. From Linde's account (which presents an overall count, in which distinctions as to sentence type, complexity of sentences and constituents, etc. are not made) it is even difficult to conclude that Latin was a verb-final language at the classical period, let alone conclude that Latin at that period was an SOV language. It is also not possible to conclude from Linde's figures, as he wanted us to believe, a constant decrease of the verb-final position (see Koll 1965: 262–3). Yet, Linde's article has become a classic and his figures about the *Peregrinatio* still play a role in the assumption of a development from a classical SOV into a SVO order in the late fourth century AD (as in Harris 1978; Renzi 1984). The existence of so much variation itself in our texts should warn us against assuming a syntactic basic order. The variation can be explained much better if we assume the existence of several different orders reserved for specific situations (text type, sentence type, constituent type, etc.) or assume other (pragmatic and/or semantic) factors to determine the order of constituents. At any rate, the statistical variation should encourage us to search for qualitative explanations of that variation. We will come to that later.

The relative order of Subject, Object, and Verb

In the last few years several scholars have published data about the relative order of S, V, and O in various texts. It is difficult to compare these data, since they differ in the way the S, O, and V constituents are defined and sometimes it is not clear at all which definition has been used. Whereas in Pinkster (1988), for example, only nominal Subjects and Objects in non-complex sentences are taken into account, Metzeltin (1987) also counts sentential complements functioning as Subject or Object. The samples used in most of these studies are very limited and the numbers of appropriate sentences very low. The low numbers can be explained to some extent by the stylistic preferences of most Latin authors. Apart from that it must also be due to the fact that sentences of the type *Dog bites man* are extremely rare. In cohesive texts nominal constituents referring back to entities mentioned earlier are usually marked by some anaphoric device. One such 'device', very frequent in Latin, especially in the case of Subject constituents, is zero-anaphora. Similarly, parallels for *I love you* are difficult to find in Latin, since Subject pronouns are only used in the case of Topic shift or Focus. However, in spite of these limitations, Table 7.1 shows the results of some {S, O, V} counts, both of classical and non-classical texts.

What can we learn from these data about the word order in Classical Latin? I suggest that the most significant aspect is the variety that appears from Table 7.1. Although even in these small numbers there is some support for claiming that S preferably takes an initial position and that O precedes V more often than the other way around, no order is excluded in principle. Notice, for example, the OVS and VOS orders in Celsus' medical treatise. So even in a well-defined sample of sentences, with many variables excluded, as is the case for the material taken from Cicero, Celsus, and Vitruvius, variation exists. It is quite different from fronting phenomena in fixed-word-order languages like Dutch and English. In these languages fronting of a specific constituent does not (or not much) affect the order of the other constituents. Once more, the data do not suggest a syntactic basic order and call for a more

Table 7.1 {S, O, V} ordering[1] (absolute numbers except in the case of Petronius)

	SOV	SVO	OSV	OVS	VSO	VOS
Cicero *Att.* 1	17	—	2	—	1	—
Caesar *Gall* 1–7+*Civ.*	360	22	120	33	6	27
Vitruvius 1.1–4	7	4	2	1	—	—
Celsus 1–6	51	4	6	15	—	7
Petronius (in %)	46	19	15	6	6	6
Claudius Terentianus	3	10	1	1	1	4
Passio Ss Scilitanorum	1	1	—	—	—	—
Peregrinatio (1)	22	35	6	4	15	22
(2), 2nd part only	10	16	3	1	14	29
Vulgata (100 sentences)	15	8	—	—	—	—
Acta conv. (direct speech)	2	—	—	4	2	—
idem (reported speech)	2	1	1	1	—	1

* 2 sets each of 200 sentences

qualitative approach to discover the rules determining the observed variation. This impression of variation is supported by the data presented by Koll (1965: 246–7) on {S, V} and {O, V} orderings. I take from his study only the figures about Cicero to illustrate this variation: (a) Cic. *Catil.*: SV/VS 30/0; OV/VO 14/7; (b) Cic. *Leg.*: SV/VS 32/6; OV/VO 18/4.

Typological inconsistency

Before turning to an examination of pragmatic and semantic correlates of word-order patterns, I briefly discuss one explanation in syntactic terms of the observed variation. Adams (1976a) has written a typological approach to Latin word order, in which he suggests that Classical Latin texts show two conflicting ordering patterns: SOV on the sentence level on the one hand, with the governed constituent O preceding V; prepositional (instead of postpositional) phrases on the other. This conflict does not exist in the Romance languages where the ordering 'preposition – NP' corresponds to the ordering 'Verb – Object'. Classical Latin data, in this approach, seem to show inconsistency. This typological inconsistency can be understood, according to Adams, by assuming at least two different registers: one of colloquial Latin, in which the typical Romance SVO pattern emerged quite early, maybe already in Plautus' time; the other one of conservative or literary language, in which the old SOV order was preserved. Representatives of the 'old order' are the *Leg. XII.* with 34 OV examples against 0 VO, and the *Sen. Cons. de Bacch.* showing 11:0 (Adams 1976a: 96ff.). Evidence for the old order may also be obtained by looking at the formation of compounds like *causidicus* ('pleader', cf. *causam dicere*) (see Oniga 1988: 88, 155ff.). Caesar should, in Adams' view, be regarded as the prime representative of the conservative register. Other authors, like Plautus and Cicero, show a mix of the old and new patterns. This approach calls forth a number of questions. One set of questions is of a methodological nature: what is the strength of typological observations for resolving problems in individual languages; what does 'typological consistency' mean? A second set of questions regards Caesar: why should he adopt this feature of the language of his ancestors; what other conservative features does his language show; how does this stylistic principle relate to his stylistic theory? And, thirdly, in Adams' approach too, it may be asked what the value is of merely statistical observations and what, if any, are the rules that can account for the statistical distribution of word-order patterns. Assuming *two* syntactic orders is no solution for the problem of Latin word order either.

A pragmatic approach

It is time now to turn to non-syntactic explanations of Latin word order. We will explore the extent to which word order in Classical Latin can be explained on pragmatic and semantic grounds. We have already seen that pragmatic factors play some role in the older literature (for example, Schneider 1912). However, they are mentioned there to explain deviations from a 'normal' word order that itself is formulated in syntactic terms, in statements such as: 'The Subject may be removed from its initial position by an emphatic constituent.' However, observing that in for example Cic. *Att*. 1.5 only three out of twenty-seven sentences start with a Subject constituent, there is not much use in pragmatically modified syntactic rules. It seems better to ask questions like: 'Where do emphatic constituents go?', or 'Which constituents occupy the initial position of the sentence?'.

At this moment several theoretical notions are available for a pragmatic analysis of Latin texts. Panhuis (1982) adopts the framework of Functional Sentence Perspective. Sentences, according to this theory, are normally ordered on the basis of the principle of communicative dynamism. This principle means that sentences usually start with a highly thematic constituent, while ending with a highly rhematic constituent, independent of the type of constituent. This can be expressed in the following formula: Theme proper > Theme > Transition > Rheme > Rheme proper. The following two examples taken from Panhuis may serve to illustrate the principle:

(1) ego   dabo   ei   talentum
    I-nom. will-give him-dat. talent-acc.
    'I will give him a TALENT' (Pl. *Mos*. 359)
(2) bonan fide? # siquidem tu   argentum   reddituru's
    good faith-abl. if   you-nom. money-acc. plan to give back
    'In good faith, you say? # If you DO plan to give the money back' (Pl. *Mos*. 670–1)

In (1) the most salient element in the discourse is the Object constituent 'talent', indicated by capitals. In (2) what is most important is the returning of the money (finite verb). In both sentences we observe a progression from a thematic constituent (*ego*, *tu*) towards a rhematic constituent. Instead of the notions

'Theme' and 'Rheme' other notions are used in other frameworks. I will henceforth use the notions 'Topic' and 'Focus', as developed in Dik's (1978; 1989) functional grammar. The main difference between the Functional Sentence Perspective (FSP) theory and other theories is the postulation of a continuum from known/given to unknown/salient in FSP and the assumption that individual constituents are ordered along this continuum. It is this aspect which I find most difficult to apply and, therefore, will avoid in this chapter.

Leaving apart connecting particles, etc., the first possible position of a declarative sentence is occupied by (i) 'framing' or 'situating' constituents of various types (examples (3) and (4), respectively);[2] (ii) Topic constituents (examples (5) and (6)); or (iii) constituents with 'contrastive' or 'replacive' (Dik 1989) Focus (example (7)):

(3) *de   forma,*   ovem   esse oportet corpore   amplo
     about form-abl. sheep-acc. be   ought   body-abl. wide-abl.
     'As to form, sheep should be full-bodied' (Var. *R.* 2.2.3)

(4) *Apud Helvetios*   longe nobilissimus   fuit . . . Orgetorix
     among Helvetians-acc. by far most-noble-nom. was   Org.-nom.
     'Among the Helvetians the noblest man by far was O' (Caes. *Gal.* 1.2.1)

(5) *Quintum   fratrem*   cotidie expectamus
     Quintus-acc. brother-acc. everyday we-expect
     'We are expecting Q. back any day' (Cic. *Att.* 1.5.8)

(6) *Terentia*   magnos   articulorum dolores   habet
     Terentia-nom. heavy-acc. joints-gen. pains-acc. has
     'Terentia has a bad attack of rheumatism' (Cic. *Att.* 1.5.8)

(7) An vero . . . Scipio . . . Gracchum . . . interfecit? #
     Q indeed   Scipio-nom. Gracchus-acc. killed
     Catilinam   nos   consules   perferemus?
     Catiline-acc. we-nom. consuls-nom. shall-tolerate?
     'Shall Scipio have killed Gracchus, and shall we, consuls, put up with Catiline?' (Cic. *Catil.* 1.3)

In example (3) we see a so-called Theme-constituent (Dik 1989), which creates the framework for the message about the bodies of sheep. In (4) the Place Adjunct *apud Helvetios* serves to introduce Caesar's episode on the Helvetians. In (5) *Quintus*, being an Object constituent, was well known to Cicero's correspondent Atticus, just as his wife *Terentia*, in (6). Both are Topics and in initial position, as is the rule in such concluding messages about his family in Cicero's letters. Sentence (7), finally, is a fine example of double contrast:

Catilinam is in contrast with *Gracchum*, but there is also a contrast between what Scipio did and what *nos consules* maybe will do. *Catilinam* is, of course, already introduced into the discourse and therefore, in a sense, topical information. Its initial position instead of the even more topical *nos consules*, however, serves the contrast with respect to *Gracchum*.

Proceeding now to the final position in sentences, we may note in examples (3)–(7) above some clear examples of the tendency for Focus-constituents to occupy the final position of the sentence. Sentence (3) is an example of a Subject Complement (*corpore amplo*). A good example of an Object constituent is (8):

(8) quem   relinquam . . .?   ratio . . .   postulat *fratrem*
     who-acc. I-shall-leave-behind? reason-nom. requires brother-acc.
     'Whom am I to leave (in command)? In principle, my brother
     is the man' (Cic. *Att.* 5.6.1)

Here, *fratrem* is the answer to the question 'who?', clearly a Focus constituent. Example (4) has a final Subject, which, however, I prefer to discuss later. Good examples of Focal Subjects are given in (9) and (10):

(9) prensat   unus   *P. Galba*
     shake hands alone-nom. P. Galba-nom.
     'canvassing is done only by P. Galba' (Cic. *Att.* 1.1.1)
(10) stomachum   autem infirmum indicant *pallor*,
     stomach-acc. but   weak-acc. indicate paleness-nom.
     macies
     meagreness-nom.
     'Weakness of the stomach is indicated by pallor, wasting'
     (Cels. 1.8.2)

In (9) Cicero is reporting about the elections, a ritual part of which is canvassing. New and important is the message that *Galba* is doing that. Example (10) is typical of the fifteen OVS instances from Celsus referred to in Table 7.1. The message can be understood as an answer to the question 'which are the symptoms for a weak stomach?' The same explanation holds for six out of seven VOS sentences.

We have seen so far nominal constituents in various syntactic functions occurring at the end of the sentence and carrying Focus function. In examples (5) and (7) the verb forms (*expectamus*, *perferemus*) may be said to carry Focus function as well. However, (6), while having a final verb form, cannot be explained along the same lines. *Habet* can hardly be Focus (meaning something like 'she has indeed'). On the other hand, (6) is not the answer to the question 'What does Terentia have?' either, which explains why the Object does not occupy the focal final position. Rather, the combination of Object and Verb constitutes the answer to a question like 'How is Terentia doing?' The pragmatic structure of (6) can be formulated in the following way:

(6') Topic (*Terentia*) Focus (*magnos articulorum dolores habet*)

In examples like (6), where Object and Verb constitute a pragmatic unit, two options are open for ordering the two constituents: either both orders (OV, VO) are possible or one order is preferred. Suppose OV were preferred: in that case the OV order would be the expression both of the combination of an Object and a focal verb, and of a verb phrase consisting of Object and verb, behaving as a pragmatic unit, as in (6). OV might thus cover Object+VERB and Object+Verb, as opposed to VO, which is only the expression of Verb+OBJECT (capitals indicating Focus). This situation would resemble what we find in noun phrases, where the order N–Adj. is the expression both of the combination of noun and non-focal adjective and of the combination of focal noun and adjective. Good examples of Object–Verb combinations acting as a pragmatic unit are expressions like *bellum gerere* ('to wage war'). They may be regarded as complex predicates in which the noun has little 'individuation' (de Jong 1989: 533) and is not likely to be focalized. At this moment, there is no detailed information available about the order of constituents in Object–Verb combinations. However, it is evident that if some order were normal in these combinations (suppose OV) authors with a high number of such combinations would also have a high overall percentage of that particular order (OV). Caesar's plain narrative may be expected to have a high percentage of Object–Verb combinations and, maybe, here is the clue for his remarkably 'stable' word order.[3]

So far I have only presented examples of sentences in which it is possible to identify some constituent as having the pragmatic function of Topic and another one having the function Focus. However, there are sentences that cannot be described as giving additional information about some topical element. One might even hold that making a distinction between topical and focal constituents in certain sentences is pointless, since the entire information is new, without being anchored in the discourse in an obvious way. Sentences of this kind are normal in answer to a question like 'What happened?'. Ulrich (1985) has studied this type of sentences in Rumanian and other Romance languages. A typical answer to the question just mentioned could be:

(11) Italian: mi ha morso un cane
Spanish: la ha mordido un perro a mi madre

Such sentences, which Ulrich calls 'thetic' sentences, look like so-called 'presentative sentences', which serve to introduce new entities into the discourse. In such sentences the Verb has a relative early position in the sentence, whereas the Subject has a relative late position. Latin seems to make the same distinction between 'all-new' and pragmatically 'split-up' information. Our example (4) could be an instance of a presentative sentence (unless one wants to call *apud Helvetios* Topic). Other examples are (12)–(15):

(12) relinquebatur *una   per   Sequanos   via*
was left   one-nom. through Sequani-acc. road-nom.
'There remained one other line of route, through the borders of the Sequani' (Caes. *Gal.* 1.9.1)
(13) erant in ea   legione *fortissimi   viri*
were in that-abl. legio-abl. very brave-nom. men-nom.
'In that legion there were two most gallant men', Caes. *Gal.* 5.44.1)
(14) intrat *cinaedus*
enters sodomite-nom.
'At last bolted in a pansy-boy' (Petr. 23)
(15) venerat iam   *tertius   dies*
had come already third-nom. day-nom.
'The third day had come already' (Petr. 26)

Notice that not only stative verbs (like *esse*) occur in this sentence type, but action verbs (*intrare*) as well. Notice also that (12) is a passive sentence. Adams (1976b) gives examples of final Subjects in passive sentences in the Late Latin text of the Anonymus Valesianus. Vincent (1988: 60–2) suggests that especially Patient NPs occur in final position. However, as example (14) shows, any Subject of a one-place predicate can be found in that position in the pragmatic setting discussed above.[4]

It is time for an interim conclusion about Classical Latin. We have seen that it is useful to make a distinction between two types of pragmatic structure. In 'split-up' sentences the initial and the final position seem to be reserved for specific pragmatic purposes. In this type of sentence special attention should be given to the relative order of constituents within larger pragmatic units. In 'all-new' sentences the order VS seems to be quite common.

WORD ORDER IN LATE LATIN AND EARLY MEDIEVAL LATIN

The *Peregrinatio* has received much attention in studies on the development of Latin word order. The number of VO instances is higher than encountered so far in Classical Latin. The number of final verb forms is low (see above). Here again the question is how the statistical findings should be evaluated. Haida (1928) and Koll (1965: 252–6) have demonstrated that many of the statistically deviant cases can be explained perfectly well. Two examples may suffice:

(16) locum,   ubi . . . montes . . .   faciebant *vallem*
place-acc. where   mountains-nom. made   valley-acc.
infinitam,   ingens,   planissima   et   valde pulchram
endless-acc. vast-acc. very-flat-acc. and very beautiful-acc.
'a region, where the mountains formed an endless valley, vast, very flat and extremely beautiful' (*Per.* 1,1)

(17) et   trans   vallem   apparebat *mons*   *sanctus*
and across valley-acc. appeared mountain-nom. holy-nom.
Dei   Syna
God-gen. Syna
'and across the valley appeared the holy mountain of God, Syna' (*Per.* 1,1)

The first of these – successive – sentences contains a relative clause with a heavy Object constituent, which also constitutes the most important information (Focus). The second starts with a locative setting constituent, also topical information, followed by a presentative-like *apparebat mons*, where the VS order was shown to be normal in Classical Latin as well. Moreover, the Subject constituent is rather 'heavy'. The conspicuously high number of final Subjects is perfectly explainable in this travel and discovery story. Other texts from roughly the same period offer a different picture as far as the order of O and V, or the position of V, is concerned. In the *Acta conventus carthaginiensis* final position of the verb is normal, followed in frequency by initial verbs (Wolffs 1987). Interestingly, this work contains verbatim reports of the conference. In these parts VO is only slightly more frequent than in the narrative parts. In the medical text *Mulomedicina Chironis*, usually regarded as a typically

Vulgar Latin text (c. AD 400), there are seventeen SOV instances as opposed to two SVO (method of counting as in note 1), a proportion that is higher than that found in Celsus. The overall picture is one of variety, just as it was in the classical period. In our texts there is no support for claiming that by AD 400 word order had changed into SVO. Koll (1965) has also examined texts from a later period including texts from the Merovingian and Carolingian period. OV order can be found until the end of the period and the picture of variety persists.

The facts reported on above are difficult to interpret. A familiar interpretation, which can also be found with respect to other topics, is that the written texts cannot be taken as reliable sources for the actual stage of the development of Latin into the Romance languages. The higher the frequency of (S)OV is in a certain text, the more, it is often claimed, the author followed the stylistic principles of classical authors. The authors mechanically put the verb in final position, applying a rule that was easy enough. There are several problematic aspects with respect to this interpretation. (i) Classical authors did not simply put the V in final position. Maybe Caesar did, but this has not yet been investigated in a satisfactory manner. (ii) There is much variety between authors and text(type)s. Here, too, more than statistical analysis has hardly been undertaken. (iii) The greatest difficulty, however, for assuming more or less successful obedience to the 'verb-final rule' is that deviations from that rule can be explained by reference to the same factors that are shown to be valid for classical authors.

MORAL

The moral to this paper in the context of 'Latin and the Romance languages in the Early Middle Ages' is the following: there is no reason for assuming a SOV order in Classical Latin, nor is there one for assuming a SVO order by AD 400. Continued pragmatic analysis will bring to light more factors that determine the orders found in our texts. The last decade has brought an increased insight into the extent to which pragmatic factors are involved in the word order of individual Romance languages. There is more than SVO order in Romance. In fact, to quote one recent statement by Lambrecht (1988: 135) about French: 'The "canonical" transitive clause of the SVO type . . . hardly ever occurs in actual speech.' It is, moreover, quite probable that the individual Romance languages developed from Latin at a different speed (see Politzer 1958). Students of Early Medieval Latin need not hurry to find SVO.[5]

NOTES

1 The data on Caesar come from Ch. Elerick (unpublished) 'Word order in Caesar: SOV/V-1'. The data on Petronius are taken from Hinojo (1985); those on Claudius Terentianus (early second century AD) from Adams (1977: 74–5). The data on the *Vulgata* are taken from Metzeltin (1987). The first count on the *Peregrinatio* is taken from Väänänen (1987: 106). Those on Cic. *Att.* 1 are from Pinkster (1990), taking only declarative non-complex sentences, only nouns and proper names as S and O, no anaphoric elements, simple finite verb forms. The same method has been applied to the other texts mentioned in Table 7.1. The *Passio Ss. Scilitanorum* dates from AD 180, the *Acta conventus carthaginiensis* are from AD 411 (alternative figures from Wolffs 1987, using a less limited way of counting are as follows: SOV 9, SVO 1, OSV 4, OVS 9, VOS 1).
2 'Framing' or 'situating' constituents may also precede Topic constituents.
3 On Subject–Verb combinations acting as complex predicates see de Jong (1989: 534). In Celsus there seems to be a slight preference for OV in Object–Verb combinations that form a pragmatic unit.
4 De Jong (1989: 536–7) gives instances of 'all-new' clauses in which the Subject takes the first position.
5 I thank Helma Dik and Luisa Collewijn for their assistance in collecting data.

BIBLIOGRAPHY

Adams, J. N. (1976a) 'A typological approach to Latin word order', *IF* 81: 70–100.
—— (1976b) *The Text and the Language of a Vulgar Latin Chronicle*, London: Institute of Classicial Studies.
—— (1977) *The Vulgar Latin of the Letters of Claudius Terentianus*, Manchester: Manchester University Press.
Dik, S. C. (1978) *Functional Grammar*, Dordrecht: Foris.
—— (1989) *The Theory of Functional Grammar*: I *The Simple Predication*, Dordrecht: Foris.
Haida, R. (1928) *Die Wortstellung in der Peregrinatio ad loca sancta*, dissertation, Breslau.
Harris, M. (1978) *The Evolution of French Syntax. A Comparative Approach*, London: Longman.
Hawkins, J. (1988) 'On explaining some left–right asymmetries in syntactic and morphological universals', in M. Hammond, E. A. Moravcsik, and J. R. Wirth (eds), *Studies in Syntactic Typology*, Amsterdam: Benjamins, 320–57.
Hinojo, G. (1985) 'Del orden de palabras en el *Satiricon*', in J. L. Melena (ed.), *Symbolae Ludovico Mitxelena Septuagenario Oblatae*, Vitoria: Vitoria University Press, 245–54.
Hofmann, J. B. and Szantyr, A. (1965) *Lateinische Syntax und Stilistik*, Munich: Beck.
Jong, J. R. de (1989) 'The position of the Latin Subject', in G. Calboli (ed.), *Subordination and Other Topics in Latin*, Amsterdam: Benjamins, 521–40.
Koll, H. G. (1965) 'Zur Stellung des Verbs im Spätantiken und frühmit-

telalterlichen Latein', *Mittellateinisches Jahrbuch* 2: 241–72.

Kühner, R. and Stegmann, C. (1912–14) *Ausführliche Grammatik der lateinischen Sprache II Stazlehre*, 2 vols, Hanover: Hahnsche Buchhandlung.

Lambrecht, K. (1988) 'Presentational cleft constructions in spoken French', in J. Haiman and S. A. Thompson (eds), *Clause Combining in Grammar and Discourse*, Amsterdam: Benjamins, 135–79.

Linde, P. (1923) 'Die Stellung des Verbs in der lateinischen Prosa', *Glotta* 12: 153–78.

Marouzeau, J. (1949) *L'Ordre des mots dans la phrase latine, III*, Paris: Les Belles Lettres.

Metzeltin, M. (1987) 'Lateinische versus romanische Satzgliederung?', in W. Dahmen, G. Holtus, J. Kramer, and M. Metzeltin (eds), *Latein und Romanisch*, Tübingen: Narr, 246–69.

Muldowney, M. S. (1937) *Word-order in the Works of Saint Augustine*, Washington: Catholic University Press.

Oniga, R. (1988) *I composti nominali latini*, Bologna: Pàtron.

Ostafin, D. M. (1986) 'Studies in Latin word order: a transformational approach', unpublished Ph.D. thesis, University of Connecticut.

Panhuis, D. G. (1982) *The Communicative Perspective in the Sentence. A Study of Latin Word Order*, Amsterdam: Benjamins.

Pinkster, H. (1990) *Latin Syntax and Semantics*, London: Routledge.

Politzer, R. L. (1958) 'On Late Latin word order', *Symposium* 12: 178–82.

Renzi, L. (1984) 'La tipologia dell' ordine delle parole e le lingue romanze', *Linguistica* 24: 27–59.

Schneider, N. (1912) *De verbi in lingua latina collocatione*, Münster: Ex officina Societatis typ. guestfalorum.

Ulrich, M. (1985) *Thetisch und Kategorisch. Funktionen der Anordnung von Satzkonstituenten am Beispiel des Rumänischen und anderer Sprachen*, Tübingen: Niemeyer.

Väänänen, V. (1987) *Le Journal-Epître d'Égérie (Itinerarium Egeriae)*, Helsinki: Academy.

Vincent, N. (1988) 'Latin', in M. Harris and N. Vincent (eds), *The Romance Languages*, London: Croom Helm, 26–78.

Wanner, D. (1987) *The Development of Romance Clitic Pronouns. From Latin to Old Romance*, Berlin: Mouton de Gruyter.

Wolffs, P. (1987) 'Woordvolgorde in de *Acta conventus carthaginiensis*', MA thesis, University of Amsterdam.

8 The collapse and replacement of verbal inflection in Late Latin/Early Romance: how would one know?*

John N. Green

In most manuals of Romance linguistics and philology, and in most histories of individual languages, one finds quite a long section on the elimination of the Latin case and declension systems, probably including discussion of the chronology of the development, the remnants it left (as in the personal pronoun system), the replacement structures, and maybe speculation on the causation of the shift (see, for instance, Elcock 1975: 69–110; Ewert 1943: 125–35; Pope 1952: 308–14). In most of the same manuals, one looks in vain for a comparable section on the loss of the Latin synthetic passive (compare Elcock 1975: 116–17; Ewert 1943: 176; Pope 1952: 332). Many, indeed, content themselves with a mere throw-away remark to the effect that the synthetic passive had disappeared without trace by the time of the first Romance texts. Yet the amount of inflectional morphology lost is at least equal to that lost from nominal declensions, and the concomitant adjustments to the grammatical system are arguably just as extensive. At a more scholarly level, there is a large literature on the loss of nominal inflection, including analysis of minute variations in epigraphic records with a view to establishing the chronology and spatial diffusion of the changes (see, for example, Gaeng 1979, 1984): but the demise of the passive is far less well documented. Is this an unjust neglect? Or is there simply no more to be said? This chapter argues that the neglect is indeed unjust, but that the challenge of interpreting the available data is quite formidable.

Table 8.1 exemplifies the five complete paradigms of the synthetic passive for typical first- and third-conjugation verbs, together, for each, with a simple morphological analysis based on the surface form. A marginally more abstract analysis would account for most of the remaining irregularities, notably those in vowel length. The five tense forms given here represent the imperfective aspect, and

Table 8.1 The Latin synthetic passive

| Past | | Present | | Future |
Indicative	Subjunctive	Indicative	Subjunctive	Indicative
am-ā-ba-r	am-ā-re-r	am-o-r	am-e-r	am-ā-bo-r
am-ā-bā-ris	am-ā-rē-ris	am-ā-ris	am-ē-ris	am-ā-be-ris
am-ā-bā-t-ur	am-ā-rē-t-ur	am-ā-t-ur	am-ē-t-ur	am-ā-bi-t-ur
am-ā-bā-m-ur	am-ā-rē-m-ur	am-ā-m-ur	am-ē-m-ur	am-ā-bi-m-ur
am-ā-bā-minī	am-ā-rē-minī	am-ā-minī	am-ē-minī	am-ā-bi-minī
am-ā-ba-nt-ur	am-ā-re-nt-ur	am-a-nt-ur	am-e-nt-ur	am-ā-bu-nt-ur
reg-ē-ba-r	reg-e-re-r	reg-o-r	reg-a-r	reg-a-r
reg-ē-bā-ris	reg-e-rē-ris	reg-e-ris	reg-ā-ris	reg-ē-ris
reg-ē-bā-t-ur	reg-e-rē-t-ur	reg-i-t-ur	reg-ā-t-ur	reg-ē-t-ur
reg-ē-bā-m-ur	reg-e-rē-m-ur	reg-i-m-ur	reg-ā-m-ur	reg-ē-m-ur
reg-ē-bā-minī	reg-e-rē-minī	reg-i-minī	reg-ā-minī	reg-ē-minī
reg-ē-ba-nt-ur	reg-e-re-nt-ur	reg-u-nt-ur	reg-a-nt-ur	reg-e-nt-ur

are supplemented for the corresponding five paradigms of the perfective by compounds of the past participle and the auxiliary *esse*. Passive morphology occurs frequently in Classical Latin texts and has a range of functions: it is naturally used in passive sentences, both with an agent expressed and without; it quite often serves as a means of intransitivizing an otherwise transitive verb; it is the shape assumed by the class of verbs known as 'deponents' which, despite their morphology, appear to have active meaning; and a subset of its forms, those of the third person singular, are used in impersonal constructions. These functions are, of course, interconnected: passive constructions are usually – and almost by definition – intransitive; the Latin deponent verbs are nearly all intransitive (though often making use of a prepositional or instrumental structure to 'disguise' what seems semantically to be a direct object); truncated passives and impersonals both carry the implicature of human agency, but decline to identify the agent; and so on. Moreover, passive morphology can also convey, for certain groups of verbs and in some tenses, both inchoativity and deontic modality. If Roman citizens had consciously planned to ditch their passive morphology, this list of functions would surely have caused them to reflect on how and where they might find acceptable substitutes. In fact, despite the potential difficulties of replacement, none of the forms in Table 8.1 did survive into any Romance language. Why not?

We might hope for enlightenment from the numerous purported explanations that have been advanced for the loss of nominal inflection. Such explanations seem to me to fall into two major categories: phonetic and structural. The older, purely phonetic, explanations assume that morphological paradigms are not protected from the ravages of phonetic reduction which regularly affect the lexical stock, and that some of the Latin case endings bearing the heaviest functional load coalesced – to the point where syncretism rendered the paradigm unworkable and alternative forms of expression had to be developed. Structural explanations tend to posit a prior morphosyntactic reorganization that left the case endings redundant. A more recent variant envisages a coherent typological shift in the language, moving grammatical information to the front of the noun phrase and allowing the endings to atrophy by normal phonetic reduction (Harris 1980, indeed, argues persuasively that NPs and VPs underwent a parallel reorganization). Aside from the fact that we now know that morphological structures can inhibit the spread of a sound change, the earlier phonetic explanation cannot be true even on its own terms: some of the case endings – notably the genitive plurals in *-arum*, *-orum* – were phonetically robust and would not have been effaced or rendered ambiguous by any known 'sound law'. There is no purely phonetic reason why the Modern Spanish for 'of the doors' should not be /poɾtaɾo/ or 'of the fingers' /dedoɾo/. True, this retention would sometimes have led to stem alternations like /pweɾta ~ poɾtaɾo/ or /θjelo ~ θeloɾo/, but such alternants would do no more than parallel the forms of many stem-changing verbs.

In the case of the synthetic passive, it is immediately apparent that a phonetic explanation could in no way account for its elimination. In Western Romance the endings would be subject to lowering of short /ĭ/ and /ŭ/ to /e/ and /o/ respectively, to voicing of the intervocalic /t/'s and to spirantization of the original intervocalic /b/'s and of the secondary intervocalic /d/'s. (There may also have been stress shifts, but these are harder to predict, especially as proparoxytonic forms survive without syncope elsewhere in the verb system.) And while these cumulative changes would certainly have had an appreciable effect on pronunciation (for instance *amabitur* > Sp. [amaβeðɔɾ]) their effect on the morphological structure of the paradigm would have been precisely nil. Indeed, when viewed purely as morphology, the passive paradigms are remarkably solid and efficient. Notice that there is no syncretism in the person endings; that one set of person endings is used for every tense form and for every conjugation; and that all the paradigms bear a regular relation to the corresponding paradigms of the active voice, including the alternation of theme vowel between the present of the indicative and the subjunctive. The only apparent weakness lies in the future, where the third and fourth conjugations use a different infix from the first and second – a distribution that exactly parallels that of the future active, and which points more securely towards the replacement of both sets of future paradigms than it does of the passive. So, the synthetic passive is morphologically very satisfactory, and immune from structural damage from regular sound change. The explanation of its loss, therefore, must be that it became redundant as a result of changes originating elsewhere in the language, and that it fell out of common usage until, at some point, a generation of speakers simply failed to learn it.

This brings us to the issue of chronology. Throughout the period from the first century AD to the early ninth, the synthetic passive is widely attested and there is no obvious attenuation either of its frequency or of its range of functions. The letters of Claudius Terentianus, dated to the early second century, show examples of passives in both classical and post-classical constructions:

(1)   occasione inuenta spero me celerius aput te uenturum (3: 9–11)

(2)   . . . bracae autem nouae postae sunt. et si quid missurus es inscribe omnia et signa mihi scribe in epistula ne quit mutetur dum adfertur (4: 22–4)

(3)   rogo te, pater, si tibi uidebitur ut mittas mihi inde caligas cori subtalare ed udones par (5: 23–5)

(4)   item litem abuit Ptolemes pater meu sopera uestimenta mea et factum est illi uenire Alexandrie con tirones . . . (8: 20–3)

(5)   Saturninus iam paratus erat exire illa die quando tam magna lites factam est. (8: 26–7)

(See Pighi 1964 for the text, and Adams 1977 for a linguistic commentary.) In (1) the passive participle /inwentaː/ is used in a classical 'ablative absolute' structure; (2) has agentless tensed passives in a classical negative final clause; (3) shows a classical deponent verb used in a slightly elliptical way; in (4) the impersonal structure *factum est illi venire* 'he was obliged to come' illustrates the extension of a more familiar classical model; and (5) contrasts two analytic passives, the first apparently resultative and the second processual.

Examples (6)–(8) are taken from the *Peregrinatio Egeriae*, usually dated to the fifth century (for a detailed commentary, see Väänänen 1987):

(6) Mons autem ipse per giro quidem unus esse videtur; intus autem quod ingrederis, plures sunt, sed totum mons Dei appellatur . . . (2: 5)

(7) Cum luce autem, quia dominica dies est, et proceditur in ecclesia maiore, quam fecit Constantinus . . . (25: 1)

(8) Ac sic ergo maximus labor in ea die suffertur, quoniam de pullo primo vigilatum est ad Anastase et inde per tota die nunquam cessatum est; et sic omnia, quae celebrantur, protrahuntur, ut nocte media post missa, quae facta fuerit in Sion, omnes ad domos suas revertantur. (43: 9)

Even a cursory reading of the text reveals that the travelling nun was very fond of passives, and some of her long sentences, like (8), overflow with them (see Winters 1984). Like Claudius Terentianus, Egeria provides ample evidence of a range of passive types: (6) has two classically deponent verbs and a third, *appellatur*, which seems virtually to have grammaticalized into a deponent; (7) shows a present-tense impersonal; while (8) has impersonals in both present and past, juxtaposed with agentless synthetic passives (*celebrantur, protrahuntur*), a present deponent (*revertantur*), and an agentless analytic passive (*facta fuerit*) which can scarcely be other than perfective in meaning.

Later pre-Romance texts continue to be replete with passive morphology. Examples (9)–(11) are taken respectively from the sixth-century *Lex Salica*, from Gregory of Tours, and from Isidore of Seville:

(9) Si quis . . . X dinarios, qui faciunt solidos Y, culpabilis judicetur.

(10) Sed credo, eum non fuisse aequalis meriti, a quo haec non merebantur audiri. (*St Martin*, 590: 6)

(11) Necesse est ergo in tantis rebus scientiae ingenium, quo proprie singula, convenienterque pronuntientur. Propterea et accentuum vim oportet scire lectorem, ut noverit, in qua syllaba vox protendatur pronuntiantis. (*De lectoribus*, 11: 4; quoted in Wright 1982: 88)

Example (9) is the canonical form of numerous injunctions, embodying a formulaic passive: 'Anyone who [does whatever] shall be judged guilty in the sum of X denarii, which make Y solidi' – in other words, 'shall be fined'. In (10) Gregory has a full passive with agent expressed, combining a passive infinitive with a classically deponent *merebantur*. In (11) Isidore uses two tensed agentless passives (*pronuntientur, protendatur*), both subjunctive, in subordinate clauses that could well have been written in Imperial times. And so on. The question is not whether the synthetic passive survived in the written language of the relevant period, but how to interpret the textual evidence.

At least two issues need resolving. Was the synthetic passive a live, productive form? And do the texts give any indication of the evolution of substitute forms? Muller (1924) takes the attestations literally, and this enables him to identify, with startling precision, the 'date of the disappearance of the synthetic passive . . ., to wit, 780–800' (1924: 85). In order to reach this conclusion, he is obliged to claim that the synthetic passive had no serious rivals, and much of his long article is devoted to dissecting and dismissing ambiguous attestations of what other scholars had taken to be instances of reanalysed analytic passives with *esse*. Likewise he pours scorn on Grandgent's view (1922) that the newer reflexive constructions provided the impetus to oust the synthetic passive. Essential to Muller's case – and he seems never to have doubted it – is a belief in the continuity of an educated spoken Latin up to the time of the Carolingian reforms.

A diametrically opposing view is taken by Politzer (1961), who employs a simple statistical comparison to show that, whereas in Late Latin inflectional endings were subject to all manner of misspellings, in seventh- and eighth-century texts from France and northern Italy, certain inflections, of both verbs and nouns, are used and spelled with total accuracy. They include both synthetic passives and the genitive ending *-orum*. Politzer concludes, from this dramatic change in levels of accuracy, not that the forms had been reinvigorated, but that they were now terminally dead and henceforth had to be learned and used as conscious archaisms.

I believe that Politzer's interpretation is essentially correct and that Muller was misguided in giving such literal credence to textual attestations. As Wright has cogently argued (1982: 41–2), indirect corroboration of Politzer's view can be found in the proportion of space allocated to inflectional morphology in pre-Carolingian grammars, suggesting that 'becoming literate' involved acquiring forms that were foreign to everyday speech. Nevertheless, Politzer's implied chronology of loss must remain tentative until a crucial piece of the jigsaw is in place. It is totally implausible that speakers of Late Latin would have allowed the synthetic passive to collapse before they had available to them a fully operative replacement structure (or structures – recall the range of functions fulfilled by passive morphology in Classical Latin). We ought not to impugn Muller's faith in the face value of attestations until we can either supply evidence of the development of these alternative structures, or, at the very least, explain why they are not attested.

If Muller is indeed wrong, it would be instructive to know why. I suggest that, underlying the radical disagreement of two data-orientated scholars, is a fairly straightforward explanation. In Western Romance, the various functions of the synthetic passive were eventually taken over by a combination of the reflexive passive and the analytic passive conjugated with the auxiliary 'to be' or one of its near-synonyms – Muller was wrong about the reflexive (1924: 86, 87, 89): it did play a structural role in the replacement. But this means that both of the replacements entailed reanalysis of forms which already existed in the language. Reanalysis by slippage is much harder to detect in fragmentary attestations than the emergence of a crisp new morphological structure. So, for instance, the forms *prindrai* and *salvarai* of the *Serments de Strasbourg* offer very solid evidence for the coalescence of an originally analytical periphrasis into a new synthetic paradigm for the future by the mid-ninth century (see Fleischman 1982). The crucial first step in the grammaticalization of reflexives, on the other hand, is their extension to *inanimate* subjects and this – as Muller correctly points out (1924: 89) – involves a metaphor. Grammaticalization cannot be considered complete until the metaphor has ceased to be conscious for the speaker or transparent for the hearer.

Pinpointing the death of a metaphor is notoriously difficult, not least because one that was dead in the mind of the writer can be 'reawakened' under the critical scrutiny of a reader. Even by the Old Spanish period, when most, if not all, of the passive functions of the reflexive had been grammaticalized, we cannot always be sure whether a metaphor is intended or not. In the much-quoted example *non se faze assi el mercado* (*Mio Cid*, 139), scholarly debate usually centres on whether the construction should be interpreted as a passive with postposed subject, or as an impersonal; but even here, it is just conceivable that the author intended a conscious metaphor: 'business deals just don't make themselves like that'. Similarly difficult to categorize are early examples of analytic passives, which usually look like adjectival structures, particularly if they employ one of the less common auxiliaries. Indeed, many of the copious examples adduced by Muller in favour of his own hypothesis that the analytic passive had not yet developed, are precisely the ones advanced by the investigators he is attacking, as proof that it had. For instance, Ernout (1909, cited in Muller 1924: 80–1) quotes a handful of fifth-century examples of *venire* used apparently as the auxiliary to a passive participle in Rhaetian texts. Since this is the very usage that eventually came to predominate in most Rhaetian varieties, such an early attestation is of great interest. But in the crucial example, *si equus de via coactus venerit*, which Ernout had interpreted as 'if the horse has been exhausted by its journey', Muller counters that *venerit* has its full semantic force – 'if the horse comes in exhausted from the road' – which in turn means that *coactus* can only be adjectival and not part of a verbal compound (for further discussion, see Green 1982: 120–1). So, back to our subtitle: 'how would one know?'.

For the history of Spanish, at least, some valuable evidence can be found in the glosses from San Millán, now generally dated to the eleventh century. As can be seen from examples (12)–(15), the original texts are quite liberally studded with synthetic passives and a good proportion of them – though not all – have been glossed.

(12) et abitationes antiquas desolabuntur [nafregarʃan] et non est cui credatur, oratoria dextruuntur [nafregatoʃ] et effunditur [uerteran] sanguinem justorum et fides nulla erit; et maledicent principes suos; et abicinabunt se [alongarʃan] jtinere. (fols 65–6)

(13) timeo ne quando boni christiani cum angelis acceperint uitam eternam nos, quod absit, precipitemur [guec ajutuezdugu] [noʃ nonkaigamus] jngeenna. (fol. 68)

(14) Non auditores legis justificabuntur [non ʃe endrezaran] apud Deum. (fol. 72)

(15) Et repleuimur [noʃ enplirnoʃamus] jn bonis domus tue. (fol. 75)

The glosses mostly involve a change both of lexical item and of morphology, and there is no instance of a synthetic passive being glossed by the synthetic passive of a different lexical item. It seems clear therefore that the passive morphology was causing problems just as much as the unfamiliar vocabulary. So, in (12), we find four agentless passives, three of which are replaced both lexically and grammatically, whereas the original reflexive *abicinabunt se* is replaced lexically but retains its reflexive shape. Most of the glosses preserve scrupulously the grammatical categories other than voice: the present subjunctive of *precipitemur* is kept in (13), and person, number and tense are preserved almost throughout, even where the original could be misleading, as in the incorrectly spelled *repleuimur* of (15). The liberties the glosser takes with the passive voice are therefore doubly noticeable. Observe that the three glossed passives in (12) are each dealt with differently: as a synthetic future reflexive; as a past participle with ellipsis of the auxiliary; and as a future active. In this third instance, the glosser may have been puzzled by the original wording, in which *effunditur sanguinem justorum* is either a high-flown impersonal 'there is a spilling of the blood of the just', or simply a mistake (the nominative *sanguis* was intended); he assumes an impersonal and chooses the vague third person plural /werte'ran/, but that construction belongs to a less formal register than the original.

Notice that five of the glosses cited employ the Romance synthetic future, and that four of them are simultaneously future and reflexive. Since the future was fully grammaticalized by this date (though still admitting intercalated clitics), this intersection of morphosemantic dimensions can only have favoured a grammaticalized interpretation of the associated reflexive. More significant, however, is the fact that three of the glosses involve the substitution of lexical items that were themselves originally metaphors: *nafregar* twice (compare the similar ambiguity of English 'wreck') and *endrezarse* (compare 'to put oneself in the right, straighten oneself out'). In all three instances, a literal reading of the etymological metaphor, though theoretically possible, would sound quirky and offhand in a context that is certainly meant to be serious, if not doom-laden. It would, in other words, provoke a clash of register, of the kind that can be consciously exploited for humorous or other stylistic effect, but which would be highly inappropriate here. The assumption that humour cannot be intended in turn allows us to say that both metaphors were either completely dead or at best in that twilight zone where the original denotation has dwindled to a faint connotation. The coincidence, in *nafregarsan* (12) and *non se endrezaran* (14), of a dead lexical metaphor with a newly synthesized future and a reflexive, argues strongly in favour of a non-metaphorical – that is, grammaticalized – interpretation of the reflexive also.

In this way, by examining the interaction of morphosyntactic and lexical change in discourse, we can hope to build up a configurational view of emerging and disappearing structures. Even so, we must expect variation. In the glosses of Silos, more extensive than those of San Millán and probably of slightly later date, synthetic passives are also widely annotated, but the glosser seems much more comfortable with an analytic passive as the substitute than a reflexive, as can be seen from example (16):

(16) Omne ſacrificium ſordidatum [nafregatu] uel uetuſtatum [obetereiſcitu oſmatu] proditum [aflatu fueret] igni comburatur [kematu ſiegat]. (*De sacrificio uel perceptione eius*, fol. 310)

A mechanism capable of explaining the transmission of a complex change such as the one under consideration, is through a system of registers. It is well known that in Modern Spanish reflexives and analytic passives have many functional overlaps; in many structures they can be mutually substituted without changing the denotational meaning or truth conditions – but that does not make them fully synonymous. The analytic passive with *ser* is virtually restricted to media reporting and to some technical registers; it rarely occurs in spontaneous speech and almost never in creative writing (Green 1975, 1979; Tobón de Castro 1986). It seems plausible that an analogous distribution was also characteristic of Classical Latin, with the morphological passive (which had developed from the Indo-European middle voice) at first neutral in register and the new reflexive constructions either consciously metaphorical or markedly colloquial. This would explain why reflexives that can be interpreted as modern in structure can be found in classical texts (for examples, see Muller 1924: 86–9), but then seem to go underground for several centuries. The later evolution from Latin into Spanish involved a gradual encroachment of the reflexive into the functions and register domains of the Latin passive, which in turn underwent a radical reorganization that eliminated the synthetic paradigms and made explicit an underlying aspectual distinction between process and state via the twin auxiliaries *ser* and *estar*. Examples (12)–(15) show beyond doubt that the reflexive passive had become acceptable in formal registers by the eleventh century (and, given the solemnity of this discourse, probably long before). By the Old Spanish period, the reflexive passive had acquired almost all its modern functions (indeed, in respect of animate subjects, it has subsequently regressed; see Brown 1930), and the later history is largely that of the decline of *ser*-plus-participle constructions, both as perfective forms of intransitive verbs and as analytic passives, to the point where the latter are now effectively confined to formal registers where 'objectivity' is consciously sought.

I suggest that a coherent register system is the missing element in the explanation offered by Politzer for the continuous attestation of the synthetic passive in Early Romance. His reasoning and dating of the effective loss of those forms from the spoken language are both convincing, but we have countered that the loss could not have taken place before adequate substitutes were available. The substitutes become visible in the eleventh-century glosses, but in Politzer's crucial period they belonged to colloquial speech and were considered inappropriate for formal, written discourse. That is the explanation for their very sparse attestation.

Returning now to Claudius Terentianus, I wish to argue that his letters – though certainly literate – are written in a spontaneous and consciously informal register that is rarely attested. This can best be demonstrated by the ease with which they slip into a slightly slangy, jokey translation:

(1a) when I get a chance, hopefully I'll get to you faster
(2a) but I've put my new pants away, and if you're going to send anything, register the lot, and write me a list, so nothing gets tampered with on the way
(3a) please, dad, d'you think you c'd send me some leather trainers and a pair of sneakers?
(4a) this is the row my uncle Tom had about my clothing allowance, and they made him come to Alex with the recruits
(5a) Sonny was all ready to go out that day when an almighty row broke out.

If the passive occurred in this kind of register, we can be virtually certain that it was still alive and well in the spoken language. The two synthetic passives in example (2/2a) especially, occur in a clause of almost throw-away banality: it is inconceivable that they were used as conscious archaisms in a deliberate attempt to 'raise the tone' of the letter. In the *Peregrinatio*, by contrast, the passives seem to play a quite different role. Though Egeria is not exactly stuffy, she is certainly aware of her dignity, and her use of the passive – especially where instances are crowded together as in (8) – seems designed to raise the level of discourse of what is, after all, a travelogue, to that of a more formal, dignified register. She is not, however, averse to an occasional homely touch, as in (17):

(17) . . . iter sic fuit, ut per medium transversaremus caput ipsius vallis et sic plecaremus nos ad montem Dei (2: 4)

This is a curious mixture: a semi-classical result clause with *ut* and two imperfect subjunctives, but embodying the decidedly unclassical reflexive verb: *plecaremus nos* 'we arrived', formerly 'we folded up (our sails)', 'we docked'. In (17) we have a lexical innovation that originally involved both metaphor and ellipsis. The reflexivization of an elliptical structure in which a different object was formerly understood, is clear proof that the original meaning has been lost and that the metaphor is now dead. We cannot be sure whether Egeria intended the construction as humorous, but if so, the humour must arise from an incongruity of structure rather than from the transparency of the metaphor. *Plecarse*, though fully lexicalized, was probably still felt to be colloquial (elsewhere she uses *pervenimus*); but it is the grammaticalized reflexive that most obviously jars – it does not belong to the appropriate register for the context. Here is one of the rare attestations of the colloquial reflexive that went underground during the period when the surviving texts are nearly all high register, and sometimes, as in the Salic Law, largely formulaic.

Of course, from a single example, we cannot infer that Egeria spoke in reflexives and wrote in passives. We can only say, after comparing her usage with that of Claudius Terentianus, that a register shift seems to have taken place and that the ground is laid for the progressive confinement of the synthetic passive to formal registers of the written language. It could have survived for a considerable period in this half-life. There are parallels in Modern Romance: the past historic and the imperfect subjunctive in French are understood and effectively manipulated by all who have been educated to write well, and both sets of forms remain understandable when seen or read aloud, but increasingly few speakers use them spontaneously. The Spanish future subjunctive has gone a stage further and is now effectively confined to a single stylized register, that of legal formulae; it is still comprehensible, but probably only because of its similarity to the imperfect subjunctive.

If the synthetic passive was indeed dead or at least moribund by the early sixth century, we are left with the intriguing question of how it might have been read aloud after it ceased to be part of the spoken language. Wright (1982: 170) suggests that remnant attestations could have been treated as lexical items and given the pronunciation appropriate to the time, though the forms may not have been meaningful. Hence, *cingitur* might have been pronounced ('tseɲedoɾ], and *audietur* [o'jedoɾ]. This is reasonable for texts that were primarily intended for silent consultation, and possibly for parts of the liturgy, which might gain mysterious power from being largely unintelligible to the populace. But the explanation will not suit all contexts: sermons, for example, and particularly those preached in monasteries, were useless if unintelligible. Consider too this example from the Nicene Creed, known to have been in use in

Spain from at least the sixth century:

(18) et [credo] in spiritum sanctum . . . qui cum patre et filio simul
     adoratur et conglorificatur

There is little point in a creed and catechism if those affirming faith
do not understand, at least in general terms, what they are claiming
to believe. By the sixth century, *adoratur* could have been given a
vernacular pronunciation as [aðoˈradɔr], but the very fact that the
lexical root remained in common use and was perfectly understandable might well have caused misunderstanding of the suffix, or even
failure to recognize its inflectional nature. It is harder to guess what
vernacular pronunciation might have been given to *conglorificatur*,
which has never been a lexeme in common use, though, of course,
its root is recognizably close to the (phonetically irregular) noun
gloria. There are a number of possibilities, some mutually
compatible: synthetic passives occurring in this kind of context could
have been repeated simply as meaningless formulae; they could
have survived as comprehensible vocabulary items long after ceasing
to be usable in new contexts; a few specific, and presumably fairly
frequent, forms may have survived with unanalysed lexical meaning;
or, most radical of all, written synthetic passives may have been
substituted wholesale by equivalent intelligible forms when read
aloud.

The evidence of the glosses is that a radical substitution was both
possible and acceptable in certain contexts (see Emiliano, Chapter
18, this volume). The best available hypothesis on the purpose of
the glosses from San Millán and Silos is that they were prompts to
aid oral performance. The sermons, in particular, had to be
intelligible, and one can easily imagine a novice, nervous in advance
of his first public reading, anxiously annotating the parts of the text
that might cause him to stumble. Indeed, it need not have been a
novice, since the concentration of forms to be substituted in some
texts could have unsettled the most experienced of readers. The
problem lies less in the abstractness of the representation than in the
non-iconic order. Many writing systems do not aim for phonemic
accuracy, and speakers of such languages learn – by dint of long
study – to associate pronunciations with abstract shapes. In
languages which do aim for phonemic representation but where a
spelling reform is long overdue, speakers intuit partial regularities,
learn some forms as unanalysable wholes, and otherwise try to avoid
being misled by accidental visual similarities; but they do not usually
have to cope with a typological reorganization as well. It is as

though we had to read *cannot* in English, not as [kɑːnt] – which we do automatically – but as *[ˈnəukən]. So, an eleventh-century Castilian monk would have had to juggle two kinds of abstraction when reading aloud: first, adding phonetic innovations that were not yet reflected in orthography and disregarding minor morphological losses that still were, so that *portas* and most probably *portae* had to be read as [ˈpwɛrtas]; and second, substituting analytic for synthetic structures, which usually involved moving grammatical material from suffixal inflections to preposed particles, so that *portarum* had to be read as [de las ˈpwɛrtas] and *cantatur* as [ɛs kanˈtado] or [se ˈkanta]. The task was proportionately more difficult when the lexical item itself had to be replaced in addition to its morphology, as in (16): *comburatur* > [keˈmado ˈsjeɣa]. The sheer mental agility required must make us wonder how consistently this feat could have been performed, but the evidence of the glosses is that, at least for certain purposes, it was attempted.

If this interpretation of the glosses is correct, we can safely assume that the written synthetic passive had long ceased to be *processed* as inflectional morphology, and much less had been available as a productive form. This accords with the earlier chronology we posited on the basis of working forwards through the surviving Late Latin texts, but it leaves an uncomfortably long period in which we can only guess at the relationship between visual and spoken media. I suggest tentatively that the synthetic passive may have had a longer half-life than is usually supposed. This could be the result of two different tendencies, one implying marginal survival, and the other marginal reintroduction.

In the first case, we have assumed – along with all previous investigators, but nevertheless perhaps wrongly – that once a fully functional alternative had evolved, the synthetic passive became redundant, then archaic, and was finally eliminated, all as a monolithic block. But suppose the temple collapsed leaving a few pillars standing? The likeliest candidates for survival were the forms of the third personal singular, which were by far the most frequent and which fulfilled one important function shared by none of the others – the impersonal. The gloss *uerteran* for the impersonal *effunditur* in (12), in a text where passives are otherwise glossed as reflexives, probably implies that the reflexive passive had not yet acquired the impersonal function – an interpretation consistent with the widespread use of *dicitur* 'it is said' in the San Millán cartularies (Blake, personal communication) and with the persistence of *diz* in Castilian up to the sixteenth century, and in parts of Central

America up to the present day. In the impersonal function, therefore, third-person passive morphology may have systematically outlived the rest of the paradigm in non-literate speech. After the demise of the paradigm, the suffix could no longer be understood as inflectional, but it would be open to reanalysis as derivational. A non-literate member of the congregation hearing the *adoratur* of the creed might accordingly have been able to match it up with a live form of approximately the right meaning. And if not by this route, a clue to meaning would be available via the phonetic similarity of *adoratur* to the flourishing past participle *adorado*, which likewise had passive value (witness the substitution of the unaccompanied past participle *nafregatos* for tensed *dextruuntur* in (12)).

In the second case, if Politzer's chronology is broadly correct, the original texts on which the glosses are superimposed must themselves have been written by clerics for whom the synthetic passive was a dead form. The clerics would have learned the inflections as part of the process of learning to write, and quite separately from acquiring their native language. How were they taught? Certainly with the aid of a grammar, but complex morphology is more easily learned in a chanting recitation than as a purely visual configuration, and it is reasonable to suppose that the learners acquired their morphology *in a contemporary pronunciation*, and that later they continued to associate this 'learning pronunciation' with what they knew to be archaic morphology. This would explain the mis-spelling in (15) of *repleuimur*, which would be the local 'learning pronunciation' of the form spelled *replebimur* in Classical Latin. If so, the passive was no longer quite dead: it had been resurrected, however marginally, as a functional component of the language. Moreover, because it could only be acquired through literacy, and literacy was the property of a small elite, it had also become a sociolinguistic marker.

So, how would one know? By careful sifting of the evidence, by refusing to take every attestation at face value, by projecting forwards from Late Latin and extrapolating backwards from Old Spanish, by relying on a coherent linguistic theory of morphosyntactic change, by hypothesizing the evolution of a complete structure to replace the one in decline, and finally, by speculation and inspired guesswork. It is far from ideal. Wright (1988) justifiably claims that we shall never be able to reconstruct the sociolinguistics of the seventh century. But both Hall (1986) and Herman (1988), from their differing perspectives, argue cogently that the notion of diglossia can be made to elucidate the linguistic perceptions of the period. And it does seem that we can make modest progress by reformulating older concepts of style and register.

NOTE

* Thanks are due to Bob Blake, Bob Coleman, Antonio Emiliano, József Herman, Carol Justus, Harm Pinkster, Sarah Thomason, Tom Walsh, and Roger Wright for helpful comments on the oral presentation at ICHL 9; for reasons of space, I have not been able to incorporate and develop all their suggestions in the detail they merit. My subtitle, of course, is owed to Dorothy Parker who, on being told that President Coolidge had died, retorted unkindly, 'How can they tell?'

BIBLIOGRAPHY

Adams, J. N. (1977) *The Vulgar Latin of the Letters of Claudius Terentianus* (*P. Mich. VIII, 467–72*), Manchester: Manchester University Press.

Brown, C. B. (1930) 'The passive reflexive as applied to persons in the *Primera Crónica General*', *Proceedings of the Modern Language Association of America* 45: 454–67.

Elcock, W. D. (1975) *The Romance Languages*, 2nd edn, rev. J. N. Green, London: Faber & Faber (1st edn 1960).

Ernout, A. (1909) 'De l'Emploi du passif dans la Mulomedicina Chironis', in *Philologie et linguistique: mélanges Louis Havet*, Paris: Hachette, 131–50.

Ewert, A. (1943) *The French Language*, 2nd edn, London: Faber & Faber (1st edn 1933).

Fleischman, S. (1982) *The Future in Thought and Language*, Cambridge: Cambridge University Press.

Gaeng, P. A. (1979) *A Study of Nominal Inflections in Latin Inscriptions* (North Carolina Studies in the Romance Languages and Literatures 182), Chapel Hill: North Carolina University Press.

—— (1984) *Collapse and Reorganization of the Latin Nominal Flection as Reflected in Epigraphic Sources*, Potomac MD: Scripta Humanistica.

Grandgent, C. H. (1922) *An Introduction to Vulgar Latin*, 2nd edn, Boston: Ginn (1st edn 1907).

Green, J. N. (1975) 'On the frequency of passive constructions in modern Spanish', *Bulletin of Hispanic Studies* 52: 345–62.

—— (1979) 'Towards a statistical delimitation of register in Spanish', *International Review of Applied Linguistics* 17: 233–44.

—— (1982) 'The status of the Romance auxiliaries of voice', in N. Vincent and M. Harris (eds), *Studies in the Romance Verb*, London: Croom Helm, 97–138.

Hall, R. A., Jr (1986) 'From bidialectalism to diglossia in early Romance', in B.F. Elson (ed.), *Language in Global Perspective*, Dallas: Summer Institute of Linguistics, 213–22.

Harris, M. B. (1980) 'Noun phrases and verb phrases in Romance',

Transactions of the Philological Society 78: 62–80.
Herman, J. (1988) 'La Situation linguistique en Italie au VIᵉ siècle', *Revue de Linguistique Romane* 52: 55–67.
Muller, H.-F. (1924) 'The passive voice in Vulgar Latin', *Romanic Review* 15: 68–93.
Pighi, G. B. (1964) *Lettere latine d'un soldato di Traiano: PMich 467–472* Bologna: Zanichelli.
Politzer, R. L. (1961) 'The interpretation of correctness in Late Latin texts', *Language* 37: 209–14.
Pope, M. K. (1952) *From Latin to Modern French*, 2nd edn, Manchester: Manchester University Press (1st edn 1934).
Tobón de Castro, L. (1986) 'El uso de la oración pasiva en español', *Thesaurus* 41: 42–58.
Väänänen, V. (1987) *Le Journal-Epître d'Egérie (itinerarium Egeriæ)*. *Etude linguistique* (ASSF, series B, 230), Helsinki: Finnish Academy of Sciences.
Winters, M. E. (1984) 'Steps toward the Romance passive inferrable from the *Itinerarium Egeriae*', *Romance Philology* 37: 445–54.
Wright, R. (1982) *Late Latin and Early Romance in Spain and Carolingian France*, Liverpool: Cairns.
—— (1988) 'La sociolingüística moderna y el romance temprano', in D. Kremer (ed.), *Actes du XVIIIᵉ congrès international de linguistique et de philologie romanes*, vol. V, Tübingen: Niemeyer, 11–18.

Part II

Latin and Romance in ninth-century France

The chapters in Part I considered whether it is plausible to hypothesize the existence of a metalinguistic Latin–Romance distinction before 800. It has long been generally appreciated that the educational and cultural reforms carried out at that time in the Empire of Charlemagne were largely based on a systematic distinction in the Romance-speaking areas, at least in some cultural centres, between two linguistic modes, which are usually identified in modern times as having been between Medieval Latin and Old French. As far as speech was concerned, it seems likely that this eventually obvious-seeming distinction was based in origin on two methods of reading aloud. In several Carolingian centres, certainly, the Church offices were performed at that time, whether or not they had also been previously, according to a method approximating to that used ever since, and probably similar to that used all along in Germanic-speaking areas, in which every written symbol was allocated a corresponding oral sound. Other texts at that time could have been, and perhaps usually would have been, read aloud in a manner more closely resembling the colloquial habits of ordinary Old French Romance vernacular. This distinction probably inspired the different writing system used in the earliest texts now said to be in Old French.

The papers in Part II consider the nature and consequences of the existence of the distinction in Old French-speaking areas in the ninth century, whenever it began and whatever it was thought to have been a distinction between. I argue myself, mainly on theoretical historical-linguistic grounds, that the distinction can only have been introduced intentionally rather than evolving naturally, and the Carolingian scholars seem the most likely people to have done that. Two chapters here go further, and doubt whether the distinction applied at all clearly even in that century. Van Uytfanghe looks at ninth-century textual evidence of ostensibly metalinguistic comments and inclines to the view that no clear distinction can have been made or felt. McKitterick considers the implications of the many edicts and decisions of administrators of the time and concludes that it seems to have been a general assumption that reading written texts aloud would have been sufficient for their content to have been intelligible to the illiterate, which suggests that (whatever the phonetics) the texts were not written in an irredeemably foreign language for Old French speakers. Heene, on the other hand, arguing from detailed hagiographical evidence in texts whose nature changes between the eighth and ninth centuries, inclines to the view that there was a clear distinction made in the ninth century. Banniard compares the Romance-speaking part with the Germanic-speaking part of the Empire, showing that even in the latter case, where the two languages concerned were obviously different, it needed a considerable effort of Rhabanus Maurus' scholarly imagination to appreciate the validity of any writing system other than the traditional one. In so far as there is a consensus in this part, it is that the existence of separate reading styles, and later of tentatively experimental new writing styles, led to ninth-century France being an area of considerable metalinguistic confusion, with the conceptual separating out of the coexisting modes into two separate languages still lying in the future.

9 The conceptual distinction between Latin and Romance: invention or evolution?

Roger Wright

Several historians have recently been arguing that early developments in human society, such as agriculture, were often consequences of human inventiveness rather than of any kind of
automatic evolutionary process (cp. Van der Leeuw and Torrence
1989). I have argued before (Wright 1983) that historians of
language need to pay more attention to the philosophy of history,
and this distinction between evolution and invention seems a crucial
one to make within our own historical discipline.

Some diachronic linguistic developments certainly occur in an
evolutionary manner, without any speakers particularly willing them
into existence. But several other developments are the consequences of a decision made by one or more speakers, and these
changes can sensibly be regarded as in origin cases of invention. The
latter are sometimes assumed to be peripheral to historical
linguistics. Lass, for example, accepted 'without argument' that
'change does not involve (conscious) human purpose' (1980: 82).
Chomsky has also exiled such phenomena from consideration *a
priori*: 'each actual "language" will incorporate a periphery of
borrowings, historical residues, inventions, and so on, which we can
hardly expect to – and indeed would not want to – incorporate
within a principled theory of Universal Grammar' (1981: 8).
Fortunately there is no compulsion for us all to be necessarily
interested exclusively in universals; and even if we are, linguistic
inventiveness can plausibly be seen as being as much of a human
universal, in the sociohistorical development of languages, as is the
linguistic creativity that Chomsky himself has so often stressed,
despite the fact that not every individual invention exists in every
language community. This chapter suggests that one such conscious
decision concerns the separate establishment of systematically
different levels of language for different social purposes; specifically,

that it still seems most likely that the conceptual distinction between Latin and the contemporary Romance languages of the Early Middle Ages can only have been the result of an innovation made on purpose in a particular historical context, that of the Carolingian renewal of Christian intellectual life, rather than the inevitable result of a gradual evolution. I disagree, therefore, with R. A. Hall's explicit view that 'A diglossic situation would have arisen anyhow, Carolingian "reform" or no "reform"' (1986: 215); there was nothing inevitable or evolutionary about the arrival of the eventually clear diglossia between Latin and the Romance languages in the later Middle Ages. The Carolingian scholars did not merely 'become conscious that Romance and Latin were different' (Michael 1988), as has often been suggested; they invented the difference.

Some historical developments can only have been invented on purpose, the creations of an individual genius rather than the result of unconscious evolutions by the mass of the human community. The wheel, the rowing boat, coinage, the bow and arrow, the internal combustion engine, for example; and within linguistic history, writing. Ong (1982: 83–5), Harris (1986), and others argue that writing can only have been an invention. Historical linguists have tended to shy away from this conclusion, using some non-committal and indeterminate phrasing such as 'the development of writing' (as in Jeffers and Lehiste 1979: 161), but writing cannot just have turned up unasked and unpremeditated. The idea of writing at all was a giant step for mankind, comparable to the invention of the wheel, and so subsequently were the successive elaborations of ideographic script based on the lexicon, syllabic and then phonemic scripts based on the phonology, punctuation, diacritics, the establishment of spaces between written words, shorthand, written tone curves, the International Phonetic Alphabet, the initial teaching alphabet, word processors, voice synthesizers, modems, etc. They were all inventions, which would not be here at all if some enterprising character had not thought of the idea. One inventor is enough, though: we can watch, in a historical atlas, how the idea of writing spread geographically from its Sumerian origins of c. 3500 BC (e.g. McEvedy and Woodcock 1967: 26, 36, 44, 56). Subsequently, new systems of recording a language do not just emerge unbidden either; for example, the distinctively non-Latinate spellings of the Romance languages were intentionally elaborated for a practical purpose (as were shorthand and the International Phonetic Alphabet, etc.). In *Late Latin and Early Romance* (Wright 1982) it was suggested that the new writing system which we now call written

Old French was consciously first elaborated for a particular purpose in a specific context; that is, to assist those speakers of Germanic who knew how to read Medieval Latin aloud to use that knowledge to read aloud in a manner that might be intelligible to speakers of Old French. Here too, as Elcock showed long ago (1961), we can see on a map how the initial invention, in this case of writing in a manner intended to give rise to an intelligible Romance reading, was imitated successively in geographical areas spreading outwards from its north-eastern French origins; one inventor followed successively by adjacent imitators.

Sinclair's 1987 article entitled 'Language: a gift of nature or a home-made tool?' suggests reasonably that language is both. Many linguistic developments are undoubtedly of an unpremeditated type that cannot seriously be thought of as invention. Most sound changes are unintentional. Indeed, if teleology is consciously invoked by speakers during the course of a sound change, the aim seems generally to be that of preventing the change taking place at all. Some phonetic changes, however, have proved to be explicable by appeal to conscious or semi-conscious phenomena such as phonosymbolism (e.g. Malkiel 1987), to conspiracies to conform to intuited phonetic templates (Pharies 1986), or to desires to escape from undesirable homonymy, and people of unusually explicit metalinguistic awareness may perhaps initiate these on purpose. But these changes are a minority, and Pagliuca and Mowrey (1987) could well be right to see most sound changes as being simply the consequences of unpremeditated relaxation of muscles round the mouth. It is thus understandable that such phenomena as the precise conditions of a conditioned change, or the detailed strength hierarchies that determine the chronology of related changes (as in Harris-Northall 1990; Cravens 1988), need to be painstakingly unearthed by specialist linguists long after the event, for they are neither the conscious inventions of a human mind nor accessible to native intuition.

Many grammatical changes are similarly unintentional. The replacement of the Latin case system with Romance prepositions, changes in statistically preferred word orders, the creation of compound prepositions from adverb + preposition sequences, for example, seem to be probably, though not necessarily, best regarded as unintended and evolutionary. And yet Ridruejo (1988) has argued rationally that morphosyntactic innovations can easily be intentional. Many semantic changes are also gradual and evolutionary; those that involve a shift in prototypical reference points, for example (e.g. Wright 1985), or those that occur when a super-ordinate term comes increasingly to be used with the reference of one of its hyponyms (e.g. Wright, 1990). Some semantic changes can be established on purpose, however. Scientists, philosophers, or social reformers often have recourse to the establishment of their own definitions of words that are already in use with a related but slightly less clear or defined meaning, and if they have sufficient authority they can in time succeed in changing the meaning of the word thereby. Einstein did not invent the word *relativity*, but he invented the definition of it that is now its central meaning. New words, that is, lexical change, are generally conceded to be, at least sometimes, inventions. The only time the word 'invention' is used in Jeffers and Lehiste is in this connection (1979: 130: 'the vocabulary of a language is continually being enriched by the invention of new words'). Borrowing of foreign words is similarly also in the first place an individual initiative.

Individual initiative, in short, has a higher place in most types of linguistic development than it is sometimes given credit for; as the Milroys say (1985: 345), 'it is not languages that innovate: it is speakers who innovate'. For every systematic feature of language, however obvious it may subsequently appear, there must have been a first time. Hurford's (1987) discussion of the psychological history and present basis of numerals is illuminating in the present context. Numerals seem a natural linguistic feature to us now. But they were not always there in language. Only up to the number three can the human brain perceive number without calculating it. Above that number, humans have invented their systems of counting, in a long sequence of successive small progressions whose complexity and rationale vary from community to community (and thus from language to language). Above three, all numeral systems are in origin invented, as was the wheel. The method of counting in tens, the *hundred*, the *thousand*, the *million*, are all inventions, and simultaneously conceptual and linguistic inventions. Hurford does not come up to date, but in our own time both the concept and the lexical item of the *light year*, the *parsec*, the *googol*, are all human inventions of the same kind. In a millennium's time the concept and the word *googol* (a 1 followed by a hundred noughts) will seem as commonplace to English speakers as the *hundred* does now. They were individual inventions once, but once invented anyone can learn them, and they come to seem self-evident.

New linguistic standardization of all types, not merely the orthographic, requires a conscious standardizer (as Marcos Marín has demonstrated for Spanish: Marcos Marín 1979; Marcos Marín and Sánchez Lobato 1988). The prescriptiveness of all prescriptive rules is invented by grammarians who think they perceive a moral order in grammatical details; the demanding peculiarities of the Latin rhetorical cursus, metrical poetry, and indeed, as Norberg (e.g. 1958) has shown, Latin rhythmical poetry, are examples of this. The detail of the morphology required of written Latin was prescribed by grammarians (especially Donatus); and so, I suggest, were the details of the peculiar and artificial Late Medieval system used for reading written texts aloud even in Romance-speaking areas, that is, producing one specified sound for each already-written letter (or digraph). All reading involved reading aloud. It seems obvious and natural to read Latin that way now, as obvious and natural as it is to count in tens. But such a method of reading aloud one's native language is totally unnatural. Anglo-Saxon speakers, however, at least since Bede, had learnt to read the same texts, in what was to them a foreign language, aloud in that way; they brought this system with them to the Continent, and there, as a result of using such pronunciations in speech as well, they were at times unintelligible to Romance speakers (as Boniface was to the Pope). Whenever and wherever this reading system began to be required of native Romance speakers, its prescriptive rules must have been in origin introduced from some non-evolutionary source. Most modern sociolinguists, including Schlieben-Lange (1982) on Romance, suggest that systems of diglossia need not only to be intentionally set up, but also to be continually reinforced subsequently – mainly by teaching the high variety in the education system – in order to exist at all, and do not arise naturally otherwise. What exist otherwise, and do indeed evolve unplanned, in a single wide speech community, are complex patterns of sociolinguistic variation.

Such patterns as modern sociolinguistic theory would lead us to expect to find anyway, particularly as concerns the relationship between speech and writing (e.g. Tannen 1982; Traugott and Romaine 1985; Pellegrini and Yawkey 1984; etc.), seem to be sufficient to explain attested phenomena from pre-Carolingian Romance Europe, largely reconciling reconstructed Romance with the (unamended) manuscript evidence. Fontaine (1981), Varvaro (1984) and others have recently been in essence envisaging such a state, in which the many and varied registers of spoken and written language were still even so part of the same language, and read texts such as sermons were given vernacular phonetics in the ordinary way, as they always are now. Sabatini (1983: 170) picked up this interpretation of the evidence with enthusiasm, since in this way the many conscientious pre-Carolingian preachers can be at last thought to have been intelligible to their audiences, the scholars who continually urged priests then to preach can be absolved from the charge of asking for the impossible; and hundreds of thousands of Early Romance-speaking individuals can recover their linguistic self-respect, their voice, their ability to understand their priests, indeed, their very participation in society in pre-Carolingian Romance Europe; as opposed to the idea, still widely held – e.g. by Coleman (1987: 50) – that, 'of course', pre-Carolingian Christian congregations found their services incomprehensible. The monolingual view of Early Romance Europe seems to be confirmed, for example, by two recent independent studies on Gregory the Great (Herman 1988; Banniard 1986), which both conclude that, unlike some of the Carolingian scholars, Gregory had no clear conceptual distinction between Latin and Romance in his mind, of the kind required for diglossia to exist; the question just did not arise, and he cheerfully wrote sermons intended to be read aloud intelligibly to the illiterate. This question apparently never arose in the mind of Isidore of Seville either (cp. Fontaine 1981: 776). If Gregory and Isidore did not know about such a distinction, it cannot have existed in the sixth and seventh centuries.

The hypothesis of Romance monolingualism also solves the problem that worried Bullough (1985: 285, 287), concerning what language Charlemagne spoke with the Italian scholars at his court in the 780s: they all spoke Romance, in a mutually intelligible, if not similar, manner. Versteegh (e.g. 1986: 426, 447) is the only historical sociolinguist I know of explicitly to disagree with this view. Versteegh, unlike most historical linguists (cp. Wright 1987: 621), sees lack of change as normal, and thus not in need of any explanation, and change therefore as necessarily externally caused. In his view 'high' status, within a postulated nascent state of diglossia, accrues inevitably to those speakers who remain unaffected by the externally caused deviations which lead to what he sees as pidginization in the speech of the socially less prestigious, such that this high level, reinforced by grammarians, naturally survives in formal situations even when the spread of the pidginized (in this case, Romance) variety means that the 'correct' variety is hardly anyone's native speech any more. Hence, to Versteegh, many societies are *de facto* diglossic, without anyone having willed that diglossia into existence. But the supposed inevitability of the survival of a Latinate level of speech alongside evolving Early Romance speech, which seems to have been based on an assumption that educated people do not get involved in sound changes, has been untenable as a supposition ever since Labov and others established that (in the words of the Milroys, 1985: 343) 'speakers who lead sound change are those with the highest status in their local communities as measured by a social class index'. That is how archaisms get stigmatized (cp. Silva 1988: 164); *pace* Versteegh, archaism rarely has automatic high prestige. (Diez rejected Versteegh's approach in 1826, in fact; see Diez 1975: 277–82.)

The tradition of reading Latin aloud as an artificial language, a sound for each written letter, in the Romance-speaking world as everywhere else, has the air of being obvious, and as though it had been forever present. But someone, somewhere, had to establish that as a standardized norm, for it could not arise naturally in a native Romance community. There was a kind of continuity through the years between Carolingian and Imperial Latin in the vocabulary and syntax of the educated, for these could always be resurrected from classical books by antiquarians (Fontaine 1981: 786), but what we now think of as traditional Latin pronunciation had no such direct continuity with that of the Empire (cp. Lüdtke 1988: 63, on [-m], for example). That is why the invention of the need for what we now call Latinate pronunciation (with the sounds determined by the spelling) is the key issue here. As the historian Hobsbawm (1983: 1) pointed out, 'traditions which appear or claim to be old are often quite recent in origin and sometimes invented'.

In *Late Latin and Early Romance* the chapter which recounted the details of the suggested source of the Latin–Romance distinction, located in the latter years of Charlemagne's reign, was entitled 'The invention of Medieval Latin'. This use of the word *invention* has been criticized (e.g., by Godman, 1985: 146). But I shall stick by it. That chapter argued in detail that the Carolingian scholars established the phonetic distinction round the year AD 800 as part of the educational reforms, in order initially to standardize the performance of the Church offices, and that the Latin–Romance distinction is only clearly felt subsequent to those innovations. Charlemagne and Alcuin knew they were introducing something revolutionary with their edict *De litteris colendis* (which added the study of *litterae* to the requirements of the already revolutionary *Admonitio generalis* of 789), in order that clerics should impress their hearers by speaking well (*bene loquendo*) when reading or singing written texts (*in legendo seu cantando*) (Wallach 1959: 204), and such reading proficiency becomes a requirement of the *litterati* thereafter (cp. Stock 1983: 27). The onus is on Godman and Versteegh, and any other scholars who are sure that the clear conceptual distinction was established earlier, to suggest who else did it, when, where, how, and why.

The elements that came to constitute Medieval Latin existed before Alcuin's arrival at Charlemagne's court – the writing system existed everywhere, the reading aloud system existed in Anglo-Saxon England – but their combination and conceptual opposition to vernacular was something new and positive. In Hurford's words (1987: 12), 'invention typically involves a creative act of putting together existing elements (which may or may not be physical) in some novel way' (also Schon 1967: 87, 192). The concept and combined attributes of Medieval Latin were thus invented out of pre-existing ingredients. Rabin's study (1985) has shown how the same kind of conscious invention of a diglossic system happened also in ninth-century Byzantine Greek, in eighth- and ninth-century Arabic, and in the Hebrew written in Moslem countries in the tenth century. This was an internationally felt psychological need; not confined to the Latin–Romance civilizations, but consciously pursued in culturally less peripheral areas also. In other socio-linguistically comparable societies, diglossia has only existed if it was consciously established, in a particular historical circumstance, and was then educationally reinforced, as with katharevousa Greek, and does not exist in any society if no one has invented it there (see e.g. Silva 1988: 178; Rotaetxe 1988: 60–1). The subsequent, and probably consequent, emergence of distinctively and intentionally non-Latinate writing systems for recording Romance vernaculars were – can only have been – experimental inventions by enterprising and innovative linguists, even if they were based on some existing approximations, and even if we do not now know who the inventors were. Perhaps they were Nithard at Strasbourg for the elaboration of the Oaths and Hucbald at St Amand for the *Eulalie* sequence; but even if not, those advances must have been made by someone, in the same way as shorthand was invented by Sir Isaac Pitman. The Riojan glosses were also elaborated for a purpose, and perhaps it was to aid a Catalan visitor to read aloud in local phonetics (Wright 1986). In any event, they did not just evolve.

CONCLUSION

Probably at all levels we have linguistic innovators of the past to thank for the invention of some of the structural distinctions that are subsequently taken for granted. Few people have the capacity to invent, but some do, and the capacity that we all have to learn from others is more plausibly seen as innate than is the actual concept demarcated by the inventor. After all, even a language-acquisition device can only acquire things that already exist. Socially purposive language planning is the result of an intentional initiative. It continues to seem probable that the Latin–Romance distinction of the Later Middle Ages was created through such language planning, and that it would not have existed if it had not been invented. I entirely take the point made by McKitterick (1989: 12–22) that through the ninth and tenth centuries the distinction took a long time to become generally felt (maybe at first it was only at Tours and centres influenced by Tours); but this is how it began.

BIBLIOGRAPHY

Banniard, M. (1986) '*Iuxta uniuscuiusque qualitatem*: l'écriture médiatrice chez Grégoire le Grand', *Colloques internationaux du CNRS: Grégoire le Grand*, Paris: CNRS, 477–88.

Bullough, D. (1985) '*Aula Renovata*: the Carolingian Court before the Aachen Palace', *Proceedings of the British Academy* 71: 267–301.

Chomsky, N. (1981) *Lectures on Government and Binding*, Dordrecht: Foris.

Coleman, R. (1987) 'Vulgar Latin and the diversity of Christian Latin', in J. Herman (ed.), *Latin vulgaire – latin tardif*, Tübingen: Niemeyer, 37–52.

Cravens, T. D. (1988) 'Consonant strength in the Romance dialects of the Pyrenees', in D. Birdsong and J.-P. Montreuil (eds), *Advances in Romance Linguistics*, Dordrecht: Foris, 67–88.

Diez, F. (1975) *La Poésie des Troubadours*, Geneva: Slatkine, reprint of 1845 edn, Paris: Lafitte (a translation of *Die Poesie Des Troubadours* (1826), Zwickau: Schumann).

Elcock, W. D. (1961) 'La Pénombre des langues romanes', *Revista Portuguesa de Filologia* 2: 1–19.

Fontaine, J. (1981) 'De la Pluralité a l'unité dans le "latin carolingien"?', *Nascita dell'Europa ed Europa Carolingia: un equazione da verificare*, Spoleto: Centro Italiano di Studi sull'Alto Medioevo, 765–818.

Godman, P. (1985) *Poetry of the Carolingian Renaissance*, London: Duckworth.

Hall, R. A. (1986) 'From bidialectalism to diglossia in Early Romance', in B.F. Elson (ed.), *Language in Global Perspective*, Dallas: Summer Institute of Linguistics, 213–22.

Harris, R. (1986) *The Origin of Writing*, London: Duckworth.

Harris-Northall, R. (1990) *Weakening Processes in the History of Spanish Consonants*, London: Routledge.

Herman, J. (1988) 'La Situation linguistique en Italie au VIe siècle', *Revue de Linguistique Romane* 52: 55–67.

Hobsbawm, E. (1983) 'Inventing traditions', in E. Hobsbawm and T. Ranger (eds), *The Invention of Tradition*, Cambridge: Cambridge

112   *Roger Wright*

University Press, 1–14.
Hurford, J. (1987) *Language and Number*, Oxford: Blackwell.
Jeffers, R. J. and Lehiste, I. (1979) *Principles and Methods for Historical Linguistics*, Cambridge, MA: MIT Press.
Lass, R. (1980) *On Explaining Language Change*, Cambridge: Cambridge University Press.
Lüdtke, H. (1988) 'Metafonía y neutro de materia', in M. Ariza, A. Salvador, and A. Viudas (eds), *Actas del primer congreso internacional de historia de la lengua española*, Madrid: Arco, 61–9.
McEvedy, C. and Woodcock, J. (1967) *The Penguin Atlas of Ancient History*, Harmondsworth: Penguin.
McKitterick, R. (1989) *The Carolingians and the Written Word*, Cambridge: Cambridge University Press.
Malkiel, Y. (1987) 'Integration of phonosymbolism with other categories of language change', in Anna Giacalone Ramat, Onofrio Carruba, and Giuliano Bernini (eds), *Papers from the Seventh International Conference on Historical Linguistics*, Amsterdam: Benjamins, 373–406.
Marcos Marín, F. (1979) *Reforma y modernización del español*, Madrid: Cátedra.
Marcos Marín, F. and Sánchez Lobato, J. (1988) *Lingüística aplicada*, Madrid: Síntesis.
Michael, I. (1988) Review of Wright 1982, *Modern Language Review* 83: 925–6.
Milroy, J. and Milroy, L. (1985) 'Linguistic change, social network and speaker innovation', *Journal of Linguistics* 21: 339–84.
Norberg, D. (1958) *Introduction à l'étude de la versification latine*, Stockholm: Almqvist & Wiksell.
Ong, W. J. (1982) *Orality and Literacy*, London: Methuen.
Pagliuca, W. and Mowrey, R. (1987) 'Articulatory evolution', *Papers from the Seventh International Conference on Historical Linguistics*, Amsterdam: Benjamins, 459–72.
Pellegrini, A. and Yawkey, T. (eds) (1984) *The Development of Oral and Written Language in Social Contexts*, Norwood NJ: Ablex.
Pharies, D. A. (1986) *Structure and Analogy in the Playful Lexicon of Spanish*, Tübingen: Niemeyer.
Rabin, C. (1985) 'Massorah and *Ad Litteras*', *Hebrew Studies* 26: 81–91.
Ridruejo, E. (1988) 'El cambio sintáctico a la luz del funcionalismo coseriano', in H. Thun (ed.), *Energeia und Ergon, II*, Tübingen: Narr, 121–33.
Rotaetxe Amusátegi, K. (1988) *Sociolingüística*, Madrid: Síntesis.
Sabatini, F. (1983) 'Prospettive sul parlato nella storia linguistica italiana', in F. A. Leoni, D. Gambera, F. Lo Piparo and R. Simone (eds), *Italia linguistica: idee, storia, strutture*, Bologna: Il Mulino, 167–201.
Schlieben-Lange, B. (1982) 'Sociolinguistique et linguistique romane', *Actes del XVIe congrés internacional de lingüística i filología romàniques, I*, Palma: Moll, 209–15 and 223–4.
Schon, D. A. (1967) *Invention and the Evolution of Ideas*, London: Tavistock.
Silva Corvalán, C. (1988) *La sociolingüística: teoría y análisis*, Madrid: Alhambra.

Sinclair, H. (1987) 'Language: a gift of nature or a home-made tool?', in S. Modgil and C. Modgil (eds), *Noam Chomsky: Consensus and Controversy*, New York: Falmer, 173–80.

Stock, B. (1983) *The Implications of Literacy*, Princeton: Princeton University Press.

Tannen, D. (1982) 'Oral and literate strategies in spoken and written narratives', *Language* 58: 1–21.

Traugott, E. C. and Romaine, S. (1985) 'Some questions for the definition of "style" in socio-historical linguistics', *Folia Linguistica Historica* 6: 7–39.

Van der Leeuw, S. and Torrence, R. (eds) (1989) *What's New?*, London: Unwin.

Varvaro, A. (1984) 'Omogeneità del latino e frammentazione della Romània', in E. Vineis (ed.), *Latino volgare, latino medioevale, lingue romanze*, Pisa: Giardini, 11–22.

Versteegh, K. (1984) *Pidginization and Creolization: the Case of Arabic*, Amsterdam: Benjamins.

—— (1986) 'Latinitas, Hellenismos, Arabiyya', *Historiographia Linguistica* 13: 425–48.

Wallach, L. (1959) *Alcuin and Charlemagne*, Ithaca NY: Cornell University Press.

Wright, R. (1982) *Late Latin and Early Romance in Spain and Carolingian France*, Liverpool: Cairns.

—— (1983) 'Unity and diversity among the Romance languages', *Transactions of the Philological Society*: 1–22.

—— (1985) 'Indistinctive features (facial and semantic)', *Romance Philology* 38: 275–92.

—— (1986) 'La función de las glosas de San Millán y de Silos', *Actes du XVIIe congrès international de linguistique et de philologie romanes, IX*, Aix-en-Provence: University of Provence, 209–19.

—— (1987) 'The study of semantic change in Early Romance (Late Latin)', in Anna Giacalone Ramat, Onofrio Carruba, and Giuliano Bernini (eds), *Papers from the Seventh International Conference on Historical Linguistics*, Amsterdam: Benjamins, 619–28.

—— (1988) 'La sociolingüística moderna y el romance temprano', in Dieter Kremer (ed.), *Actes du XVIIIe congrès international de linguistique et de philologie romanes, V*, Tübingen: Niemeyer, 11–18.

—— (1990) 'Semantic change in Romance words for "cut"', *Papers from the Eighth International Conference on Historical Linguistics*, Amsterdam: Benjamins, 553–61.

10 The consciousness of a linguistic dichotomy (Latin–Romance) in Carolingian Gaul: the contradictions of the sources and of their interpretation*

Marc Van Uytfanghe

'Confusion reigns in the spirits and the most opposite theses are defended with the greatest faith in the world.' With this undeceiving statement Robert de Dardel characterized, thirty years ago, the scientific debate about the periodization of the transition of Latin into diverse Romance languages (Dardel 1958: 24). We can only adhere to his judgement when we find that some let the 'birth' of the Romance languages go back as far as the epoch of the Roman colonization of the concerned territory, whereas others (particularly Henry Francis Muller and his school) extended the (Latin) linguistic unity of Romania till the beginning of the ninth century (Van Uytfanghe 1976: 23–35).

Granted, Dag Norberg found an apparently happy compromise formula, by which the spoken language was certainly Latin before 600, and certainly Romance after 800; for the intermediate period, as he says, we have the choice, as long as we are aware that a precise limit appears to be impossible to fix. Afterwards, however, the second tendency has been fortified again in so far as several scholars (e.g. Helmut Lüdtke, Francesco Sabatini, D'Arco Silvio Avalle, Oronzo Parlangéli) have not only rejected the idea of a precocious formation of Romance languages separate from Latin, but also admit a continuity, on the level of the written language, between the *scriptae latinae rusticae* of the seventh and eighth centuries and the first Romance *scriptae* (Van Uytfanghe 1976: 30–1, 86–8; 1977: 79–84).

The book of Roger Wright (1982) that lies at the basis of our 'special session' drives home all this in an original way, by proposing that Latin and Romance never stopped being identical, purely and simply, before the Carolingian Reform had literally 'invented' Medieval Latin by the imposing of new norms of elocution for the reciting in public of religious texts. In the long run this decisive step would lead to a Latin–Romance dichotomy that, in France, would only set in at the end of the eleventh century.

Although it is true that the phonetic relevance of Alcuin's reforms has been doubted, especially by Michel Banniard (1985), one thing remains certain: the famous question of Henry Francis Muller (1921), of Ferdinand Lot (1931), of Dag Norberg (1966), and of Joseph Herman (1967: 114–21) – 'at what time did they cease speaking Latin (in Gaul)?' was, as Michael Richter (1983) said, 'a question that was put in the wrong way', and which had to be replaced by this one: 'at what time did they cease *understanding* Latin?'. I would like to add, for my part: 'and have they become conscious of speaking a *language* different from Latin, and not only another *level* of language?'

If we put aside the conviction that the so-called Carolingian Renaissance has something to do with it, we find again a fundamental diversity in the answers given to this question inspired by historical sociolinguistics. For some, indeed, the *reformatio in melius* designed by Alcuin brought to light a linguistic situation that had developed in the preceding period. For some others, on the contrary, the reform is to be situated exactly at the starting-point of a new linguistic evolution. Thus, already according to Paul Zumthor (1959: 217), the texts of the eighth and ninth centuries still express an opposition of styles, that only very slowly changed into an opposition of languages (Latin–vernacular Romance). Roger Wright's book shares the same perspective, but it has the originality of concentrating everything on the effect of the 'alienation' caused by the new norms of elocution.

My own thesis is that the diversities mentioned come quite naturally from the evidence itself that is able to inform us about the sociolinguistic situation of Gaul in the ninth century, because it lends itself to contradictory interpretations. I will examine some with you.

1 Let us begin with the name itself of the Romance language. The syntagm *lingua Romana* (*eloquium Romanum, facundia Romana,* etc.) has always meant the Latin language, even 'a sort of better Latin' and then 'the language that everybody claimed to speak' (Muller 1923: 10; Vercauteren 1932: 82; Díaz y Díaz 1951: 36–7, 41–3). But in 813, Canon 17 of the Council of Tours attests for the first time the formula *rustica Romana lingua*, a language that it puts on the same footing as the *Thiotisca lingua*, i.e. the Old German

spoken by the Franks. The Council of Mainz in 847 (Canon 2) takes up this passage, whereas, in a verse of the poem he composed on the death of Saint Adelard of Corbie (d. 826), Paschase Radbert (d. about 860) puts both the *rustica Romana* and the *Latina lingua* side by side.[1] For Nithard the syntagm *lingua Romana* by itself means the language in which, on 14 February 842, Louis the German pronounced 'his' Oath of Strasbourg in order to be understood by the soldiers of Charles the Bald. Here, the *lingua Romana* seems to be sufficiently different from the *lingua Latina* to be translated commonly by 'Romance language'.[2]

There are, however, other texts in which *lingua Romana* continues to be used with the sense of 'Latin language'. In his biography of Charlemagne (about 833), Einhard still understands that *Latine scribere* is done in the *Romana locutio*.[3] There are two versions of the 'Life of Saint Mummolenus' (d. 686?), successor of Saint Eligius (d. 660) in the see of the bilingual diocese of Noyon-Tournai. From the historical examination of the hagiographical sources, we know that they evidently bear witness to the epoch of their authors rather than to the epoch of the hero himself. The episcopal election of the saint, who was a native of Constanz, a Teutonic-speaking area, is related to his linguistic knowledge, indicated as follows in one of his 'Lives' (BHL 6025): 'praevalebat non tantum in Theutonica, sed etiam in Romana lingua'. And in the other one (BHL 6026): 'et Latina et Theutonica praepollebat facundia'.[4]

Whatever may be the sense of *Romana lingua* in the first *Vita*, it has been shown that it dates from the eleventh or the twelfth century, and that the second is the older one, i.e. going back as far as the ninth century (Van der Essen 1907: 375–84). It is true that this author of the end of the ninth century adds the following explanation: 'Ecclesia siquidem Noviomensis Romana vulgariter lingua, Tornacensis vero Theutonica, maiori ex parte utitur.'[5] Provided that this passage is not a later interpolation, as the Bollandists thought, it is clear that *Romana lingua uti* cannot purely and simply mean 'to use the Romance language', for otherwise the hagiographer could have done without the adverb *vulgariter*, which exactly means the *way* the Christian people of Noyon speak this *lingua Romana*.

This synonymy or quasi-synonymy of *Latinus* and *Romanus* is also felt by authors who themselves do not belong to the *Romania*. A monk of Werden, who in the second half of the ninth century wrote the third 'Life of Saint Liudger' (d. 809), first Bishop of Münster, makes the equation quite clearly: 'Habuit et genera linguarum, quas etsi omnes non nosset, Thiudiscam tamen et Latinam, ne plures dicamus, id est barbaram et Romanam, non ignoravit.'[6] It is also worthy of mention that, even in the first half of the eleventh century, Arnold of Saint-Emmeran, in his 'Miracles of Saint Emmeran of Ratisbon' (d. about 650), still evokes a 'curtis regia, quam Germana lingua Helfandorf vocitat, Romana vero Adiutorii-vicum latinizat'.[7] Thus, for him, transposing a proper name into the *lingua Romana* still means 'latinizing'.

We do have, on the other hand, some complementary evidence when, in a relevant sociolinguistic context, the *lingua Latina* is opposed to the *lingua barbara*, without any question of a 'Romance language'. Thus, in the ninth century, Bishop Haito of Basel (d. 836), whose diocese included territories of the two linguistic communities, required of his priests the ability to teach the Lord's Prayer and the Apostles' Creed 'tam Latine quam barbarice'.[8] In the third 'Life of Saint Gall' (d. about 636), written about 834, Walahfrid Strabo says about this disciple of Saint Columban who had travelled through parts of Romania as well as of Germania, that he had received from the Lord the grace 'ut non solum Latinae sed etiam barbaricae locutionis cognitionem non parvam haberet'.[9]

So the least we can say is that the ambiguity in the sense of *Latinus/Romanus* did not disappear quickly. Was it to solve this problem that, in order to refer to vernacular Romance, they invented the adverb *Romanice* and the substantively used adjectives *Romanicum*, *Romancium*, *Romancia* (*lingua*)? However, the appearance of these terms is far later than the Carolingian epoch, although the adjective *Romanicus* in the sense of 'Roman, made in Rome', was already used, just like *Romaniensis*, by Cato (Tagliavini 1972: 169–70).

But let us return for a moment to the *rustica Romana lingua* of the Synod of Tours. The addition of the adjective *rusticus* exactly constitutes an argument not to translate *Romana* by 'Romance', the whole expression being better rendered as 'rustic Roman language' ('la langue romaine rustique'; Fontaine 1981: 796–7). Indeed, *rustice loqui*, using the *sermo rusticus* (as opposed to the *sermo urbanus*) has always indicated the social origin or condition of the speaker, the level of his language, or his way of speaking (and, above all, of pronouncing) or of writing Latin (Väänänen 1981: 23). This meaning always explains sufficiently the use of these terms in the eighth and ninth centuries, e.g. the 'eloquium simplex et rusticanum' as mentioned in the Carolingian remake of a sermon of

Saint Eligius.[10] Moreover, there are writers of saints' 'Lives' who attack the *vitium rusticitatis* of their predecessors, who were often guided, in their stylistic choice, by a pastoral purpose (Riché 1972: 131, 540). But in the ninth century, while getting a more negative connotation, this *rusticitas* still refers to a type of *Latin*, that of the Merovingian hagiographers in this case.[11]

A scholion of Vergil (*Georg.* II, 446), due to Berno of Tours (in the early part of the ninth century), declares that 'ratis rustice dicitur reth', which points to a question of pronunciation. 'I shall leave it to Romanic philologists to determine whether *rustice* here means Old French or vulgar Latin', J. J. Savage (1928: 405) commented concerning this. A shift towards the sense of 'vernacular distinct from Latin' (whether it is Romance or Germanic) might well follow from a monastic legislation document, namely the *Statutum* said to be of Murbach (816), which imposes on the monks the 'usus Latinitatis potius quam rusticitatis'.[12] It seems suitable to add an extract from a Carolingian story (ninth century) of the transfer of the relics of Saint Germain of Paris, which mentions a person who not only spoke the *lingua rustica* perfectly, but who, once he had joined the clergy, started learning the *litterae* ('litteras discere coepit'), i.e. Latin;[13] although this passage might be good evidence in favour of the thesis of Roger Wright (1982: 104–18), according to which these *litterae* mean above all the *recte loqui* (i.e. reading by articulating the letters and the syllables).

There remain the adverb *vulgo* and the adjectives *vulgaris* or *vulgaricus* (joined to *lingua*, *locutio*, etc.). These last two introduce, in a Passion written by Arbeo of Freising (d. about 783), a Germanic proper name.[14] On the other hand, Willibald of Mainz, in his 'Life of Saint Boniface' (d. 754) composed about 763–5, tells us that Pope Gregory II (d. 731) was surnamed 'Iunior' in the 'vulgarica Romanorum lingua'.[15] But in Italy and in Rome there is evidently even less reason than elsewhere for such an expression to signify anything else but Latin as it was spoken by people then (Richter 1979: 26–32).

As to Romance Gaul, I myself have recently carried out research into the expressions of the type *quod vulgo vocant* in texts of the seventh and eighth centuries (Van Uytfanghe 1989). I have come to the conclusion that the very diverse cases of words indicated in this way hardly permit us to deduce the existence of a vulgar language perceived as distinct from Latin, *vulgo* instead denoting a particular lexical register or simply meaning 'commonly'. A rapid sounding in Carolingian sources has shown that there is a continuity in this matter. The following are involved here: proper names which are commonly used (as with Nithard (d. 845): 'in saltum qui Pertica' [> *la Perche*] vulgo dicitur');[16] then words of non-Latin origin (e.g. in the (ninth-century) 'Life of Saint Sadalberga' (d. 664?), Abbess at Laon: 'in vas quod lingua vulgari [var.: *lingua communi*] tunnam [> Fr. *tonne*] vocant);[17] Latin words to which attention is drawn because they are effectively of more or less popular creation, or because they are rare, or because they refer to a rather particular or 'technical' meaning (e.g. in Anso, who in the second half of the eighth century composed a 'Life of Saint Ursmarus', Abbot–Bishop of Lobbes: 'infirmitas . . . seva nimis, quae vulgo dicitur guttreria' (cf. GUTTURIO > Fr. *goitron, goitre*); Deacon Donat who wrote at about the same time a 'Life of Saint Trudo', priest in Hesbay (d. 690?): 'vir habitans prope ecclesiam . . . quem nos vulgo matricolarium [> Fr. *marguillier*] vocamus'; in the 'Life' (end of the ninth century) of the hermit Saint Vodoal (d. about 720): 'febris, quae tertiana vel quartana [FEBRIS TERTI(AN)A, QUART(AN)A > Fr. *fièvre tierce, quarte*] vulgo dicitur'; 'pallium suum, quod vulgo cappa [> Fr. *chape*] vocatur'; in a letter from the monk Elpricus, which is part of the epistolary dossier of Lupus of Ferrières (d. after 862): 'praecedentibus eadem natalicia diebus, quos vulgo vigilias (> Fr. doublet: *veille/vigile*] eorum appellamus').[18]

Latin terms like these generally have a quite 'normal' French derivative, and they are in no way comparable to those words that were reborrowed much later from the vernacular languages (of the type *chariettum*, for example).[19] However, there is a passage in the grammatical work of Gottschalk of Orbais (d. 867/9), where the meaning of *ergo, itaque*, and *igitur* is explained by 'quod vulgo dicitur "gers"' [< *de ea re, ea de re*], which is already very near the ancient French *giers, gieres*.[20] And there is also Chapter 77 of the 'Life of Saint Adelard' (d. 827) by Paschase Radbert, mentioned earlier. The author evokes as follows the triply melodious eloquence of the Abbot of Corbie: 'Quod si vulgo audisses, dulcifluus emanabat, si vero idem barbara, quam Teutiscam dicunt, lingua loqueretur, praeeminebat claritatis eloquio; quod si Latine, iam ulterius prae aviditate dulcoris non erat spiritus.'[21] Here, at any rate, a formal distinction seems to operate between *vulgo* (which would not refer to a Germanic idiom, this one being called by its own name) and *Latine*.

The least that one can say, in consequence, is that, whatever may be the terminology that is analysed, the contradictions remain.

2 Michael Richter wondered when Latin ceased being *understood* in Gaul. This question, which refers to 'vertical communication', is important. Indeed, as long as even those who only use the popular register of a language still understand the learned register, the organic link between the two remains, and in this case we cannot speak of bilingualism, only of 'diglossia'.

We know that in 813 some synods asked the bishops and priests to preach 'iuxta quod intellegere vulgus possit' (Mainz, Canon 15) or 'prout omnes intellegere possent, secundum proprietatem linguae' (Rheims, Canon 15). In Tours (Canon 17) and later at Mainz (847, Canon 2), it is stipulated 'ut easdem omelias quisque aperte transferre studeat in rusticam Romanam linguam aut Thiotiscam, quo facilius cuncti possint intellegere quae dicuntur' (Richter 1983: 441; Wright 1982: 118–22). Hence, it follows that the comprehension, by the illiterate, of these homilies of the Church Fathers (Rheims, Canon 15: 'omelias sanctorum patrum') caused a problem, although the adverb *facilius* tempers the phrasing somewhat.

There is, as a matter of fact, also a discussion about the meaning of *transferre*. This verb certainly means 'to translate' in the case of the *Thiotisca lingua*, but in the case of the *rustica Romana*, it might as well signify 'to transpose'[22] or 'reading by means of the non-reformed pronunciation', according to Wright. We repeat, as to this matter, that the phonetic interpretation of the directives contained in the *De orthographia* of Alcuin has been contested, although certain chapters of the work of Raban Maur (d. 856) seem to corroborate at least partly the opinion of Wright.[23] The Alcuinian reform was certainly not only a matter of pronunciation, far from it; but taking into consideration, on the one hand, the Carolingian tendency to standardization in all areas of public life, and, on the other hand, the strong phonetic reduction of French with regard to Latin, I would be surprised, just like Thomas J. Walsh (1986–7: 214) in his review of Wright's book, if the reform did not have phonetic implications.

But it is not only the sermons that are of interest to us here; it is suitable also to pay attention to the hagiographical stories. I have shown elsewhere (Van Uytfanghe 1985) that up to the end of the Merovingian epoch, extracts of 'Lives' of saints were recited in the presence of the Christian people (the *catervae populorum*), especially on the feast-day of the saint, and that the hagiographers wanted to be understood by the *rustici* and the *illiterati*. Now, the research of Heene into Carolingian hagiography (summarized in this volume, Chapter 12) shows a considerable dwindling of the hagiographers' audience, the *audientes* of the people shrinking in comparison to the *legentes*, who are evidently mostly clerks and monks. One will hardly be surprised about that since, under and after Charlemagne, both cult and liturgy (from now on Roman and no longer 'Gallican') take on in general a more 'sacral' aspect and so become less close to the common faithful (Le Goff 1972: 798–800).

To be sure, hagiography remains an important sector of literary production (of which, however, it has no longer the quasi-monopoly it had in the Merovingian centuries), but very often it concerns 'remakes in a better style' of former *Vitae* (of which some have been saved and some have been lost today). These authors, it has already been said, do not like the 'unrefined' language of their predecessors, or they blame the poor quality of the hand-written transmission of the hagiographical texts.[24] This struggle against the *vitium scriptorum*[25] should, in principle, improve the clearness and the intelligibility of the text,[26] but as a matter of fact, the elevated and not infrequently complicated style of many of these recast *Vitae* prevents them from being accessible to an illiterate audience, whatever the pronunciation may be with which they would have been read aloud.

However, this does not mean that the Latin of hagiography is completely 'incommunicable' from now on. At the end of the eighth century, the monks of Saint-Riquier (Centula) ask Alcuin to rewrite for them the ancient *Vita Richarii*; but as to the collection of miracles of their holy patron, they want to leave it as it is, exactly because it is still meant to be read out to the people: 'cuius simplex et minus polita locutio quia fratribus ad recitandum in populo aptior videbatur'.[27] I do not agree with Walter Berschin (Berschin and Berschin, 1987: 16) when, in a critique of Roger Wright's book (which has definitely thrown a big stone in the scientific pool), he sees in Alcuin's prologue evidence, more or less comparable to the Council of Tours, of a new conscience of the autonomy of the *Volkssprache*. In my opinion, this statement of Alcuin, as well as a similar allusion of Hincmar of Reims (d. 882) to the *Miracula* of Saint Remigius (d. about 530),[28] simply proves that a certain Merovingian Latin was still considered to be understandable to the *populus*.

That even applies, to all appearances, to certain readings in Carolingian Latin. Thus, the author who, in the first third of the ninth century, wrote the second 'Life of Saint Balthild' (d. 680), still wanted, on the occasion of the feast of this Queen of the Franks, to communicate to the *audientes* and to obtain the 'aedificatio plurimorum' by a 'verbum simplex'.[29] And in his own *Vita Remigii*, Hincmar himself marks with an *asteriscus* the passages 'quae populo recitanda sunt', and with a *paragraphus* those 'quae per Dei gratiam illuminatis legenda reservari debent'.[30] And again in the second half of the ninth century, Bishop Adalhelm of Séez, author of the 'Life of Saint Opportuna' (d.

770), confirms the fact that, on the occasion of the feast of the Abbess of Almenèches, the 'plebs' comes to listen to the 'revelatio' of his miracles (although Adalhelm too seems to direct the *Vita* in question only at his 'dilectissimi filii').[31] Testimonies like these – we repeat – are rare in the Carolingian epoch, but none the less they show that, as to the maintenance or the disappearance of diglossia in the ninth century, all the evidence is certainly not of the same kind.

3 Finally, I want to draw attention, briefly, to a third contradiction. The philologists and the historians have always liked to oppose the 'decadent' Merovingian Latin to the 'restored' Carolingian Latin, i.e. returning to the patristic and classical tradition. Now, we know today that Carolingian Latin is a plural latinity, a *latinitas mixta* (Fontaine 1981: 802). A lot of study remains to be done in this domain, but texts such as the description of the basilica of Saint-Denis near Paris, the *Liber Manualis* of Dhuoda, the Charters of Cluny and of Conques-en-Rouergue show that there is a variety of levels between the most chastened style of some poet or some hagiographer and the *rustica Romana lingua* of the Strasbourg Oaths (842). Michel Banniard has analysed the Latin of Alcuin himself and he has found that certain works of the reformer, meant for a more modest audience, betray the 'phrasé roman' and show off what he calls 'un effleurement sensible du *sermo simplex*', a *sermo simplex* that sometimes touches the *sermo vulgaris* (Banniard 1986: 586, 597).

   As to the text of the Oaths conserved by Nithard, there is quite a scientific literature about his latinisms and his romanisms and on the question of knowing whether it is vulgar Latin or semi-Romance or already French. I pass it by, but the least we can say is that the answer is not clear. It is all the less so, because it has been shown in a study by Helmut Lüdtke that, from the Glosses of Reichenau to the Saint Eulalia Sequence, including the Strasbourg Oaths, the texts become 'Romance' step by step (*stufenweise*) (Lüdtke 1964: 12; also Avalle 1983). Add to this the fact that the generalization of certain Proto-Romance linguistic phenomena stretches, in reality, over a good part of the Middle Ages (think of the floating use of the definite article, which appears early in Latin texts in the shape of 'articloid', but which is missing, for instance, in the Strasbourg Oaths; Selig 1987). So, the Latin–Romance diachronism has really not developed *recta linea*.

It is time to conclude. Whether we approach it by the way of the denomination of the languages, of the activity of vertical communication, or of the stratification of the language and style levels, the problem raised in the title of this volume is not easily to be solved, because of the contradictions of the sources themselves and/or of their potential interpretations. As I have just said, we will have to continue studying the Carolingian 'Latins' (Fontaine 1981: 802), and also the prolongation of the polymorphism of which Michel Banniard (1986: 589) has clearly seen the importance, and of its relation with the *Vorlesesprache* and more generally with the four mental operations of communication: hearing, speaking, reading, writing (Fontaine 1981: 793, n. 38).

But we can affirm already that the consciousness of the linguistic dichotomy, Latin–Romance, and of the transition from diglossia to bilingualism in Gaul, has known a rather different evolution according to individuals, regions, and sociolinguistic situations. The analysis that I have just made, confirms, it seems to me, the remark that Jacques Fontaine made in a footnote to his beautiful contribution to the *Settimana* of Spoleto of 1979 about Carolingian Europe: 'La distinction entre latin et roman n'était sans doute pas aisée pendant une longue phase de transition où la différence de degré n'était pas encore parvenue à se constituer en véritable différence de structure linguistique' (Fontaine 1981: 797, n. 43). I deduce from it, for my part, that those who attribute to the ninth century (and more particularly to its first half) a catalysing role in the linguistic crisis that eventually led to the duality of Romania (learned language against vernacular languages), are closer to the truth than those who only consider it – if I may take the liberty of using a metaphor taken from medicine – as the moment when the abscess that has long been ripening burst at last.

NOTES

* I wish to express my cordial thanks to my former teacher, Urbain Triest, who translated my text into English.

1 *Carm.*, I, 7–8 (*MGH, PLAC*, III, p. 45): 'Rustica concelebret Romana Latinaque lingua, Saxo quibus pariter plangens pro carmine dicat.'

2 *Historiae*, III, 5 (ed. Ph. Lauer, 2nd edn, Paris, Les Belles Lettres, 1964, p. 102): 'et sacramenta que subter notata sunt, Lodhuvicus Romana, Karolus vero Teudisca lingua, iuraverunt. Ac sic, ante sacramentum, circumfusam plebem, alter Theudisca, alter Romana lingua alloquuti sunt'; also ibid., p. 104: 'Cumque Karolus [i.e. Charles the Bald himself] haec eadem verba Romana lingua perorasset . . .'

3 *Vita Caroli Magni, prol.* (ed. L. Halphen, 3rd edn, Paris, Les Belles Lettres, 1938, pp. 4–5):

> En tibi librum praeclarissimi et maximi viri memoriam continentem, in quo praeter illius facta non est quod admiraris, nisi forte quod, homo barbarus et in Romana locutione perparum excitatus, aliquid me decenter aut commode Latine scribere posse putaverim . . .'

4 *Bibliotheca Hagiographica Latina* (*BHL*) 6025: *V. Mummoleni*, 9 (*AASS Oct.*, VII, 2, p. 983); *BHL* 6026: *V. Mummoleni*, 18 (*AASS Belgii*, IV, pp. 403–4). On this subject, see the older and largely outdated studies (listed in the bibliography) of F. Novati, A. Pellizzari, V. Crescini, F. d'Ovidio, and P. Rajna.

5 The author continues: 'utraque autem eruditiori latinorum eloquio sicut gratia haec concessa fuerit, ad plenum respondere dinoscitur. Quia ergo tot et tantarum linguarum peritum eum noverat . . .' On the conflicting interpretation of this text, see Muller (1923: 12–13) and Avalle (1965: 5–7).

6 *Vita tertia S. Ludgeri*, 40 (ed. W. Diekamp, Münster 1881, p. 108).

7 *De miraculis S. Emeramni*, 7 (*MGH, Script.*, IV, p. 552).

8 *Hettonis Capitulare*, II (Migne, *PL*, 105, col. 763): 'Secundo iubendum, ut Oratio dominica. . . . Symbolum apostolorum . . . ab omnibus discatur tam Latine quam barbarice: ut quod ore profitentur, corde credatur et intelligatur.'

9 *V. Galli*, 6 (*MGH, SRM*, IV, p. 289).

10 *Homilia XI in Coena Domini* (Migne, *PL*, 87, col. 630): 'Boni homines, quia vestram fraternitatem aliter necesse est alloqui quam consacerdotes et cooperatores nostros, quibus datum est nosse mysteria regni coelorum.' (*Matt.* XIII, *Marc.* IV, *Luc.* VIII): 'ideo ad vos simplici et rusticano utentes eloquio convertamur, ut tantae solemnitatis sacramentum iuxta parvitatem nostri sensus exponamus vobis rusticitate verborum'.

11 For example, Ardo (d. 843), *V. Benedicti Anianensis, prol.* (*MGH, Script.*, XV, 1, p. 200): '. . . non rusticitatis vicio redolentes peritorum adgravent aures, set urbanitatis salefacentiae condita proferant verba politis sermonibus, ut ita dixerim, derogantium demulceant aures'; Heiricus (d. 876), *Miracula S. Germani Autissiodorensis, prol.* (Migne, *PL*, 124, col. 1207–8):

> quandoquidem vulgaris inurbanitas tum se optime credit diuturnitati prospicere, cum illustria quaeque et maxima, succidua solum narratione ad posteros fecerit emanare. Res ista non insana minus quam improvida, perniciosa sanctorum praeconiis interdum peperit detrimenta, quod qui imperitae rusticitati fidem astruat, rarum quemque reperias.

12 *Actuum praeliminarium Synodi primae Aquisgranensis, commentationes sive statuta Murbacensia* (816), *Corpus consuetudinum monasticarum*, I, Siegburg 1963, p. 449: 'Usum latinitatis potius quam rusticitatis qui inter eos scolastici sunt sequuntur. In tali enim confabulatione notitia scripturarum aliquoties magis quam lectione penetratur et dictandi usus discitur et ad discendum sensus acuitur.'

13 Quoted (without any precise reference) by Du Cange, *Glossarium*, I, *praef.*, XIII, p. xiv: 'Unde factum est, ut tam auditu quam locutione, in brevi non solum rusticam Linguam perfecte loqueretur; sed etiam literas, in ipsa Ecclesia Clericus effectus, discere coepit.'

14 *P. Haimhramni*, 37 (*MGH, SRM*, IV, p. 513): 'Dum autem pervenisset in solitudinem, quae mutata vulgarica locutione [version B: *locutione vulgari*] Feronifaidus appellatur, incidit in latronem.' Elsewhere in this text (22, ibid., p. 493), the author gives the 'vulgar' name of a plant (the *spina alba* or 'hawthorn'), which already occurs in classical Latin: 'His namque transactis, incole huius loci, collectis abscissis sacri martyris membris, in quodam arbore vulgari locutione spine albe [version B: *spina alba*] condentes abierunt.'

15 *V. Bonifatii*, V, 14 (Migne, *PL*, 89, col. 613): 'qui et vulgarica Romanorum lingua dicitur Iunior . . .'

16 *Hist.*, III, 4 (ed. Ph. Lauer, 2nd edn, Paris 1964, p. 98). See also ibid., III, 5, p. 100: '. . . in civitatem, que olim Argentaria vocabatur, nunc autem Strasburg vulgo dicitur, convenerunt'.

17 *V. Sadalbergae*, 20 (*MGH, SRM*, V, p. 61).

18 *V. Ursmari*, 6 (ibid., VI, p. 459); *V. Trudonis*, 27 (ibid., p. 295); *V. Vodoali*, 6 and 10 (*AASS Febr.*, I, col. 691 and 692); *Epistulae Lupi abbatis Ferrariensis, additamentum*, 9 (*MGH, Epist.*, VI, p. 123). For other examples, see Chapter 12 of this volume.

19 See also the use of *vulgo* by the scholiasts in an eleventh-century manuscript of Vergil (Savage 1928: 405).

20 C. Lambot (ed.), *Oeuvres théologiques et grammaticales de Godescalc d'Orbais*, Louvain, Louvain University Press 1945, p. 407: ' "ergo", "itaque", "igitur" coniunctiones inlativum habent sensum et illud significant, quod vulgo dicitur "gers". Iam quia sic est: "gers faciam" '

21 *V. Adalhardi*, 77 (Migne, *PL*, 120, col. 1546).

22 Notice that, e.g. Paschasius Radbertus, in the prologue of his *Passio SS. Rufini et Valerii* (Migne, *PL*, 120, col. 1489) uses the expression 'ad emendatioris styli formam transferre'.

23 Cf. *De clericorum institutione*, II, 52 (*De lectionibus*); III, 30 (*Quod facili locutione uti in vulgus debeat*); III, 37 (*De discretione dogmatum iuxta qualitatem auditorum*) (Migne, *PL*, 107, cols 363–4, 408, 413–15). But the interpretation of these passages is not easy, as Raban partly quotes Augustine and Isìdore of Seville. Notice however that, when he treats of the *permixtiones* and *translationes verborum*, Raban speaks about the filiations between Hebrew, Greek, Latin, and *lingua Thiotisca*, but does not take into account any Romance vernacular (*De rebus ecclesiasticis*, ibid., 114, cols 926–7).

24 For example, Hincmarus, *V. Remigii, praef.* (*MGH, SRM*, III, p. 252): 'Sicque prefatus liber cum aliis partim stillicidio putrefactus, partim soricibus conrosus, partim foliorum abscisione divisus in tantum

deperiit, ut pauca et dispersa inde folia reperta fuerint'; Paschasius Radbertus, *P. SS. Rufini et Valerii, prol.* (Migne, *PL*, 120, col. 1491):

> . . . quoniam studuimus depravata corrigere, inveterata reparare, quandoquidem per haec utilitati legentium deservire quaesivimus. Non enim gestorum fidem corrupimus, sed nostro sub eloquio priorum scriptorum texuimus historiam. Quod si quis nostram spreverit editionem, legat si maluerit antiquam. . . . Caeterum imperitorum calumnias, malitia seu livore conflatas, surda debemus aure transire.

This passage betrays some nervousness about the question of the opportuneness of rewriting saints' 'Lives'.

25 See already the *Vita Eligii* (about the middle of the eighth century), *prol.* (*MGH, SRM*, IV, p. 665): 'Haec idcirco, quia plerumque videmus nonnulla volumina et praecipue sanctorum gesta ita scriptorum vitio depravata, ut studiosis quibusque non solum lectitare, verum etiam manibus sit contingere fastidium.

26 Paschasius Radbertus (*Passio* n. 24, col. 1490): 'Non quod virtutum insignia et gesta sanctorum stupenda, fucos verborum atque ornamenta requirant orationis, sed quod simplex eorum atque naturalis prolatio, distincta tamen et honesta debet specie enitere, ne sermo confusus et horridus non instruat, sed offendat auditorem.

27 *V. Richarii, prol.* (*MGH, SRM*, IV, p. 389).

28 *V. Remigii*, n. 24, p. 251) (about the text of which he deplores the poor material quality:

> petiit de eodem libro coturno Gallicano dictato aperto sermone aliqua miracula, quae in populo recitarentur, excipere, quatinus ea sine tedio audire et mente recondere atque per ea ad amorem et honorem atque devotionem Dei et ipsius protectoris sui idem populus excitari valeret. . . . Et cum ipsa exceptio cepit lectione in populo frequentari et a multis propter brevitatis suae facilitatem transcribi, ipse magnus codex a neglegentibus neglegentius cepit haberi, usque dum tempore Karli principis . . .

29 *V. Balthildis* (version B), *prol.* (*MGH, SRM*, II, p. 482):
> 'Qui licet inpolito sermone uti videamur, magis tamen volumus studere patentem aedificationem plurimorum, qui velut apes prudentes dulce requirunt ex floribus nectar, id est ex verbo simplici veritatis dulcedinem, que magis aedificet audientes, quam inflet . . .'; ibid., 1 (p. 483): sicut in hac venerabili Dei cultrice, domna Balthilde regina, cuius hodie, exultantibus animis, festa recolimus, ad multorum augmentum fidelium completum esse cernimus.

30 *V. Remigii, op. cit.* (n. 24, p. 258).

31 *V. Opportunae, prol.* (*AASS Ordinis S. Bened.*, III, 2, p. 322):

> Et si non pro meis meritis, tamen pro utilitate diem festum B. Opportunae celebrantium, distillet in nobis vel parvissimam sui roris guttam . . . ita haec plebs, quae modo huc advenit pro amore dominae nostrae Opportunae gaudens recedat cum sua iucunditate audita virtutum eius revelatione. Nunc vobis, dilectissimi filii, prout

Dominus ministraverit, narraturi sumus, quanta divina gratia in famula sua, virgine Opportuna, operari dignata est mirabilia. Sed vos non pigeat audire, quod in ea Dominus perficere voluit . . . ut operum illius imitatores effecti . . . possimus cum illa caelestis regni perfrui gaudia.

BIBLIOGRAPHY

Avalle, D. S. (1965) *Protostoria delle lingue romanze*, Turin: G. Giappichelli.
—— (1983) *Latino 'circa Romançum' e 'rustica Romana lingua'. Testi del VII, VIII e IX secolo*, Padua: Antenore.
Banniard, M. (1985) 'Vox agrestis: quelques problèmes d'élocution de Cassiodore à Alcuin', *Trames. Etudes antiques (Limoges)*: 195–208.
—— (1986) 'Théorie et pratique de la langue et du style chez Alcuin: rusticité feinte et rusticité masquée', *Francia. Forschungen zur Westeuropäischen Geschichte* 13: 579–601.
Berschin, H. and Berschin, W. (1987) 'Mittellatein und Romanisch', *Zeitschrift für romanische Philologie* 103: 1–19.
Crescini, V. (1909) 'Del passo relativo a' linguaggi nella biografia di san Mummolino', *Memorie storiche Forogiuliesi* 5: 1–12.
Dardel, R. (de) (1958) *Le Parfait fort en roman commun*, Genève: E. Droz.
Díaz y Díaz, M. C. (1951) 'Latinitas. Sobre la evolución de su concepto', *Emerita* 19: 35–50.
D'Ovidio, F. (1910) 'San Mommoleno e il volgare romanzo di Gallia', *Rendiconti della Reale Accademia dei Lincei, Classe di scienze morali 5*, 19: 185–200.
Fontaine, J. (1981) 'De la Pluralité à l'unité dans le "latin carolingien"?' in *Nascita dell'Europa ed Europa carolingia: un'equazione da verificare. Settimane di studio sull'alto medioevo 17 (1979)*, II, Spoleto: Centro Italiano di Studi sull'Alto Medioevo: 765–805.
Herman, J. (1967) *Le Latin vulgaire*, Paris: Presses Universitaires de France.
Le Goff, J. (1972) 'Le Christianisme médiéval en Occident du Concile de Nicée (325) à la Réforme (début du XVIᵉ siècle)', in *Histoire des religions (Encyclopédie de la Pléiade)*, II, Paris: Gallimard, 749–868.
Lot, F. (1931) 'A quelle époque a-t-on cessé de parler latin?', *Archivum Latinitatis Medii Aevi* 6: 97–159.
Lüdtke, H. (1964) 'Die Entstehung romanischer Schriftsprachen', *Vox Romanica* 23: 3–21.
Muller, H. F. (1921) 'When did Latin cease to be a spoken language in France?', *Romanic Review* 12: 318–34.
—— (1923) 'On the use of the expression *lingua Romana* from the first to the ninth century', *Zeitschrift für romanische Philologie* 43: 9–19.
Norberg, D. (1966) 'A quelle époque a-t-on cessé de parler latin en Gaule?', *Annales ESC* 21: 346–56.
Novati, F. (1900) *Due vetustissime testimonianze dell' esistenza del volgare nelle Gallie esaminate e discusse*, Milano: Reale Istituto Lombardo di

Scienze e Lettere.
—— (1906) 'Per la mia interpretazione', *Studi Medievali* 2: 98–100.
Parlangéli, O. (1970) 'Tra latino "parlato" e romanzo "scritto"', *Studi A. Corsano*, Manduria: Lacaita, 553–66.
Pellizari, A. (1906) 'Su la più antica testimonianza dell' esistenza del volgare nelle Gallie', *Studi Medievali* 2: 93–7.
Rajna, P. (1910) 'S. Mommoleno e il linguaggio romanzo', in *Mélanges de philologie romane et d'histoire littéraire offerts à M. Wilmotte*, II, Paris: Champion, 541–67.
Riché, P. (1972) *Education et culture dans l'Occident barbare, VIe–VIIIe siècles*, 3rd edn, Paris: Le Seuil.
Richter, M. (1979) 'Latina lingua – sacra seu vulgaris?', in W. Lourdaux and D. Verhelst (eds), *The Bible and Medieval Culture*, Leuven: Leuven University Press, 16–34.
—— (1983) 'A quelle époque a-t-on cessé de parler latin en Gaule? A propos d'une question mal posée', *Annales ESC* 38: 439–48.
Savage, J. J. (1928) 'Lingua romana', *Speculum* 3: 405.
Selig, M. (1987) 'Die Entwicklung des Determinantensystems im Spätlateinischen', in W. Raible (ed.), *Romanistik, Sprachtypologie und Universalforschung. Beiträge zum Freiburger Romanistentag 1987*, Tübingen: Narr, 99–130.
Tagliavini, C. (1972) *Le origini delle lingue neolatine*, 6th edn, Bologna: Pàtron.
Väänänen, V. (1981), *Introduction au latin vulgaire*, 3rd edn, Paris: Klincksieck.
Van der Essen, L. (1907) *Etude critique et littéraire sur les Vitae des saints mérovingiens de l'ancienne Belgique*, Louvain: Bureaux du Recueil; Paris: A. Fontemoing.
Van Uytfanghe, M. (1976) 'Le Latin des hagiographes mérovingiens et la protohistoire du français. Etat de la question, première partie: à quelle époque a-t-on cessé d̃ parler latin?', *Romanica Gandensia* 16: 5–89.
—— (1977) 'Latin mérovingien, latin carolingien et *rustica romana lingua*: continuité ou discontinuité?', *Revue de l'Université de Bruxelles* 1: 65–88.
—— (1984) 'Histoire du latin, protohistoire des langues romanes et histoire de la communication. A propos d'un recueil d'études, et avec quelques observations préliminaires sur le débat intellectuel entre pensée structurale et pensée historique', *Francia. Forschungen zur Westeuropäischen Geschichte* 11: 579–613.
—— (1985) 'L'Hagiographie et son public à l'époque mérovingienne', *Studia Patristica* 16, 2: 54–62.
—— (1986) 'Après les "morts" successives du latin: quelques réflexions sur son avenir', in F. Decreus and C. Deroux (eds), *Hommages à Jozef Veremans*, Brussels, Collection Latomus 193: 328–54.
—— (1989) 'Les Expressions du type *quod vulgo vocant* dans des textes latins antérieurs au Concile de Tours et aux Serments de Strasbourg: témoignages lexicologiques et sociolinguistiques de la "langue rustique romaine"?', *Zeitschrift für romanische Philologie* 105: 28–49.
Vercauteren, F. (1932) 'Le "Romanus" des sources franques', *Revue Belge de Philologie et d'Histoire* 11: 77–88.
Walsh, T. J. (1986–7) 'Latin and Romance in the Early Middle Ages',

Romance Philology 40: 199–214.

Wright, R. (1982) *Late Latin and Early Romance in Spain and Carolingian France*, Liverpool: Cairns.

Zumthor, P. (1959) 'Une Formule galloromane du VIIIe siècle', *Zeitschrift für romanische Philologie* 75: 211–33.

11 Latin and Romance: an historian's perspective

Rosamond McKitterick

At first sight, the Latin–Romance debate is encouraging in its lack of conclusiveness. If the linguists cannot agree then the historians can presumably think what they like. But in practice, because the issues of Latinity and literacy are so intertwined in the Early Middle Ages, and because the survival or revival and uses of Latin in particular political and ecclesiastical contexts have so much symbolic resonance, the lack of agreement is disconcerting, if not disturbing. If clarity cannot be achieved concerning the status and communicative potential of our texts, how are we to interpret these texts in their historical context? From the historian's point of view it has been a move in the right direction that the questions raised in the past by such scholars as Lot (1931) and Muller (1921), and re-examined by Richter (1983), have now begun to move away from attempts to define the languages being spoken and written in western Europe in the seventh, eighth, and ninth centuries as 'Latin' or 'Romance' or as a learned written language and a spoken register of that written language. That is not to say that this aspect of the problem does not continue to preoccupy some Latinists, nor that it does not retain its importance. Questions about Latin and Romance, however, are now being rephrased, by such scholars as Van Uytfanghe (1983) and Banniard (1975, 1980: 104–12) in terms of communication and the relationship between orality and literacy. It is not so much the name and nature of the language that is important, but whether or not it could be or was used effectively as a means of communication.

The discussion has also been bedevilled by negative assumptions about communication and the use of language in the Early Middle Ages that belittle the cultural achievements of the Carolingian period. The answer to the blunt question 'What did the Franks speak in the ninth century?' may be as elusive as ever, and so, I fear, is that to the question 'When did the Franks stop speaking Latin?'; but there are many answers, some more plausible than others, in response to the more subtle questions: 'What did the Franks understand in the eighth and ninth centuries and what did they use Latin for?' That there are so many answers is a reflection of the difficulties of the evidence and the necessity for an interdisciplinary tackling of the problem such as is being attempted in this book. Although I have already ventured to contribute to the debate in the past (McKitterick 1977, 1989, 1990), I shall explore here a little more fully first the implications of the Latin–Romance debate for our assessment of the levels and functions of literacy and education in the Frankish kingdoms in the Carolingian period, and second the Franks' use of written discourse in terms of the written texts that survive.

There are a number of obvious difficulties which merit note at the outset. I have already made the point (McKitterick 1989) that the arrival of the ninth century cannot be heralded as the solution to linguistic problems, in which Latin emerges triumphantly purified in its written form by the scholars of the Carolingian Renaissance, and the vernacular or spoken form can now be safely labelled 'Romance'. Chronological imprecision has marred some contributions to the debate over the last twenty years. While written forms of a recognizable 'Romance' are exceedingly rare before the tenth century in the West Frankish regions north of the Alps, this does not prevent even the most distinguished linguists from lumping the ninth century together as but a passing moment in the history of linguistic change. Historians, well aware of the ferment of activity in the late eighth and the ninth centuries, not least the pride and care taken in the improvement and refinement of the written language, the realization of the symbolic potential of Latin as a unifying element in the diverse regions of the Frankish kingdoms (Guerreau-Jalabert 1981), and the dramatic increase in the use of writing itself, (Ganshof, 1951; Ganz 1987; Nelson 1990) find this mental leap very difficult to understand. Above all, it fails to take into account the Carolingians' perception of the importance of the written word, presented to us entirely in the form of Latin texts (McKitterick 1989). Linguistic change can be very rapid, as we well know, but in as disparate a realm as the Carolingian one it was certainly not uniformly rapid chronologically, geographically, or within the different social groups.

I also stressed that the sociolinguistic research of scholars such as Richter (1975, 1976, 1979), Itkonen (1978), and others indicates that the emergence of Romance, perceived as different by hearers and speakers, should be posited ever later, into the ninth and tenth centuries. I accepted too, and still accept, the arguments put forward by Wright (1982) concerning Merovingian Latin texts being the written representations of a language that may have sounded very different from what we think, though the extent to which the refinement of written Latin under the Carolingians was accompanied by pronunciation reforms is distinctly questionable. It is clear, moreover, that Alcuin's *De orthographia* was crucial for the production of written, not only spoken Latin (it was probably a text designed to assist scribes in the scriptoria when copying Latin texts from defective exemplars), and cannot be invoked in support of arguments concerning the pronunciation practice of Latin in the ninth century. Further, I invoked the evidence of the surviving grammars from the Carolingian period. These, the work of the Latin-speaking ancient world designed for native Latin speakers, not grammars adapted for non-Latin speakers such as the insular grammars identified and defined by Vivien Law (1982), support the view that Latin was not learnt by the Franks in the ninth century as a foreign language but as the formal written form of the language they used every day. Even as far as the non-Latinate East Frankish regions were concerned, I suggested that it was imperative for the ruling social groups to conduct their business affairs in Latin, to express their Christian religion in Latin, and to play their part in Carolingian administration in the language of government, namely, Latin, and that we should therefore be careful not to underestimate the ability of the East Franks to acquire the necessary linguistic facility to do so.

Behind the scepticism concerning the Franks' linguistic capacity, let alone their original knowledge of Latin, there are a number of unspoken assumptions, and a certain ignoring of Frankish history, which it may be as well to bring out into the open. There is a lingering understanding of Early Medieval Latin as a degenerate form of a once pure and glorious tongue, and that later evolved forms witness to a decline and a debasement rather than a living language adapting itself to new circumstances and needs. Such pejorative assessments are unhelpful. They reflect unfairly on the intellectual capacities of the people allegedly responsible in some deliberate way for letting Latin get into such a state of disrepair. Although it is conceded that the Carolingians at least earn their Brownie points by their efforts to correct the written form of Latin, and, indeed, by their astounding use of the written word itself, should we award them because they appear to have returned to classical norms or because they perceived that the written language was in danger, through lack of clarity and error, of failing to communicate as it should? To praise the Franks for getting closer to Classical Latin than they were in the eighth century is an essentially humanistic judgement, a reaction against 'Gothic barbarism', and anachronistic. The Carolingians could only gauge correctness in the context of the books they read and the content of their education. These had not altered in essentials since the fifth and sixth centuries. The Franks' written models were more likely to be legal, biblical, and patristic than classical, and their guides were the Late Antique grammarians.

Lupus of Ferrières is certainly striking in his identification of a particular Latin, that of Cicero, as his inspiration. He writes: 'I subsequently began to do some reading in the authors and the works of our period displeased me, especially since they lacked the grandeur of Cicero and the rest of the classical writers which our distinguished Christian authors emulated', and praises Einhard for his *Vita Karoli*, a work in which there were 'noble sentiments, a moderate use of conjunctions, which I have observed in the classical writers and sentences not too long and involved but of moderate length' (Lupus, ed. Levillain, 1964, trans. Regenos, 1966). Yet Lupus' reaction to classical authors is to their style rather than to their correctness. Undoubtedly, Latin was redolent of the Roman past and Roman civilization; it had an essential role to play in the continuities from late Roman to Carolingian culture, but there is no indication in the written sources that Latin was adopted because of its associations. Its associations being remarked upon and exploited is quite another matter, much as we make capital out of still speaking the language of Shakespeare. As far as Carolingian scholars are concerned, indeed, we are observing a fundamental pride in a shared heritage that they possessed and had inherited through many generations, not one they had recently acquired. Its most self-conscious manifestation is the poetry emanating from the royal court (Godman 1985, 1987), but its most solid expression is the laws and the legislation of the Franks and their subject peoples (McKitterick 1989: 23–75).

It should not be forgotten that the Franks in the so-called Romance regions had been settled in Roman Gaul since the mid-third century and had merged with the population quite considerably, certainly in northern Gaul, by the sixth century, and that the Gallo-Roman population south of the Loire played key roles in the

Frankish church and politics from the late fifth century onwards as members of the Frankish kingdom. Nor had the Franks east of the Rhine been totally cut off from the Roman world (James 1982, 1988; Wightmann 1985). The historical circumstances of the Franks' first encounter with the Latin language in the last centuries of the Roman Empire thus have to be borne in mind. As possible federate troops in Toxandria, in their relations with Roman military officials and merchants in the Austrasian region round Trier and Cologne, as *laeti* in Gaul as far south, it is thought, as the Loire river valley, the Franks from the mid-third century encountered Latin. When Clovis and his heirs took over Gaul they ruled over a mixed population of Gallo-Romans and Franks. As an essentially (though not wholly) illiterate people themselves it might be assumed that it was only natural for the Franks, when codifying their laws or converting to Christianity, simply to use as their written language the language of law and religious texts of the Romans they emulated. Yet Ulfilas had devised an alphabet so that the Bible might be rendered into vernacular Gothic for the Goths (Friedrichsen 1926, 1939; Thompson 1966). Such an enterprise was presumably unnecessary for the Franks because, while apparently retaining a sense of their cultural identity, Latin had long since become their normal language of communication. They thus aligned themselves, whether consciously or unconsciously, with a whole new cultural tradition. As sixth, seventh, and eighth century texts show, this Latin did not remain static. It modified its syntactical structure and its orthography: new linguistic forms emerged in due course, as they do in any language over a number of years. Some of the texts in which such forms occur may reflect an attempt to correspond with the current spoken forms of the language. That formal written Latin remained a norm throughout the Merovingian period is evident from the continued copying of patristic, biblical, and legal texts and the production of Latin documents and letters in the private and public, local and central domains (Wood 1990).

Latin in the Merovingian and Carolingian realms, therefore, had long been accepted as part of the fabric of public life along with Frankish rule. It was the language of government, law, and religion. Its very prevalence, especially in Alemannia, Rhaetia, and Bavaria, should perhaps encourage us to readjust our notions of the durability of the Roman Empire in these regions. Clearly, old habits died hard. Such linguistic unity as the dominance of Latin promoted (something akin to the status of English in the old British Empire and new Commonwealth) was, of course, appreciated and fostered by the Carolingians for the purposes of government, religion, and learning. In so doing, they created a firm bridge between Frankish Germanic and Roman Latin culture, so strong that it united the two cultures and each enriched the other. We cannot assume, therefore, as many do, that because the Franks were originally German, they could not speak Latin, let alone regard Latin as their first language. The experience of English alone should warn us to exercise some common sense when it comes to appreciating the enormous variety of linguistic patterns resulting from settlement and conquest of a people from one linguistic type with those of another.

The Carolingian Franks thus inherited the customary and the learned uses of Latin from the Gallo-Romans and Merovingian Franks. Because it was used as a matter of course, it makes no sense to interpret the growing 'decadence' of Latin and its reform in the ninth century in terms of the refinement of a written language by learned and clerical scholars for their own exclusive use, as distinct from organization from the top to reform the written language of everyone, along with the provision of education generally. Latin, with all its resonances of the Roman past, was not reserved for the clergy as a learned language. False analogies with the status of Latin in Europe in the Later Middle Ages *vis-à-vis* the vernaculars are entirely inappropriate in relation to the period before c. 1000.

The possible difference between the different grades of text, the different audiences for whom they may have been intended, and the range of levels of literacy, have been insufficiently respected. Further, we must remember that if we confine ourselves to written literary texts, as distinct from legal and administrative material, we are bound to get a distorted and rarified view of Carolingian culture and language. It is one of Wright's virtues (1982; quite unfairly criticized by Adams 1989) that he exploited the documentary material of the seventh and eighth centuries in his analysis. How valid would an assessment of twentieth-century British culture be if it were confined to the output of the Cambridge and Oxford University Presses? Certainly, it is true that the better educated an early medieval writer was, the closer his Latin comes to patristic Latin; but does this give us a right to dismiss the legal documents and their staunch testimony to a tradition of a living language recognizably related to Latin? The legal documents are crucial if we want to see what the range of current and unlearned linguistic practice was. We cannot lump all texts together as one type of evidence and dismiss the ones in 'decadent' Latin as irrelevant. What we have to realize is that the texts demonstrate the different registers of the written language in the eighth and ninth centuries, the different educational levels of their authors, and the different functions written language could perform.

The attitude of Lupus of Ferrières cited above also serves as a reminder that we must be careful not to extend the written evidence from a few individuals in particular localities to make general statements about the current written and spoken language of the population at large, their attitudes towards it, and its correctness. We are guilty of crassness if we judge the cultural and linguistic expressions of a people on the basis of examples randomly selected from the past by the passage of time and the chance of survival.

That said, let us adopt, for the sake of argument, the stance of the traditionalist and consider Latin for a moment as the learned written language of an elite bearing little relation to the speech and concerns of the Franks. If we should indeed insist on calling the spoken Latin forms of the ninth century 'Romance', does this really present major obstacles to those learning to read Latin in its written form? There seems to be an assumption that it would be more difficult for the Franks, being barbarians and Germans to boot, to learn to read than it is for us. Would not the difference between Late Antique Latin and Carolingian 'Latin/Romance' be something akin to our understanding of Elizabethan, or at most Chaucerian, as opposed to Modern English?

Another assumption is that the Frankish clergy, despite being Frankish, by means of divine grace no doubt, are for some reason exempt from the difficulty of learning Latin. Carolingian clergy undoubtedly wielded their written language as a potent cultural and religious force, but they had no exclusive monopoly of written Latin. Their remarkable achievements are praised, but praised as those of an elite operating in a foreign language rather than, as they should be, as an elite of academics expressing themselves in the formal written language of their culture, whatever their native speech may have been. If one learnt to read in the ninth century in Europe one learnt to read in Latin.

Interpretations which insist on Latin being the elite learned language of the clergy and a few exceptional laymen create a false paradox. There is a great abundance of Latin texts on all manner of subjects from all kinds of milieus, from charters recording land transactions and granting manumission, wills bequeathing property, letters issuing instructions to secular officials, capitularies setting out agenda for discussion, royal directives for administration and an enormous range of governmental texts, complex theological tracts, sophisticated, if somewhat mannered poetry, sermons, liturgy, and texts on estate management. In fact, the entire written culture of Frankish civilization is represented by texts in the Latin language. It is not Classical Latin but it is Latin and it is their language, used for every kind of written text in both secular and ecclesiastical contexts. These observations are not intended to decry the importance of the linguistic categories provided for eighth- and ninth-century texts. However one may wish to categorize their Latin – as a learned written language transmitted in the schools or as a learned register or style of a vernacular – there is acknowledgement of the syntactical and orthographic transformations underway and the division between what we choose to call Romance, recognizable in texts in the tenth century (with one or two famous precursors such as the Strasbourg Oaths and Eulalia Sequence in the ninth) and Latin in their written forms at least by the tenth century. But what the historian has to try and understand is what these linguistic categories meant in terms of an individual in the ninth century and how they affected that individual's ability to learn to read and conduct his or her daily affairs with some resort to literate modes of communication.

Let us look at a selection of texts within their particular and local historical context. The first of these is the Council of Tours decree of 813; not, it should be noted, echoed by any of the other Reform council decrees of that year, and not included in the digest of the decrees forwarded to Charlemagne in Aachen (McKitterick 1977). The extent to which this may have been a problem peculiar to the metropolitan province of Tours, to my knowledge, has not yet been examined. It is always taken to mean widespread problems over the entire Carolingian Empire rather than, as seems more likely, an indication of the particular problems presented by a mixed population in the region of Tours. If a piece of Latin with learned morphology, syntax, and vocabulary could not be made comprehensible to an uneducated 'vernacular speaker' by being pronounced in vernacular phonetics, (no one yet has proved that it could not, and Wright (1982) suggests that it could), should we envisage a rapid paraphrase into everyday speech, as it were, on the part of the preacher? Does this markedly weaken the point that the text for guidance remains the written Latin one and it is this text which is the historian's (and the linguist's) only means of knowing the purport of what was actually spoken to the people? The Tours decree can be interpreted, regardless of whether translation, paraphrasing, or pronunciation is required for either the German or the Romance, as being proposed with a mixed congregation in mind. There were obviously beginning to be problems in communication between priests and linguistically diverse congregations in the churches in the archdiocese of Tours in the second decade of the ninth century, but they were far from insuperable if such a simple remedy as this could be proposed to deal with them. This passage's importance has been blown out of all proportion because it is the first one actually to refer to *lingua romana et teudisca*. Should we not register all the other texts of similar and subsequent date which make no reference to language being a problem, rather than build such cumbersome edifices on the one text that does?

The famous Oaths of Strasbourg are also pertinent here. Nithard, writing both private and public history (Nelson 1986; Rau 1974) for his lay colleagues in the entourage of Charles the Bald, composed his account in vigorous and intensely personal Latin. The meeting of Charles the Bald (king of the West Franks and thus a 'representative' of the Romance regions) and his brother Louis the German (king of the East Franks and representative of the German regions) in 842 is usually limited in published discussions to the texts of the oaths in Latin, 'lingua Romana' and 'lingua teudisca'. The circumstances of the oath in the political crisis of the years 840–3 and the complex motives of Nithard in presenting his narrative as he does receive little attention. It is even often forgotten that Louis the German addressed Charles' army in Romance and Charles addressed Louis' army in German, that Louis swore his oath in Romance and Charles his in German, whereas their followers are described by Nithard as speaking in their own languages respectively: that is, Charles' men spoke Romance and Louis' warriors swore their oaths in German. The implications first of all is that these were mutually intelligible, certainly to the leaders, for the kings could speak both languages. So, surely, could many members of each army. Our knowledge of the supporters of Louis the German and Charles the Bald certainly makes any restriction of their origins to Romance regions for the West Frankish supporters and German regions for the East Frankish supporters totally absurd. The consequent triumphant conclusion that the Oaths of Strasbourg prove that Romance had emerged definitively, was unintelligible to other members of the Frankish Empire, and that the differences were clearly defined is untenable, at least in terms of this text. Even if it were, the usual assumed corollary that Latin had become unintelligible is simply not proven. Nithard, as Nelson (1986) has argued, had to present the alliance between Louis and Charles in a favourable light. He therefore made striking use of difference in language, exchanged by the brothers but maintained by their troops, to enhance both the difference he wished to stress and the necessity for reconciliation. Nithard had to continue to address fellow supporters of Charles the Bald and could do so by letting them symbolically speak the same language, just as followers of Louis the German spoke a different one. By giving each army a tongue each he was able to stress the unity and coherence of each. But in putting the language of the other army in the mouth of their leaders he could at the same time underplay the difference. He did this also through the medium of the text of the oath, so that it is repeated three times, in all three languages of the Franks, the two current spoken languages and the formal written one. The collective nature of the commitments is heightened by this clever and essentially literary use of language; it is a rhetorical device in the traditions of the great classical history writers. It certainly cannot be understood as an accurate reflection of the linguistic capacities or affiliations of either the nobles or the rank and file in either army. We are not justified in extrapolating from these oaths the linguistic situation in the whole of France, for in so doing we underestimate the sheer diversity of linguistic knowledge in the Carolingian world and ignore the different local and family origins of the supporters of the two Frankish rulers. Certainly, Nithard's attempt to render the words of the oath as spoken by his symbolically unified group indicate what had happened to the spoken language and might be compared, as an attempt to record the spoken word, to Otfrid of Weissenburg's efforts outlined in the preface to his *Evangelienbuch* (Erdmann 1973); but it does not prove at all either that a follower alleged to have said the oath in this manner would have recognized it as such, or that Latin when spoken out loud would not have been intelligible to the army of either side.[1] Awareness of language difference, which we can find scattered throughout the sources, cannot be taken to mean lack of comprehension of Latin as a whole.

The charter evidence, all of it in Latin, from Latinate (Wickham 1986; Nelson 1986), Germanic (McKitterick 1989: 77–134) and Celtic (Davies 1986, 1988) regions of the Carolingian Empire witnesses to the everyday use of Latin to establish rights to property on the part of the free land-owning population. Although often dependent on monastic and clerical charter redactors as well as lay notaries attached to local comital and judicial courts, their participation in Latin literacy in this way indicates how pervasive the use of written Latin documents was in the Early Middle Ages and the nature of social adjustments made to accommodate the uses of the written word.

We may also reflect on the implications of the capitulary evidence (Mordek 1987; McKitterick 1989: 25–40; Nelson 1990). These directives are all formulated in Latin, and provision in some instances is made for reading them aloud. Yet there is seldom reference made to the need to translate the capitularies into a spoken vernacular. There is, for example, the capitulary made and consigned to Count Stephen of Paris so that he might make these manifest in the city of Paris in the public assembly and so that he might read them out before the *scabini* (*MGH Cap.* 1, no. 39, pp. 111–12). Louis the Pious ordered archbishops and counts to

> collect copies of capitularies from the chancellor and to have these copied for the bishops, abbots, counts and other faithful men throughout the diocese, and to read them out in their countries before everyone so that our orders and our wishes can be made known to all.
>
> (*MGH Cap.* 1, no. 150. c. 26, p. 307)

Charles the Bald at Pîtres in 864 insisted that his decisions were to be made known to his faithful men in writing, 'so that you can hear them more fully', and also by constant reference back to the written text 'may more firmly keep in mind what we have ordered to be given and read out and kept in every county'. In Hincmar of Rheims' description, written in 882, of the manner in which Carolingian assemblies functioned, moreover, many were organized in terms of written agendas and issued capitularies containing decisions made at the meeting, all of them in Latin; there is no hint that translation was either required or necessary. Hincmar states clearly that 'all the important men, both clerics and laymen, attended the general assembly and that the important men came to participate in the deliberations, and those of lower station were present in order to hear the decisions and occasionally also to deliberate concerning them, and to confirm them not out of coercion but by their own understanding and agreement' (Hincmar, *De ordine palatii*, ed. Gross and Schieffer 1980, c. 29, pp. 82–4, trans. Herlihy 1970, p. 222). He then adds information which sheds light on the interchange between oral and written modes of communication:

> The important persons and the senior advisers of the realm were given by royal authority, for their discussion and consideration, the decisions which the king through the inspiration of God had made, and the information which he had learned from every

quarter since their last meeting. These documents were titled and arranged in chapters. Having received the chapters, the great men deliberated sometimes one day, sometimes two, three, or more days, according to the importance of the affair. With the aid of the messengers chosen from the servants of the palace mentioned above, they proposed questions to the king and received responses on all matters which seemed appropriate to them.

(ed. Gross and Schieffer 1980, c. 34, p. 91
and trans., Herlihy 1970, p. 225)

It is essential to stress, therefore, that Latin was the language of government, apparently in its spoken, as well as its written form (compare Richter 1982). It transcended any linguistic divide between West and East Franks. Latin united the Franks, and the facts that the few references to translation concern the Germanic vernaculars, and the small number of extant translations of capitularies or oaths are in Germanic texts of East Frankish provenance, suggest that it was between Latinate speech and German that the linguistic divide was perceived, not between Latin and Romance (*Annales Fuldenses*, s.a. 876, ed. F. Kurze, *MGH SS in usum scholarum*, p. 89, and Werner 1980: 99, n. 27). In addition to the absence of references to the need for translation we can note the assumption of literacy or access to literate assistance, and the exploitation of literate modes consistently in the processes of Carolingian administration.

Assessments of the degrees and ranges of literacy in Merovingian and Frankish Gaul have been hamstrung in the past by the apparent insistence that Latin was unintelligible, in whatever form, to the mass of the population. Although linguists and historians may not be able to agree on the extent to which either spoken Latin or written Latin was generally understood, there ought to be an acknowledgement of the awkwardness, in face of all the evidence to the contrary, of insisting on duality of language and the confined access to Latin, and of the difficulties of generalizing about the languages known to the Franks in both the western (so-called Romance) and the eastern (Germanic) portions of the Frankish kingdom. In other words, the eighth and ninth centuries were a culturally as well as linguistically diverse period, in which the one common element, Latin, has to be acknowledged in its proper context. Latin, whatever it may have sounded like when it was spoken, and however much it may have been refined and reformed in order to bring it closer to idealized norms by Carolingian scholars, was the dominant language. The Franks were a Germanic people who conducted their administrative, legal, and intellectual affairs in Latin. The Franks, in short, represent a unique blend of linguistic factors as a people that had embraced the language and thus some of the cultural assumptions of the Roman world in which the status of Latin as the primary means of communication in writing was maintained. The very absence of discussion of linguistic problems should be interpreted at their face value. There were no major linguistic problems other than those encountered in the efforts to spread literacy and learning.

The literacy of the Franks in the Carolingian period has received full attention in McKitterick (1989: 211–70). It should be evident from what I have said in that discussion that even if Latin is to be understood as the second, acquired, foreign and learned language of the Franks in the ninth century, it is abundantly clear that the Franks used it extensively nevertheless, and that the ability to read was quite widespread among the upper groups of society, and, as is indicated by the charter evidence, writing and its importance were understood and exploited by many of the lower groups as well. Nithard, Dhuoda, Eberhard of Friuli, and Eccard of Mâcon and members of the Carolingian family, acclaimed in the past as the exceptions which proved the rule of general Frankish lay illiteracy, have now been joined by many other literate lay Franks, Alemans, Saxons, Bavarians, Rhaetians, and Aquitainians, male and female, all over the Carolingian world. They indicate that literacy in Latin was not confined to a clerical elite and that legislative and judicial activities and the reception of the written word in Frankish society were things in which lay Franks did indeed have a part to play.

The character of lay literacy, moreover, reflects the kind of transformations that literacy effected in lay culture. Significant consequences of literacy can be observed in lay religious observance, for it was expressed and directed in relation to specific Latin texts. We have become accustomed to the association of the reproduction of Books of Hours in the Late Middle Ages with lay literacy and piety, especially among the women in families that could afford books. So too, in the eighth, ninth, and tenth centuries we may associate the Psalter, accompanied by other prayers, as well as theological texts, laws, histories, and practical manuals on military affairs and estate management, with particular well-to-do lay owners. A copy of the Octateuch, now Vat. pal. lat. 14, for example, is to be associated with a Countess Hoda, probably the wife of Zwentibold of Lotharingia (Bischoff 1974: 85), and there are many other examples of book ownership, with a consideration of its implications for lay literacy, provided by McKitterick (1989: 135–64, 244–61). There is evidence too of the borrowing of books in Latin in both Germanic and Romance regions (ibid.: 261–6). Yet the indications of the current trends in the Latin–Romance debate are that there is no longer certainty, and still less agreement, that Latin was a foreign language reserved for a clerical elite in the eighth, ninth, and tenth centuries. It may have been so in the eleventh and twelfth centuries, but what is true of the High Middle Ages in no sense can be taken as applying to the Early Middle Ages. In short, the exposure of the weaknesses of old assumptions about the linguistic situation in early medieval Europe have made possible a radical reassessment of the degree of lay literacy among the Franks, and with it, a positive reappraisal of the Carolingian achievement as a whole. Despite many remaining problems and the need for much further research on a wide range of issues, the full extent to which the Franks realized the potential of the written word can now properly be appreciated.

NOTE

1 It is inconceivable in any case that Nithard is faithfully recording the actual words spoken. What he is doing is giving literary form to what was an extempore promise (though, given the familiarity of the Carolingians with oath-taking, it may not have differed all that much in content). In other words, we do not necessarily have what anybody actually said, only what Nithard says they said. Only one copy of Nithard's 'Histories' survives; Paris, Bibliothèque Nationale 9768, dated to the end of the ninth century, whose provenance is St Médard of Soissons. Whether this copy was made from an autograph of Nithard is impossible now to establish, but we may have to reckon with a scribe adjusting the spelling of the Romance and German words to accord with his own late ninth-century practice rather than those of the mid-ninth century in the original. (A fuller discussion of this is in preparation.)

BIBLIOGRAPHY

Adams, J. N. (1989) Review discussion of Roger Wright, *Late Latin and Early Romance* (Liverpool, 1982), *Liverpool Classical Monthly* 14, 1: 14–16 and 14, 2 and 3: 34–48.
Banniard, Michel (1975) 'Le Lecteur en Espagne wisigothique d'après Isidore de Seville: de ses fonctions à l'état de la langue', *Revue des Etudes Augustiniennes* 21: 112–44.
—— (1980) *Le Haut Moyen Age Occidental* (Que sais-je? 1807), Paris: Presses Universitaires de France.

Bischoff, Bernhard (1974) *Lorsch im Spiegel seiner Handschriften* (Münchener Beiträge zur Mediävistik und Renaissance-Forschung, supplement), Munich: Arbeo.

Davies, Wendy (1986) 'People and places in dispute in ninth-century Brittany', in W. Davies and P. Fouracre (eds), *The Settlement of Disputes in Early Medieval Europe*, Cambridge: Cambridge University Press, 65–84.

—— (1988) *Small Worlds: the Village Community in Early Medieval Brittany*, London: Duckworth.

Erdmann, Oskar (1973) *Otfrids Evangelienbuch*, Tübingen: Max Niemeyer.

Friedrichsen, G. W. S. (1926) *The Gothic Version of the Gospels*, Oxford: Clarendon Press.

—— (1939) *The Gothic Version of the Epistles*, Oxford: Clarendon Press.

Ganshof, F. L. (1951) 'Charlemagne et l'usage de l'écrit en matière administrative', *Le Moyen Age* 52: 1–25; English version, 'The use of the written word in Charlemagne's administration', in F. L. Ganshof, trans. J. Sondheimer, *The Carolingians and the Frankish Monarchy*, London: Longman, 1971, 125–42.

Ganz, David (1987) 'The preconditions for caroline minuscule', *Viator* 18: 23–44.

Godman, Peter (ed.) (1985) *Poetry of the Carolingian Renaissance*, London: Duckworth.

—— (1987) *Poets and Emperors*, Oxford: Clarendon Press.

Gross, T. and Schieffer, R. (1980) *Hincmarus de ordine palatii* (Monumenta Germaniae Historica, Fontes Iuris Germanici Antiqui in usum scholarum separatim editi), Hanover: Hahnsche Buchhandlung.

Guerreau-Jalabert, A. (1981) 'La "Renaissance Carolingienne": modèles culturels, usages linguistiques et structures sociales', *Bibliothèque de l'Ecole des Chartes* 139: 5–35.

Herlihy, David (1970) *History of Feudalism*, London: Macmillan.

Itkonen, E. (1978) 'The significance of Merovingian Latin to Linguistic Theory', *Four Linguistic Studies in Classical Languages*, Helsinki: Department of General Linguistics, 9–64.

James, Edward (1982) *The Origins of France*, London: Macmillan.

—— (1988) *The Franks*, Oxford: Basil Blackwell.

Law, Vivien (1982) *The Insular Latin Grammarians*, Woodbridge: Boydell & Brewer.

Levillain, Leon (1964) *Loup de Ferrières, Correspondance*, Paris: Société d'Edition "Les Belles Lettres".

Lot, Ferdinand (1931) 'A quelle Epoque a-t-on cessé de parler Latin?', *Archivum Latinitatis Medii Aevi (Bulletin du Cange)* 6: 97–159.

McKitterick, Rosamond (1977) *The Frankish Church and the Carolingian Reforms, 789–895*, London: Royal Historical Society.

—— (1989) *The Carolingians and the Written Word*, Cambridge: Cambridge University Press.

—— (ed.) (1990) *The Uses of Literacy in Early Mediaeval Europe*, Cambridge: Cambridge University Press.

Mordek, Hubert (1987) *Überlieferung und Geltung normativer Texte des frühen und hohen Mittelalters* (Quellen und Forschungen zum Recht im Mittelalter, 4), Sigmaringen: Jan Thorbecke.

Muller, Henry F. (1921) 'When did Latin cease to be a spoken language in

France?', *The Romanic Review* 12: 318–24.

Nelson, Janet L. (1986) 'Public Histories and private history in the work of Nithard', *Speculum* 60: 251–93.

—— (1990) 'Literacy in Carolingian government', in R. McKitterick (ed.), *The Uses of Literacy in Early Mediaeval Europe*, Cambridge: Cambridge University Press, 258–96.

Rau, R. (1974) *Quellen zur Karolingischen Reichsgeschichte* 1, Darmstadt: Wissenschaftliche Buchgesellschaft.

Regenos, Graydon W. (1966) *The Letters of Lupus of Ferrières*, The Hague: Martinus Nijhoff.

Richter, Michael (1975) 'A socio-linguistic approach to the Latin middle ages', *Studies in Church History* 11: 69–82.

—— (1976) 'Kommunikationsprobleme im lateinischen Mittelalter', *Historische Zeitschrift* 222: 43–80.

—— (1979) 'Urbanitas–rusticitas: linguistic aspects of a mediaeval dichotomy', *Studies in Church History* 16: 149–57.

—— (1982) 'Die Sprachenpolitik Karls des Grossen', *Sprachwissenschaft* 7: 412–37.

—— (1983) *Sprache und Gesellschaft im Mittelalter. Untersuchungen zur mundlichen Kommunikation in England von der Mitte des elften bis zum Beginn des 14. Jahrhunderts* (Monographien zur Geschichte des Mittelalters, 18), Stuttgart: Anton Hiersemann.

Thompson, E. A. (1966) *The Visigoths in the Time of Ulfila*, Oxford: Clarendon Press.

Van Uytfanghe, Marc (1983) 'Histoire du latin, protohistoire des langues romanes et histoire de la communication. A propos d'un receuil d'études, et avec quelques observations préliminaires sur le débat intellectuel entre pensée structurale et pensée historique', *Francia* 11: 579–613.

Werner, Karl-Ferdinand (1980) 'Missus, Marchio, Comes. Entre l'administration centrale et l'administration locale de l'empire carolingien', in W. Paravicini and K. F. Werner (eds), *Histoire comparée de l'administration (IVe–XVIIIe siècles)* (Beihefte der Francia, 9), Munich: Artemis, 190–239.

Wickham, Chris (1986) 'Land disputes and their social framework in Lombard–Carolingian Italy', in W. Davies and P. Fouracre (eds), *The Settlement of Disputes in Early Mediaeval Europe*, Cambridge: Cambridge University Press, 105–24.

Wightmann, Edith (1985) *Gallia Belgica*, London: Duckworth.

Wright, Roger (1982) *Late Latin and Early Romance in Spain and Carolingian France*, Liverpool: Cairns.

Wood, Ian (1990) 'Administration, law and culture in Merovingian Gaul', in R. McKitterick (ed.), *The Uses of Literacy in Early Mediaeval Europe*, Cambridge: Cambridge University Press, 63–81.

12 *Audire*, *legere*, *vulgo*: an attempt to define public use and comprehensibility of Carolingian hagiography[*]

Katrien Heene

Until some years ago it was almost common, for those who opted for a relative late disappearance of Latin as a spoken language, to believe that the language of the ordinary 'French' people north of the Loire was Latin before AD 600 and Romance after AD 800. The Merovingian period thus constituted a period of diglossia (Lüdtke 1964: 5–6) and was crucial for the drifting away of the popular language from 'Classical' Latin (Van Uytfanghe 1976: 23–31; 1984: 597–8; Banniard 1980a: 109 and 118; 1980b: 11–12; Löfstedt 1983: 260). The awareness of the existence of two different language systems, a Romance on the one hand and a Latin on the other hand, would have arisen for the first time in the year 813, under the influence of the Carolingian linguistic reformation (Van Uytfanghe 1976: 78–83; 1984: 601–2; Richter 1979: 21; Banniard 1980a: 109–10; 1980b: 18; Löfstedt 1983: 262; Berschin 1987: 16). Recent research, however, focuses on the Carolingian Age (Van Uytfanghe, as early as 1975: 285–6), the ninth century in particular, and presents new perspectives (Van Uytfanghe 1976: 86–9; 1984: 602). In particular, R. Wright's quite innovating study (1982) has kicked up much scientific dust (Banniard 1985).

In our dissertation on aspects of femininity, particularly maternity and maternal feelings in the edifying literature of the Carolingian Age, we are searching for the communicative bearing of this kind of literature (cf. Richter 1979: 22–3). This means that we are trying to grasp the nature of the public and the degree of comprehensibility of our main source: the *vitae* and *miracula sanctorum*.

Our research emphasizes the hagiographical literature which constitutes an important sociolinguistic (Richter 1975: 70) witness for the Merovingian period (Banniard 1980b: 19–24), and focuses on the ninth century (Van Uytfanghe 1985: 57–60; 1984: 598–612). By using the information from our corpus of texts, which all originated in the regions north of the Loire (Romance as well as Germanic), we hope that we can contribute our modest part towards the discussion.[1]

Our approach was mainly twofold. First, we have tried to work out whether the written Latin of the Carolingian hagiographical texts could still function as 'Horchsprache' (Sanders 1982: 412, n. 2).[2] On the basis of external elements as well as information from the texts themselves (*inter alia*, the terms *legere* and *audire*), we have attempted to highlight the direct role of the hagiographical literature in what we would call 'pastoral' communication (Fontaine 1981b: 364).[3] Second, we have paid attention to turns of phrase of the 'quod vulgo dicitur, quod vulgo vocant' kind. We were not only interested in the extent to which these phrases might refer to the linguistic situation, but also particularly in possible changes in comparison with the testimony of the Merovingian sources.[4]

Despite the linguistic reformation there are several linguistic and stylistic levels in the Carolingian *vitae* as there were in Merovingian ones (Fontaine 1981a: 798–802; Van Uytfanghe 1984: 608–9). It seems possible that the descriptions of the miracles – by actualizing *hic* and *nunc* God's power working in his saints (Heinzelmann 1981a: 245–8) – were much more important for the edification of the ordinary believers (Collins 1981: 25–30). We would have liked to examine the language and style of the separate *miracula* collections (a typical ninth-century phenomenon), since these possibly reflect this desire for popular edification (Heinzelmann 1981a: 244–6). Unfortunately, time did not permit us to elaborate this aspect, but we will try to formulate our general impression. Eventually we will try to connect our data with the diverse opinions concerning the linguistic situation.

It is obvious that in the Merovingian Age the hagiographical texts were used with direct pastoral objectives. Several texts mention that parts of the *vitae* were being read aloud during Mass or other celebrations performed on the saint's feast-day (Collins 1981: 19). The hagiographers themselves indicate that they are writing for an illiterate audience by whom they want to be understood (Banniard 1980b: 20–1; Collins 1981: 22–3; Van Uytfanghe 1985: especially his conclusions, 60–2).

The Gallican rite (Jungmann 1962: 59–62) – which had a rather loose shape – did, as a matter of fact, provide the possibility of replacing one of the Gospels for the day by a fragment from the life of the saint whose *nativitas* was being celebrated (*DACL* VI s.v.

(Gallicane) liturgie: 540–75; Jungmann 1962: 510; Vogel 1966: 262; de Gaiffier 1954: 145–51).[5]

The more rigid Roman rite was gradually substituted for the Gallican type of liturgy from the middle of the eighth century onwards (Vogel 1966: 118–19; Salmon 1967: 21–3). In the Frankish lands, however, this liturgy form was contaminated with many autochthonic elements (Jungmann 1962: 98–122; *DACL* IX, s.v. Liturgies néo-Gallicanes: 1636–7 and 1646–8). Also from the eighth century onwards there is very little information on the use of hagiographical texts in the Mass, and this habit even seems to have disappeared completely with the introduction of the Roman rite (Philippart 1977: 113–14).[6] In contrast, there is evidence that this kind of text continued to be used in the clerico-monastic hours (de Gaiffier 1954: 141–2 (Rome); Salmon 1967: 39–40; Philippart 1977: 109, 114–15). Ordo XVI – written at the end of the eighth century by a Frankish monk for religious communities (*coenobia*) in Gaul and in the Germanic territories – explicitly mentions the reciting of hagiographical texts during the nocturnal office, the *vigiliae*, on the saint's feast-day (Andrieu 1948: 135, 147).

Scholars (Chélini 1956: 173–4; Devailly 1973: 53–4; McKitterick 1977: 144–5, 147) are still investigating the ordinary people's churchgoing and their participation in the celebration of Mass. It is therefore certainly not farfetched to question their attendance at the other offices on holy days. The cult of saints was nevertheless very popular in the Carolingian Age and Charlemagne – although he reacted against its excesses – gave permission for cloisters and parishes to celebrate their local saints (this means the saint whose relics they owned) (von Schubert 1916: 669–72).

Moreover, several authors of *miracula* collections describe the people crowding to the church on the holy festival day, and even state that common people were present during the nocturnal celebrations. Many healings took place at the saint's grave while the monks (or clerics) were saying the *vigiliae*.[7]

Attendance and even listening, however, did not necessarily include understanding of the texts which were being recited.[8] It is not surprising that the author of the *M. Goaris* c. 35 expresses the importance of *spectare*, of watching the ceremonies, in Germanic territory. But it is surprising that similar information is found in texts from Romance regions: the *M. Carileffi* c. 5 (written in northern France) stress the importance of the seeing of the *lector* and the author of the *M. Cassiani* c. 12 pities a blind woman even though she is able to attend (and hear) the celebration.[9] This is certainly not evidence in favour of their understanding the texts. Skimming through the texts – the prologues in particular (de Gaiffier 1947: 159–61) – for their function and public, it is striking that those texts which mention terms such as *legere* or *lectores* outweigh to a considerable extent the ones referring to *audire* or *auditores*.[10] These references do not, of course, clarify the kind of public. Many texts give no additional information on this subject. Besides, several authors clearly aim at a monastic or clerical audience, not at the common believers. There are various texts pointing to the improving individual reading of *vitae* by monks or clerics living in a community (e.g. *V. Adalhardi* c. 19 (*PL* 120, 1507– 57, here 1517), *V. Benedicti* c. 41 (*MGH SS* XV, 200–20, here 218); *V. Maldelbertae* c. 9 (*ASS* Sept. III, 109–11, here 110)), to the reading aloud of parts of the texts in the *refectorium* (*V. Aegili* c. 22 (*MGH SS* XV, 222–33, here 232)) or in the chapter (*Diadema monachorum*, prol. (*PL* 102, 593–690, here 593)), or during the divine offices on the saint's feast-day (*V. Willibrordi* c. 32a (*MGH SS rer. merov.* VII, 81–141, here 139)).[11] Reference to the festal day is, nevertheless, not as common as one would expect.[12]

Few authors from the Romance-speaking territory of the realm explicitly state that they are aiming at, or that they are understood by, the ordinary believers, the *plebs*, the *populus*, the *fideles*, or the *multi*.[13] This, of course, does not exclude the possibility that the texts were used indirectly to edify these people by incorporating elements in sermons (Riché 1973: 239 (rarely); Philippart 1977: 107; McKitterick 1977: 98, 108). There are, indeed, many allusions to the edifying purpose of the text, but such an utterance belongs to the standard *topoi* of the hagiographical prologue (Strunk 1970: 90–2).[14]

The prologue of the *V. Richarii*, however, written in AD 801 by Alcuin, is clear evidence for the existence of a situation of diglossia at the end of the eighth century, albeit unconsciously. Alcuin mentions that the monks of St Riquier still use the Merovingian text of the *miracula* to edify the common people, while they want a new and more 'polished' text of the *vita* for internal use: there are clearly two written levels distinguished, each with their own public.[15] Yet, after some years, a new collection of miracles was written (*M. Richarii*, *ASS* April III, 446–85), the older collection having undoubtedly lost its topicality (Heinzelmann 1981a: 244, 285). Possibly the less sophisticated language too became unacceptable as the Carolingian linguistic reformation progressed.

The other texts indicating a pastoral use chronologically corroborate Alcuin's testimony. Most of them originated in the second half of the eighth century or at the beginning of the ninth. I here present some examples: the author of the *V. Eligii* (a rewritten text of the second half of the eighth century) clearly expresses the text's public function: 'Quotiens ergo sanctorum sollemnia anniversario curriculo caelebramus, aliqua ex eorum gestis ad aedificationem christianae plebis convenientia in Christi laudibus recitare debemus.'

The author of the *V. Balthildis B* is less explicit: he mentions the saint's festal day and says he wants to write 'ad multorum aedificationem et profectum', be it 'imperito sermone'. The writer of the *V. Vulframni* introduces a miracle he is going to tell as follows: 'illud quoque stupendum rarissime alicui concessum miraculum, verax scribentis stilus pandat auribus fidelium'.[16]

Similar utterances are found in other texts of the beginning of the ninth century at the latest, but not exclusively. There are two *vitae* written at the end of this same century which possibly support the supposition that even texts written in 'good' Carolingian Latin were addressed to the illiterate believers: the *V. Opportunae*, written around AD 880 by Adalhelm, Bishop of Séez; and the *V. Remigii* composed at about the same time by Hincmar of Reims.

Hincmar distinguishes two kinds of public: the *legentes* on the one hand and the *audientia populi* on the other hand. He also indicates that he has divided the text into lessons to be recited on the festival of the saint's deposition and transfer and that he has separated and marked the parts intended for the 'minus scientes (populo audiente)' from those for the 'illuminati (que instructioribus et studiosioribus . . . legenda serventur)'.

Analysing the different parts of the text, we are under the impression that the difference is merely one of content, not of syntax or style.[17] An elaborate linguistic and stylistic study, however, is required to throw more light on the question of whether this text could indicate the survival of a form of diglossia at Reims even at the end of the ninth century.

The preface of the *V. Opportunae* sets 'haec plebs', of whom the author hopes that they 'gaudens recedat audita virtutum eius revelatione', against the 'dilectissimi filii', for whom he is going to recite the virtuous acts of Opportuna as an example: 'ut operum illius imitatores effecti, ei mereamur in caelestibus sociari'.[18]

As the text gives no other references to the public (except for *audientes* (c. 22)) and as the *miracula* (c. 9) mention the fact that it often pleases to relate (not to recite) the miracles of saint Opportuna ('saepius placet beatae Opportunae miracula referre'), one could assume that there are two possible approaches: reporting the miracles of the saint to the ordinary faithful, on the one hand; and reading aloud the description of her life to the priests of the cathedral church, on the other hand.

In either case, without attributing the situation to linguistic incomprehensibility (as does Berschin 1987: 16), one cannot deny that the direct use of hagiographical texts for an illiterate audience becomes restricted after the beginning of the ninth century and that many texts seem to have been written for internal monastic use, not out of liturgical needs (Phillippart 1977: 31–2, 119).

This restriction is in line with the fact that the authors constantly express their desire to improve the language of their predecessors ('secundum regulas loquendi', according to Jonas of Orléans (*V. Hucberti*, II, prol. *ASS* Nov. I, 806–18, here 806)) and with their efforts to write as correctly as possible according to the norms of the linguistic reformation (Van Uytfanghe 1975: 275; Richter 1983: 443) and especially to avoid the *vitium rusticitatis* (Banniard 1986: 584–5 (concerning Alcuin)).[19]

In this context, expressing one's inability to write proper Latin without God's help is a well-known *topos* of modesty which fits in with Christian *humilitas* (Strunk 1970: 116–29 and 137–61).

Only the author of the *V. Eligii* (prol. *MGH SS rer. merov.* IV, 634–761, here 664) tells us that he deliberately adapts his style to an illiterate audience. But at the same time he tries not to offend his learned readers and attaches great importance to the correct transcription of his text. The authors of the *V. Trudonis* and *V. Hucberti* I, for example, do declare that they are writing in a *sermo rusticus*, but they ask anyone who knows better to make the necessary corrections.[20]

It is obvious that the Carolingian hagiographers do not always use 'better' Latin than the best of their Merovingian colleagues (Van Uytfanghe 1975: 276–8), but, in opposition to the latter, they do not seem to write a *lingua rustica* with pastoral aims. If they do so, it seems rather to be due to their lack of education or an 'unconscious and involuntary influence' of the spoken language (Strunk 1970: 146, 149–51; Banniard 1986: 587–96, 601).

Let us now consider the occurrence of the syntagma *quod vulgo dicitur* and its possible sociolinguistic scope.[21] It is not here possible to discuss each passage separately, but we will point to the general tendencies.

As in the early Carolingian attestations, we rarely find the phrase *quod vulgo dicitur* explaining a more difficult antecedent; we often find it used merely in order to define the general meaning of this antecedent (Van Uytfanghe 1989: 47).

The author of the *V. Ermenlandi* c. 8 (*MGH SS rer. merov.* V, 674–710, here 696) mentions that, while the saint is resting on the bank of the Loire, one of the brothers tells him: 'Namnetensem episcopum abuisse piscem, qui vulgo naupreda dicitur.' A few moments later God gives them a similar fish in answer to the saint's prayer. *Naupreda* merely is the name of a specific kind of fish.

In the *V. Vodoali* c. 8 (*ASOSB* IV2, 544–50, here 548; also dated to the end of the eighth or the beginning of the ninth century) the hagiographer recounts that the saint is attacked by fever on one of his wanderings: 'Factum est autem ut in itinere medio invaderet eum febris, quae vulgo tertiana vel quartana dicitur.' This substantivized term already occurred in the works of Cicero (Díaz y Díaz 1952: 208–9).

It is clear that in these examples, as well as in those where *vulgo* is connected with the name of a town or cloister, it only means 'commonly'.[22] There are, however, many cases where the phrase introduces a term which has a French derivative and which consequently belongs to the spoken language.[23] The *M. Opportunae* c. 14 (*ASOSB* III2, 231–9, here 237), for example, relate how a poor woman comes to the oratory of Opportuna without any gifts. At the last moment she sees a little bird and she asks the saint if the bird would be acceptable as her donation, a wish which the saint, of course, fulfils: 'vidit aviculam [notice the diminutive, cf. *FEW* I, 170–2 (*avicellus*), Fr. *oiseau*] nomine acredula, quam vulgus vocavit Alaudam'. *Alauda* is already mentioned in Pliny as a Gallic word; it gives the Old French *aloe* and its diminutive gives the French *alouette*.

Another example with the paraphrase *vulgari nomine* (*M. Richarii* c. 6, *ASS* April III, 446–56, here 454): thanks to the piety of his mother, who sends candles to Saint Richard, a paralysed boy can walk with a crutch after three years. Another three years later he is totally cured during Mass on the saint's feast-day: 'Et ubi trium tempus annorum peractum est, coepit iam sustentaculo iter suum agere, quod vulgari nomine crocia vocatur.' *Crocia* (*REW*, 344) comes from the Germanic word *krukkja* and gives the old French *crosse* (English *crutch*).

A third example, the *V. Leutfredi* c. 21 (*ASOSB* III1, 582–92, here 590) tells us that while the brothers are working on the field, one of them drops his sickle in the river: 'illud autem feramentum vocant rustici bidubium, quod a quibusdam falcastrum vocatur, eo quod in falcis similitudinem curvum sit'. The saint puts his stick in the water and it attracts the sickle like a magnet. *Bidubium* or *vidubium* (*FEW* XIV, 434–5) is a Gallic word which becomes *vooge* in Old French, *vouge* in Modern French.

There are similar cases where *quod vulgo dicitur* is introducing words which have a normal French derivative. Since the anteceding words often also have a normal derivative, one cannot simply conclude, on the basis of such data, that in the Carolingian Age *vulgo* would refer to the Romance vernacular. Consequently the situation of 'diglossia' need not necessarily have become one of bilingualism in the ninth century (Wright 1982: 90–5; Van Uytfanghe 1989: 48).

As there is a material separation between *vita* and *miracula*, especially in the ninth century, thirdly we assume that miracles could be more important to edify the ordinary faithful, while the more biographical aspects of the saints' life were intended for a more literate audience. This different communicative function could influence the linguistic level of the texts. We unfortunately can only express our general impressions: the authors of *miracula* collections do not refer more to an illiterate audience than do the writers of the *vitae*. They do sometimes use a simple narrative style, but so do the authors of some *vitae* also (*V. Geremari, MGH SS rer. merov.* IV, 626–36). More than once they address their *lectores*, but the kind of miracles they narrate are often very popular: e.g. the punishment of a mistress who forbids her servants to go to Mass (*M. Opportunae* c. 7 (*ASOSB* III1, 232–9, here 235)), or of a woman who prefers to continue her weaving activities instead of attending the liturgical celebration of the feast-day (*M. Richarii* bk II c. 4 (*ASS* April III, 446–56, here 453)), the healing of animals (*M. Vedasti* c. 5 (*ASS* Feb. I, 801–2, here 802)), the healing of innumerable little children (*M. Germani* c. 11 and c. 113 (*PL* 124, 1207–72, here 1213 and 1260)).[24] In order to be able to draw conclusions, however, each text should be studied for its language and style. It is a pity that many miracle collections are not yet critically edited.

In conclusion: since the pastoral and communicative function of Carolingian hagiography seems to be reduced after the beginning of the ninth century, the sociolinguistic information offered by this literature is not as easy to interpret as the information from Merovingian sources.

It is tempting to ascribe the devaluation of the texts' pastoral function to Carolingian written Latin becoming incomprehensible; but that is not necessarily so. There are indeed two testimonies of the end of the ninth century which could be used to defend a situation of diglossia at that time. Moreover, this devaluation was possibly provoked by the liturgical evolution. In the frame of the standardization of public and liturgical life (Wright 1982: 103–5), the liturgical rites and the language of their texts gradually became more formalized and the exclusive domain of the clerics. This was in spite of Charlemagne's efforts to adapt the language of the church to the people in some specific cases (Richter 1976: 53–7; Dekkers 1979: 12; Richter 1982: 413–14). The ordinary believers play no really active part (Richter 1976: 52; 1982: 428); it is the priest who addresses God in their name (Jungmann 1962: 106–14, 312).[25]

The Merovingian written language had several levels of influence from colloquial speech, which depended on the author's schooling or on the extent to which he was interested in pastoral communication: then he made his texts comprehensible for the average laymen, when they were read aloud. The different registers of Carolingian written Latin were probably mainly dependent on the author's level of education, and not on his pastoral aims. The language of the highest levels (e.g. the *omilias patrum*) was not comprehensible for all illiterate faithful and had to be adapted.

Alcuin undoubtedly had a certain reform of pronunciation in mind (Lüdtke 1964: 13–21; Van Uytfanghe 1975: 279; 1984: 608; Wright 1981: 345–51; 1982: 105–16; Walsh 1986–7: 213–14), and was certainly followed in this by some of his pupils.[26] We personally prefer to join those scholars (Banniard 1980b: 23; 1985: 196, 203; Fontaine 1981a: 794–5; Van Uytfanghe 1984: 612; Walsh 1986–7: 205–7, 212–14; Berschin 1987: 6–7) who find it hard to accept that a mere adaptation of the way of pronouncing would first have caused, and afterwards have solved, the understanding of the normalized written Latin; and that *transferre in rusticam Romanam linguam* would only have meant adapting the pronunciation (Wright 1981: 355–7; 1982: 118–21).[27]

At the beginning of the ninth century the situation certainly still was one of diglossia: the same Alcuin in the preface of the *V. Richarii* gives a clear testimony: the 'Merovingian' level of the language ('Latin à la mérovingienne', Dekkers 1979: 11) was still apt for recitation before an illiterate audience.

The current research on the *vitae* and *miracula sanctorum* only provides limited evidence concerning the issues of whether the evolution towards a formalized (written) Latin language accelerated the rupture between the learned and the popular level of the language, and whether the awareness of this already occurred in the course of the ninth century or was postponed for still another century. The fact that hagiographical texts, which seem to have been an important pastoral medium in the Merovingian Age, almost totally ceased to be used as such after the beginning of the ninth century, could, however, be at least partly due to the fact that reformed Latin became the language of communication of a restricted group, while it was then incomprehensible for the man in the street (Dekkers 1979: 11; Fontaine 1981a: 797).

ABBREVIATIONS

ASOSB	L. D'Achéry and J. Mabillon (1668–1701) *Acta sanctorum ordinis Sancti Benedicti*, Paris.
ASS	*Acta Sanctorum* (collegit Bollandus) (1643–1894), Antwerp and Brussels.
FEW	von Wartburg (1922).
MGH SS (1826–)	*Monumenta germaniae historica. Scriptores*, Hanover.
MGH SS rer. merov. (1885–)	*Monumenta germaniae historica. Scriptores rerum merovingicarum*, Hanover.
PL	J. P. Migne (1844–64) *Patrologiae cursus completus. Series latina*, Paris.
REW	Meyer-Lübke (1911).

NOTES

* I would like to thank the 'Vlaamse Wetenschappelijke Stichting' for its financial support allowing me to take part in this conference.

1 We have compiled a corpus of some 130 Carolingian *vitae* and *miracula sanctorum* (AD 750–900). Unfortunately, many hagiographical documents have not yet been critically edited nor precisely dated. In anticipation of the results of the dating project of M. Heinzelmann and J. C. Poulin (Heinzelmann 1981b), we mainly followed the dating proposed by the *Bibliotheca Sanctorum* (1961–4). We have also used the non-critical editions of texts relevant to our research.

2 On the important intermediary function of the *lector*: Lüdtke (1964: 12); Banniard (1975); Sanders prefers the term 'Horchsprache' to the term 'Vorlesesprache' (Lüdtke 1964: 4), since the former stresses the position of the uncultivated hearer, while the latter is connected with the viewpoint of the professional *lector*.

3 This article is partly a continuation and elaboration of the ideas phrased in a lecture delivered at the Tenth International Conference on Patristic

Studies at Oxford (Heene 1989).

4 On this subject we are following Van Uytfanghe (1989).

5 There are, however, few saints with a proper office (de Gaiffier 1954: 149–50; Salmon 1967: 39).

6 According to Hilduin, the author of the *V. Dionysii* (around AD 835), it was precisely the transition from Gallican to Roman rite that caused the disappearance of the old Latin *passio* which had been used in the Gallican rite; *V. Dionysii* cc. 5–6 (*PL* 106, 14–50, here 17): 'hunc missae tenorem de Gallica consuetudine recessisse, et hanc passionis martyrorum istorum memoriam . . . inolevisse'.

7 For example, *M. Liudgeri* c. 7 (*ASOSB* III1, 48–61, here 51):

> sancti sacerdotis ambit sepulcrum, ipsa nocte sopori dedisset, beati ei confessor . . . per visum apparuit, et membra illius tangens abscessit in sopore ipso relicto. Post cuius discessionem dum mox signa ad nocturnas vigilias sonarent, et his ipse expergefactus esset, sanus surrexit . . . una cum aliis laetus et incolumis templum intravit.

See also *M. Remacli* c. 28 (*ASS* Sept. I, 696–703, here 702); *M. Richarii* c. 8 (*ASS* April III, 446–56, here 448); *M. Vedasti* c. 2 (*ASS* Febr. I, 801–2, here 802).

8 One must, however, listen attentively (Jungmann 1962: 318). Cf. *M. Richarii* c. 8 (*ASS* April III, 446–56, here 449), where the author gives the testimony of a man who was cured at the saint's tomb: 'cum vobis <monachis> almifici officii celebrantibus magnificas laudes ingressus fuissem hanc venerabilem domum . . . subito ingens me invasit sopor. Et ecce duo venerabili canitie viri . . . his me vocibus alloquuntur: "Cur piger dormitas, et non audis ea quae recitantur?".'

9 *M. Goaris* c. 35 (Stiene 1981: 82): 'Eodemque die cum missarum sollemnia populus *spectaret* et divina a sacerdote mysteria agerentur . . .'; *M. Carileffi* c. 5 (*ASS* Iul. I, 98–102, here 100); and *M. Cassiani* c. 12 (*ASS* Aug. II, 59–69, here 67):

> accurit et mulier cum ceteris quidem solennem diem celebrare, sed non cum ceteris sollennitates *videre. Audire* cum ceteris poterat, *videre* non poterat, quam saeva caecitas olim damnaverat. . . . Videbatur tamen ei sat esse, si ei contingeret interesse: . . . efficitur aequalis ceteris, quae ex propria miseria venerat dissimilis. Solvuntur enim palpebrae ad instar evigilantium oculorum.

Moreover, several texts appear to indicate that the celebrating monks are separated from the common people praying at the saint's tomb, e.g. *M. Leutfredi* c. 2 (*ASOSB* III1, 582–93, here 593); *M. Remacli* cc. 1 and 27 (*ASS* Sept. I, 696–702, here 702); *M. Richarii c. 8 (ASS* April III, 446–56, here 448).

10 Some references are listed below (the exhaustive list will be incorporated in our forthcoming dissertation):

> *Legere, lectores*: *V. Adalhardi* c. 26 (*PL* 120, 1507–57, here 1522); *V. Anskarii* cc. 1 and 18 (*MGH SS* II, 689–725, here 689 and 700); *V. Bavonis* c. 16 (*MGH SS rer. merov.* IV, 534–46, here 545); *V. Harlindis et Reinulae* c. 25 (*ASOSB* III1, 654–62, here 662); *V. Hucberti* II praef. (*ASS* Nov. I, 806–18, here 806); *M. Leutfredi* (*MGH SS rer. merov.* VII,

1–18, here 18); *V. Lupi* c. 9 (*ASS* Oct. XI, 670–4, here 672); *V. Medardi*
c. 2 (*ASS* Iun. II, 82–6, here 82); *M. Remacli* c. 30 (*ASS* Sept. I,
696–703, here 703); *V. Rigoberti* cc. 3, 15, and 24 (*MGH SS rer. merov.*
VII, 54–80, here 64, 70, and 75), etc.
Audire, auditores: *V. Anstrudis* cc. 3 and 10 (*MGH SS rer. merov.* VI,
64–78, here 64 and 70); *V. Erminonis* prol. (*MGH SS rer. merov.* VI,
461–70, here 461); *V. Maxellendis* c. 1 (*ASSB* III, 567–87, here 580); *V.
Vulframni* prol. and c. 8 (*MGH SS rer. merov.* V, 657–73, here 662 and
666); *V. Willibrordi* prol. (*MGH SS rer. merov.* VII, 81–141, here 113),
etc.

There are also texts which mention individual reading as well as reading
aloud or listening: *V. Aldegundis* I c. 18 (*legentibus vel audientibus*),
(*ASOSB* II, 807–15, here 812); *V. Balthildis B* prol. (*audientes*) and c. 7
(*legentes*), (*MGH SS rer. merov.* II, 475–508, here 482 and 489); *V.
Eligii* prol. (*audire*) and prol. and c. 38 (*legere*) (*MGH SS rer. merov.*
IV, 634–761, here 664 and 723); *V. Filiberti B* prol. (*legentibus . . .
audientibus*) (*MGH SS rer. merov.* V, 568–606, here 583); *V. Laudomari*
II c. 1 (*audientes*), c. 6 (*lecturi*), and c. 17 (*lecturi*), (*ASOSB* I, 335–8,
here 335, 336, and 338); *V. Maximini* c. 1 (*legentium atque audientium
sensibus*) and c. 20 (*legentes vel audientes*), (*ASOSB* I, 591–7, here 592
and 596), etc.

11 For example, *V. Adalhardi* c. 19 (*PL* 120, 1507–57, here 1517):
'sanctorum vitas, quorum sedulo ruminabat exempla virtutum'. References to a clerico-monastic audience: *V. Aldegundis* I c. 1 and cc. 17–18
(*ASOSB* II, 807–15, here 807 and 812); *V. Anstrudis* cc. 3 and 10 (*MGH
SS rer. merov.* VI, 64–78, here 64 and 70); *V. Corbiniani* prol. (*MGH
Ep.* IV, 498); *V. Filiberti B* prol. (*MGH SS rer. merov.* V, 568–606, here
583); *V. Gregorii* c. 7 (*MGH SS* XV, 63–79, here 74); *V. Maxellendis*
c. 1 (*ASSB* III, 567–87, here 580); *V. Medardi* c. 22 (*ASS* Iun. II, 82–6,
here 86); *V. Richarii* prol. (*MGH SS rer. merov.* IV, 381–401, here 381);
V. Rictrudis prol. (*PL* 132, 829–48, here 830), etc.
12 For example, *V. Aldegundis* I, c. 1 (*ASOSB* II, 807–15, here 807); *V.
Balthildis B* prol. (*MGH SS rer. merov.* II, 475–508, here 482); *V.
Opportunae* prol. (*ASOSB* III2, 222–31, here 222); *V. Sollemnis* c. 13
(*MGH SS rer. merov.* VII, 303–21, here 321), etc.
13 It is not always apparent which public is meant by *fratres* (cf. e.g. *V.
Sollemnis* c. 13 (*MGH SS rer. merov.* VII, 303–21, here 321); *V.
Hucberti* I prol. (*MGH SS rer. merov.* VI, 471–92, here 482). Sometimes
the term clearly refers to a clerico-monastic audience (cf. de Gaiffier
1947: 153).
14 For example, *V. Balthildis B* c. 1 (*MGH SS rer. merov.* II, 475–508,
here 482): 'ad multorum aedificationem et profectum . . . volumus
studere patentem aedificationem plurimorum'; *V. Corbiniani* prol.
(*MGH Ep.* IV, 498): 'ad aedificationem audientium'; *V. Findani* prol.
(*MGH SS* XV, 502–6, here 503); 'nobis haec legentibus et posteris
aliquid ad profectum suum . . . utilitatis'; *V. Gregorii* prol. (*MGH SS*
XV, 63–79, here 66): 'ad aliorum aedificationem'.
15 *V. Richarii* prol. (*MGH SS rer. merov.* IV, 381–401, here 389):

oraverat . . . Angilbertus . . . quendam libellum stilo simpliciori digestum de vita ... Richarii cultius adnotare ... innotuit Angilbertus ... haberi apud se, quin et apud diversas ecclesias, codicem alium grandioris quantitatis in quo scilicet illa miracula legebantur, ... cuius simplex et minus polita locutio quia fratres ad recitandum in populo aptior videbatur, sufficere sibi eandem descriptionem consenserunt.

16 *V. Agnofledis* prol. (*MGH SS rer. merov.* VII, 429–37, here 432): 'ad profectum populo christiano'; *V. Balthildis B* prol. (*MGH SS rer. merov.* II, 475–508, here 482): 'volumus studere patentem aedificationem plurimorum'; *V. Eligii* prol. (*MGH SS rer. merov.* IV, 643–761, here 653 and 664): 'aedificationis historiam pandere plebi ... ad aedificationem christianae plebis'.

See also *V. Carileffi* c. 1 (*multi*), (*ASS* Iul. I, 85–98, here 90); *V. Ermenlandi* c. 28 (*fideles, plurimi*), (*MGH SS rer. merov.* V, 647–710, here 709); *V. Eucherii* prol. (*fideles*), (*MGH SS rer. merov.* VII, 41–53, here 46); *V. Glodesindis* c. 3 (*credentes*), (*ASS* Iul. VI, 198–205, here 203); *V. Lamberti* II prol. (*christiani*), (Canisius 1601: 172); *V. Maximini* prol. (*fideles*), (*ASOSB* I, 581–97, here 592); *V. Vulframni* c. 8 (*fideles*) (*MGH SS rer. merov.* V, 657–73, here 667). (All of these texts originated at the beginning of the ninth century at the latest.)

Similar utterances occur in texts from Germanic territory: e.g. *V. Liudgeri* prol. (*multis ad aedificationem*), (*MGH SS* II, 404–19, here 404); *V. Pirminii* c. 9 (*fideles*) (*MGH SS* XV, 17–35, here 28).

17 *V. Remigii* prol. (*MGH SS rer. merov.* III, 250–341, here 258–9):

> His miraculorum premissis capitulis, quedam sunt in sequenti opusculo de sanctis scripturis et catholicorum dictis sed et de hystoriis ad instructionem et exortationem legentium interposita. Que ut ad recitandum omnia in populi audientia non increscant, cui pro captu audientium mensuram verbi convenit ministrari, et excerpta per se alia lectioni studiosorum non depereant ... per lectiones ad legenda in duabus festivitatibus, scilicet depositionis et translationis huius domni et patroni nostri, determinatas, ut in depositionis sollempnitate novem lectiones ab exordio usque ad obitum eius legantur, et in eius translationis festivitate sex lectiones de his que post obitum illius ostensa sunt et tres de omelia lectionis euvangelicae legantur, subsiciva distinctione notis antiquorum peritia inventis quantum inde, populo audiente, legantur, et que instructioribus et studiosioribus, quando sibi licuerit vel libuerit, legenda serventur, designare curavi: eo videlicet modo, ut illa que populo recitanda sunt nota quae asteriscus vocatur∗, non ut ea que omissa fuerant illucescant, sed ut quasi stelle radii minus scientes illuminent, prenotentur; eis vero quae per Dei gratiam illuminatis legenda reservavi debent nota paragraphus Γ preponatur.

In the *praefatio* Hincmar apologizes to the *lector* for the *stili diversitas* of his text, caused by the fact that he has quoted fragments from older sources (253).

18 *V. Opportunae* prol. (*ASOSB* III2, 222–31, here 222):

> ut sicut tunc populus sitiens satiabatur aquis illius petrae, ita et haec

plebs, quae modo huc advenit pro amore dominae nostrae Opportunae, gaudens recedat cum sua iucunditate, audita virtutum eius revelatione. Nunc vobis dilectissimi filii, prout Dominus ministraverit, narraturi sumus, quanta divina gratia in famula sua, virgine Opportuna, operari dignata est mirabilia. Sed vos non pigeat audire, quod in ea Dominus perficere voluit: quia dum ancillam suam glorificat, nos ad eius invitat exempla: ut operum illius imitatores effecti, ei mereamur in caelestibus sociari, et vestigia virginis imitando, atque praecepta dominica observando, possimus cum illa caelestis regni perfrui gaudio.

19 *M. Germani* c. 1 (*PL* 124, 1207–70, here 1207–8):

Constat namque ad sancti Censurii episcopi tempora . . . intentatum omnibus id perstitisse negotium, dum per successus temporum iuniores quique simplici seniorum relatione contenti, nunquam haec arbitrabantur a memoria posse obolescere; quandoquidem vulgaris inurbanitas tum se optime credit diuturnitati prospicere, cum illustria quaeque et maxima, succidua solum narratione ad posteros fecerit emanare. Res ista non insana minus quam improvida, perniciosa sanctorum praeconiis interdum peperit detrimenta, quod qui imperitae rusticitati fidem astruat, rarum quemque reperias.

Cf. *V. Benedicti* prol. (*MGH SS* XV, 200–20, here 200): 'scribentibus vitam precedentium . . . curandum est . . . non rusticitatis vicio redolentes peritorum adgravent aures, set urbanitatis salefacentiae condita proferant verba politisque sermonibus, ut ita dixerim, derogantium demulceant aures'.

20 *V. Trudonis* prol. and c. 32 (*rustico sermone* (298)) (*MGH SS rer. merov.* VI, 264–98, here 298):

Supplico itaque per eundem Dominum eos, qui lecturi sunt hoc meae parvitatis opusculum, quique acriori pollent ingenio et auctoritate eximiae lectionis vigent, ne audatiae me culpa redarguant, dum magnae auctoritatis iussione coactus hoc opus me adire cognoverint, nec gracilis rudique sermonis dicta contempnant, sed magis mediocriter a me relata eorum redundante scientia suppleantur.

See also *V. Hucberti* I prol. (*MGH SS rer. merov.* VI, 471–96, here 482).

21 We are skipping the early Carolingian documents which were elaborately treated by Van Uytfanghe (1989).

22 Cf. *M. Goaris* c. 8 (cited in n. 9, here 52–3): 'duo non modici pisces, quos vulgo seluros dicimus, repperti sunt'. Also *V. Vodoali* c. 3 (*ASOSB* IV2, 544–50, here 545): 'nunc usque Picti vulgo vocantur'. See also, e.g. *V. Harlindis et Reinulae* c. 4 (*ASOSB* III1, 654–62, here 656): 'commendarunt eas confestim pariter pater et mater Abbatissae cuiusdam Monasterii, quod vulgo Valencina vocatur'; *V. Opportunae* c. 7 (*ASOSB* III1, 222–31, here 224); *V. Waldetrudis* c. 5 (*ASSB* IV, 439–48, here 442).

23 Additional examples, not necessarily using the term *vulgo*, are: *V. Filiberti B* c. 19 (*MGH SS rer. merov.* V, 568–606, here 594): 'vas

vinarium quod tunna dicitur', Fr. *tonne* (*FEW* XIII, 414–18); *M. Filiberti* cc. 13 and 20 (*ASOSB* IV1, 539–60, here 542 and 543): 'in vase, quod vannus vulgo dicitur', OFr. *ven*, Fr. *van* (*FEW* XIV, 157–62); 'in quodam vasculo, quod corbes dicitur', Fr. *Corbeille* (*FEW* II2, 1181–2); *V. Haimhramni* A and B c. 22 (*MGH SS rer. merov.* IV, 467–523, here 493): 'in quodam arbore vulgari locutione spine albe' (B: 'spina alba'), OFr. *espine*, Fr. *épine* (*FEW* XII, 176–9); *V. Leobae* c. 6 (*MGH SS XV*, 118–31, here 124): 'signum aecclesiae quod vulgo cloccum vocant', Fr. *cloche* (*FEW* II, 790–2); *M. Opportunae* c. 8 (*ASOSB* III2, 231–9, here 236): 'baculum, quem vulgus furcam vocant', OFr. *forche*, Fr. *fourche* (*FEW* III, 884–95); *V. Sadalbergae* c. 20 (*MGH SS rer. merov.* V, 49–66, here 61): 'ius tritici vel ordei, quod cervesam nuncupant', Fr. *cervoise* (*FEW* II, 612–13); *V. Trudonis* c. 27 (*MGH SS rer. merov.* VI, 264–98, here 295): 'vir habitans prope ecclesiam s. Trudonis . . ., quem nos vulgo matricolarium vocamus', OFr. *marrugler*, Fr. *marguillier* (*FEW* IV, 352–4); *V. Ursmari* c. 6 (*MGH SS rer. merov.* VI, 445–61, here 459): 'infirmitas in collo . . ., quae vulgo dicitur guttreria', OFr. *goitron* < **gutturione*, Fr. *goitre*; *V. Vodoali* c. 11 (*ASOSB* IV2, 544–50, here 548): 'pallium . . ., qui vulgo cappa vocatur', Fr. *chappe* (*FEW* II, 269–79); *V. Willehadi* c. 7 (*MGH SS* II, 378–90, here 382): 'patenam ligneam, quae vulgo scutella vocatur', OFr. *escuele*, Fr. *écuelle*.

24 Phillippart (1977: 76) stresses that, for the average believers, the living oral tradition concerning the saint's miraculous powers is much more important than the written tradition.

25 It is remarkable that Alcuin, even in his *homilia Willibrordi*, does not directly address the ordinary faithful but only talks about them: *V. Willibrordi* c. 32a (*MGH SS rer. merov.* VII, 138–40, here 139): 'gaudeamus, dilectissimi fratres, gaudeat et nobiscum omnis populus, qui ad natalicia sanctissimi patris hodie concurrit'. Cf. the prologue to the *V. Opportunae* (cited in n. 18).

26 Hrabanus Maurus certainly appears to have supported Alcuin's efforts to reform the pronunciation: *De institutione clericorum* c. 52 (*De lectionibus*) (*PL* 107, 295–420, here 364): 'ut suis quaeque litterae sonis enuntientur, et unumquodque verbum legitimo accentu decoretur'. This passage is inspired by Alcuin's *Dialogus de rhetorica* (*PL* 101, 916–46, here 942 (*de pronuntiatione*)). The correct accentuation, however, was apparently at least as important as the new pronunciation (ibid.: 'multae sunt dictiones quae solummodo accentu discerni debent a pronuntiante, ne in sensu earum erretur. Sed haec a grammaticis discere oportet.') and could have had a similar alienating effect (cf. Lüdtke 1964: 21, n. 26).

27 As opposed to R. Wright's point of view (1981: 355–8; 1982: 120–1), *transferre* can mean 'to translate' in the usage of the time: Berschin (1987: 8 n. 2). See also *MGH Ep.* VII, 5, 224–5 (*ep.* 255).

BIBLIOGRAPHY

Andrieu, M. (1948 [1974]) *Les Ordines Romani du haut moyen âge III*, Louvain: Spicilegium Sacrum Lovaniense, fasc. 24.

Banniard, M. (1975) 'Le Lecteur en Espagne wisigothique d'après Isidore de Séville, de ses fonctions à l'état de la langue', *Revue des Etudes Augustiniennes* 21: 112–44.

—— (1980a) *Le Haut moyen âge occidentale*, Paris: Presses Universitaires de France.

—— (1980b) 'Géographie linguistique et linguistique diachronique. Essai d'analyse analogique en occitano-roman et en latin tardif', *Via Domitia* 24: 9–43.

—— (1985) 'Vox agrestis. Quelques problèmes d'élocution de Cassiodore à Alcuin. I: Une situation diglossique de quatre siècles?', *Trames, Etudes antiques*: 195–208.

—— (1986) 'Théorie et pratique de la langue et du style chez Alcuin: Rusticité feinte et Rusticité masquée', *Francia* 12: 579–601.

Berschin, H. and Berschin, W. (1987) 'Mittellatein und Romanisch', *Zeitschrift für Romanische Philologie* 103: 1–19.

Bibliotheca Sanctorum (1961–4) Rome: Instituto Giovanni XXIII nella Pontifica Università Lateranense.

Canisius, H. (1601) *Antiquae lectiones* II, 1, Ingolstadt.

Chélini, J. (1956) 'La Pratique dominicale des laïcs dans l'Eglise franque sous le règne de Pépin', *Revue d'histoire de l'Eglise de France* 42: 161–74.

Collins, R. (1981) 'Beobachtungen zu Form, Sprache und Publikum der Prosabiographien des Venantius Fortunatus in der Hagiographie des römischen Gallien', *Zeitschrift für Kirchengeschichte* 92: 16–38.

de Gaiffier, B. (1947) 'L'Hagiographe et son public au XIᵉ siècle', *Miscellanea historica in honorem L. Van der Essen*, Brussels and Paris: Editions Universitaires.

—— (1954) 'La Lecture des Actes des Martyrs dans la prière liturgique en Occident', *Analecta Bollandiana* 72: 134–66.

Dekkers, E. (1979) 'L'Eglise devant la Bible en langue vernaculaire', in W. Lourdaux and D. Verhelst (eds) *The Bible and Medieval Culture*, Louvain: University Press: 1–15.

Devailly, G. (1973) 'La pastorale en Gaule au IXᵉ siècle', *Revue de l'Histoire de l'Eglise en France* 64: 23–54.

Díaz y Díaz, M. C. (1952) 'Sobre formas calificadas de vulgares o rústicas en glosarios. Contribución al estudio de *Vulgo*', *Archivum Latinitatis Medii Aevi* 22: 193–216.

DACL = *Dictionnaire d'archéologie et de liturgie* (1907–53), ed. F. Cabrol and H. Leclercq, Paris: Letouzey & Ané.

Fontaine, J. (1981a) 'De la Pluralité à l'unité dans le "latin carolingien"?', *Settimane di Spoleto* 27, 2: 765–805.

—— (1981b) 'La Naissance difficile d'une latinité médiévale (500–744)', *Bulletin de l'association Guillaume Budé* 27: 360–8.

Heene, K. (1989) 'Merovingian and Carolingian hagiography: continuity or change in public and aims?', *Analecta Bollandiana* 107: 415–28.

Heinzelmann, M. (1981a) 'Une Source de base de la littérature hagiographique latine: le recueil de miracles', in E. Patlagean and P. Riché (eds), *Etudes Augustiniennes. Hagiographie, cultures et sociétés (IVᵉ–XIIᵉ siècles). Actes du Colloque organisé à Nanterre et à Paris (2–5 mai 1979)*, Paris: 235–59.

—— (1981b) 'Ein neues Forschungsvorhaben: erzählende hagiographische Quellen in Gallien vor dem Jahr 1000. Ein kritischer Katalog', *Francia* 9: 887–90.

Jungmann, J. A. (1962) *Missarum sollemnia. Eine genetische Erklärung der Römischen Messe*, vol. I: *Messe im Wandel der Jahrhunderte, Messe und Kirchliche Gemeinschaft, Vormesse*, vol. II: *Opfermesse*, Freiburg and Basle: Herder.

Löfstedt, B. (1983) Review of R. Wright (1982), *Vox Romanica* 42: 259–64.

Lüdtke, H. (1964) 'Die Entstehung romanischer Schriftsprachen', *Vox Romanica* 23: 3–21.

McKitterick, R. (1977) *The Frankish Church and the Carolingian Reforms (789–895)*, London: Royal Historical Society.

Meyer-Lübke, W. (1911) *Romanisches etymologisches Wörterbuch*, Heidelberg: Winter.

Philippart, G. (1977) *Les Légendiers latins et autres manuscrits hagiographiques*, Turnhout: Brepols.

Riché, P. (1973) *La Vie quotidienne dans l'Empire carolingienne*, Paris: Hachette.

Richter, M. (1975) 'A socio-linguistic approach to the Latin Middle Ages', *Studies in Church History* 11: 69–82.

—— (1976) 'Kommunikationsprobleme im lateinischen Mittelalter', *Historische Zeitschrift* 222: 43–80.

—— (1979) 'Latina lingua sacra sive vulgaris?', in W. Lourdaux and D. Verhelst (eds), *The Bible and Medieval Culture*, Louvain: Louvain University Press: 16–34.

—— (1982) 'Die Sprachenpolitik Karls des Grossen', *Sprachwissenschaft* 7: 412–37.

—— (1983) 'A quelle Epoque a-t-on cessé de parler le latin? A Propos d'une question mal posée', *Annales. Economies. Sociétés. Civilisations.* 38: 439–48.

Salmon, P. (1967) *L'Office divin au Moyen Age*, Paris: Editions du Cerf.

Sanders, G. (1982) 'Le remaniement carolingien de la "Vita Bathildis" mérovingienne', *Analecta Bollandiana* 100: 411–28.

Schubert (von), H. (1916 [1962]) *Geschichte der christlichen Kirche im Frühmittelalter*, Hildesheim: Georg Olms.

Stiene, H. E. (1981) *Wandelbert von Prüm. Vita et miracula sancti Wandalberti*, Frankfurt am Main and Bern: Peter D. Lang.

Strunk, G. (1970) *Kunst und Glaube in der lateinischen Heiligenlegende (zu ihrem Selbstverständnis in den Prologen)*, Munich: Wilhelm Fink.

Van Uytfanghe, M. (1975) 'De zogeheten Karolingische Renaissance, een breekpunt in de evolutie van de Latijnse taal?', *Handelingen Kon. Zuidned. Maatschap. Taal, Lett. & Geschied.* 29: 267–86.

—— (1976) 'Le Latin des hagiographes mérovingiens et la protohistoire du français. Etat de la question', *Romanica Gandensia* 16: 5–89.

—— (1984) 'Histoire du latin, protohistoire des langues romanes et histoire de la communication', *Francia* 11: 579–613.

—— (1985) 'L'Hagiographe et son public à l'époque mérovingienne', *Studia Patristica* 16: 54–62.

—— (1989) 'Les Expressions du type *quod vulgo vocant* dans des textes latins antérieures au concile de Tours et aux serments de Strasbourg: témoignages lexicologiques et sociolinguistiques de la "langue rustique romaine"?' *Zeitschrift für Romanische Philologie* 105: 28–49.

Vogel, C. (1966) *Introduction aux sources de l'histoire du culte Chrétien au moyen âge*, Spoleto: Centro Italiano di Studi sull'Alto Medioevo.

von Wartburg, W. (1922) *Französisches etymologisches Wörterbuch. Eine darstellung des galloromanischen Sprachschatzes*, Bonn and Leipzig: K. Schroeder.

Walsh, T. J. (1986–7) 'Latin and Romance in the Early Middle Ages', *Romance Philology* 40: 199–214.

Wright, R. (1981) 'Late Latin and Early Romance: Alcuin's *De orthographia* and the Council of Tours (813 AD)', *Papers of the Liverpool Latin Seminar* 3: 343–61.

—— (1982) *Late Latin and Early Romance in Spain and Carolingian France*, Liverpool: Cairns.

13 Rhabanus Maurus and the vernacular languages

Michel Banniard

LINGUISTIC CONSCIOUSNESS: LATIN, GERMANIC, AND ROMANCE

Carolingian Europe aimed to be Christian, Latin, and Imperial. Languages and cultures that played no direct role in this tripartite intention rarely came to the conscious attention of the intellectuals of the time, and only gradually came to play a part in their activities (Wolff 1982). As a result, the eventual surfacing of the Romance languages and cultures happened along very complex paths. The study of the phenomena that led to this evolution (or revolution) has progressed significantly over the last thirty years or so. The holding of the ICHL workshop serves to show simultaneously the novelty of the recent methods used to explore these centuries of sociolinguistic change, the success that has come from the development of new theoretical approaches, and the gaps which our present state of knowledge still faces the challenge of filling.

The characteristic property of this period, in which the Middle Ages were born, is that it offers us parallel fields of research that are different in the different cultural areas, according to whether we are considering the Germanic-speaking or Latin-speaking world. It has seemed valuable, for the present volume, to highlight some points of comparison and reference from the other half of the Frankish political and cultural world. The three connected problems of the birth of a new language, the realization of the existence of this previously unknown entity, and the consecration of this change via the elaboration of a *scripta* that breaks with traditional modes of writing, can be posed in much simpler terms when we consider the Germanic languages than when we consider the Romance languages. In this case the second and third aspects of the change are the relevant ones. In other words, since it was already clear that a different language existed, the next step was for the intellectuals to give some kind of status to this language that was neither Latin nor sacred (cp. Borst 1961) in the heart of Latin culture, before they confirmed their acceptance of its status by working out a written form.

I would argue here that, given the cultural, religious, and intellectual unity that characterized the start of 'Europe' (Banniard 1989), studying the sociolinguistic situation there was across the Rhine can help us understand better the initial stages of the development of the written Romance languages in general, and of the 'langue d'oil' in particular. In my view, political fragmentation raises no obstacle to there being reciprocal influences between the Germanic and Romance worlds. Anglo-Saxon was the first western language that was neither sacred nor Latin to be given (by Bede) its cultural consecration and intellectual status (see Manitius 1965: 74). Three centuries later, Otfrid of Weissenburg was to do the same for Old High German, which he promoted, in practice but also especially in theory, to the rank of a literary language (Haubrichs 1982: 188).

Between these two dates are placed the official birth of the Romance languages, proclaimed, as everyone knows, to have happened at Tours in 813, and the appearance of the first texts prepared in a Romance *scripta*, at Strasbourg in 842. Broadly speaking, it is in this first half of the ninth century that the intellectual developments occur which lead to the development of the vernacular *scriptas*, the first manifestations of Romance literature, and also the first texts of Germanic literature. The first great strictly Germanic learned figure of the age was Rhabanus Maurus, the *praeceptor Germaniae* (Brünholzl 1982), who was intellectually active during this period of maturation, to which he contributed directly, for important documentary evidence of his teaching in *lingua theotisca* has survived (Manitius 1965: 301). His choices of language seem, therefore, to be quite different from those made a little earlier by his teacher, Alcuin, who expresses almost no interest in the vernacular languages he is aware of, neither his native language nor his adopted one (Banniard 1990: Ch. 6). Neither of them, however, show the creative courage of Otfrid. They correspond to the earlier phase, when the French *scripta* was being developed within the scriptoria, and more particularly within people's minds, of which we have no evidence.

Can we learn something useful to our purpose by looking at Rhabanus? I think we can, if we consider his personality as a whole.

To put it another way, does his written work (which was, of course, in Latin) include any indications, even if only indirect, to suggest that his mental furniture was in the process of changing, relative to that of his teacher, as regards the status of the vernacular languages? This is equivalent to asking whether his attitude, as a *litteratus*, and his sociolinguistic practice were in harmony.

TENDENCIES TO LINGUISTIC ISOLATIONISM?

Alcuin's intellectual legacy, characterized by the desire for forced marches back to a *norma rectitudinis* in every area of Christian teaching, plays such a dominant role in Rhabanus' thoughts that we cannot help being tempted to conclude that his frame of mind must have impelled him to cut himself off entirely from the linguistic realities of his people and time. In general, the Abbot of Fulda has been criticized for a total lack of innovative spirit and for having been no more than a compiler of the works of others; according to this view, his pastoral activities would have been entirely like this (Knöpfler 1900, followed by Manitius 1965; Bisanti 1985, however, disagrees), and in his *De clericorum institutione* (819) he would have been merely following in the wake of Augustine, Cassiodorus, and (in particular) Isidore, offering no new ideas of his own.

And yet he continually praises a discipline which the Fathers of the Church had effectively deposed from any position of intellectual importance, that is, *grammatica*. Echoing Alcuin, Rhabanus responds across the centuries to the comments of Gregory the Great, when he says that 'inculpabiliter enim, immo laudabiliter hanc artem discit' (*De cler. inst.* 3.19). He even praises the art of classical metrics (in the same paragraph), despite the fact that Augustine had abandoned it in his desire to communicate to the uneducated. And then he sings the praises of venerable masters such as Varro (ibid., 3.24). His admiration is not merely theoretical, either, since he composed a lengthy *Excerptio de arte grammatica Prisciani*, where I would go so far as to say that the key point is a detailed account of classical metrics, in which he had himself composed many poems (now in *MGH*, PAC, vol. II). Priscian was the most learned, the most demanding, and the most complicated of the Latin grammarians, and a reliable inspiration for high-minded linguistic purism.

This conclusion is reinforced by the comments that Rhabanus adds to his appraisal of the texts where Augustine prescribes the manner in which a preacher ought to express himself when addressing his congregations. Modern scholars have, indeed, noticed that Rhabanus does not follow his mentor all the way here; indeed, his requirement of the preacher is the very opposite of Augustine's, that he should express himself in the most perfect Latin that he can (Blumenkranz 1951). Any idea of compromising with a level of Latinity approximating the *sermo humilis*, and above all the *rusticus*, is hereby banished from his own teaching. Was Rhabanus then, in his turn, engaging in oral communication through a kind of linguistic isolationism?

We can also, on the other hand, find in his work special praise of *rusticitas* ('Sancta rusticitas solum sibi prodest', *De cler. inst.*, 3.27). This seems here to be a moral quality rather than a stylistic one, but its implications (which are confirmed by the accompanying commentaries) are close to being stylistic. In any case, he has read carefully Augustine's recommendations that the preacher should adapt his language to the ability of his public to understand (*De cler. inst.*, 3.30; *De eccl. disc.*, 1, *De sacris ordinibus*, in *PL* 112, c. 1193–6). Altogether, the reorganization and rewriting that he gives to his sources show that he was actively thinking himself about the problems discussed.

This is corroborated by another of Rhabanus' great works of synthesis, his *De rerum naturis* (also called *De uniuerso*): far from merely being the servile follower of Isidore and the Encyclopedists, here he reshapes the fabric of what he inherited to come up with a new pattern; similarly, instead of beginning in the traditional way with an account of the *artes liberales*, he starts his work with theological matters (Heyze 1969). It has also proved possible to show that, in an area that was essentially a sideline of his pastoral activity, Church Law, Rhabanus was able to choose, from within the traditions of Church Law, the regulations that were relevant to the needs of his own time (Kottje 1982).

In these circumstances it would be much too simple a solution to explain the contradictions, or failures to adapt, that we think we can find in his work, merely as the result of intellectual inertia. They are really the result of an inappropriate level of reading on our part; it is precisely the combination of this apparent lack of adaptation with Rhabanus' own creative abilities that can lead us to detect in him a new mental attitude, both caused by and giving rise to new cultural structures.

ONE CULTURE, FACING TWO WAYS

We can resolve this difficulty if we accept that this attested dichotomy corresponds in reality to a deep mental division between the two aspects of a new Christian culture, one of which looks back to the legacy of the Latin tradition, and the other forward to the first signs of a vernacular literature. Rhabanus is aware of the need to adapt himself to modern times. Significantly, even the word, *modernus*, has a place in his vocabulary. He does not aim for this characteristic in cases where it is important to underline the antiquity of an edifying work (*De vita b. M. Magdalenae, PL* 112, Prologue, c. 1573); but on the other hand he does consider this important when he addresses to Lothar a treatise on the art of war, inspired by Vegetius, but recast specifically 'ne forte ea scribere uiderer quae tempore moderno in usu non sunt' (*Tract. de anima, Praef., PL* 110, c. 1109). When he is addressing his king, he replaces the traditional terms *imperium* and *regnum* with the contemporary word *Europa*, thereby consecrating a new geopolitical perspective (*De uniuerso, Praef.*).

As well as his search for an erudite Latinity, Rhabanus also finds room for a certain curiosity concerning less elevated cultural concerns. He is happy to give house room to the word *paganus*, of the spoken vernacular (*De cler. inst.*, 1.27; *De uniuerso, Praef. altera, Ad Haymonem*), rather than using the classical terms *rustici, gentiles*, because, in his own words, 'pagi <sunt> conuenticula rusticorum' (*Excerptio, PL* 111, c. 668). With the aim of making his pastoral instructions clearer, he replaces terms that are slightly technical with their 'vulgar' equivalent: 'Magi sunt qui uulgo malefici . . . nuncupantur' (*De magicis art., PL* 110, c. 1097); 'hi sunt qui uulgo mathematici dicuntur' (ibid., c. 1098). This fondness for *realia* also breaks through into his Encyclopedic work (*De rerum naturis*: 'Burgos uulgo uocant', 16.2; 'hunc uulgus aureum solidum uocat', 18.1). The meaning of the word *uulgus* in Rhabanus is clear; it means the whole mass of the people without any distinctions; 'Vulgus est passim inhabitans multitudo' (16.4). That means that, occasionally, he was happy to give a cultural 'safe-conduct' pass to the popular spoken language.

Naturally, Rhabanus, like all the *potentes* of his time, can only have had ambivalent feelings towards the masses. He also happened to hear a sign of irritation let slip by his king: Lothar described himself as 'uulgari tumultu caesis auribus circumseptus' in 842 (*Comm. in Ezec., PL* 110, c. 493). But his serious-minded awareness of his apostolic mission, which led him to direct the programmes of the various councils that he convened as Archbishop of Mainz (Hartmann 1982) towards a more reforming approach, gave him the intellectual abilities needed to overcome this prejudice. When he came to analyse in due course the origins at Babel of the linguistic fragmentation of the human world (*De cler. inst.*, 3.8: *De uniuerso*, 16.1), Rhabanus drew out the evangelical consequences of this divine punishment, insisting on the obligation to make the words of salvation accessible to those of other tongues ('Linguis omnium gentium loquerentur <discipuli>, ut nulla illis gens extera, nulla lingua barbaris inaccessa uel inuia uideretur', *De cler. inst.*, 2.56). So he took a close interest in the practical conditions of Christian communication, and described in detail the necessity of translation, 'ut ex his unaquaeque gens et natio propriae linguae adminiculo intellectum sibi salubrem adtraheret, interpretando ac colloquendo sensum eundem canonicum propriis uerbis' (*De cler inst.*, 3.8). The insistence on the words *propria lingua*, *propriis uerbis* (even if Rhabanus is following here Augustine and Isidore) is particularly noticeable.

Indeed, these are the very words used, in Anglo-Saxon or Germanic-speaking areas from the eighth century on, by synods and councils requiring preachers to teach the illiterate faithful (Lentner 1963). Now, we have every reason to believe that when the Abbot of Fulda writes these words he usually has in mind the vernacular of the eastern part of the Empire, since he happens to add in his remark an unexpectedly specific comment based on the existence of the language in which he himself and his addressees expressed themselves: 'omnes nobiscum linguae Latinae homines' (*De cler. inst.*, 2.8). Even when copying word for word the *De doctrina christiana*, where Augustine used the phrase *lingua nostra* (opposed to Hebrew and to Greek), Rhabanus clarifies it with the words 'id est latina' (ibid., 3.9). This modest addition means that the writer is aware of the ninth-century context, despite following a fourth-century source: for the monks and clerics of Germania *lingua nostra* would here have meant *lingua theotisca*. Both as abbot and as archbishop, Rhabanus never forgets the unique cultural circumstances of his own area. Even when he is preparing his *De catechizandis rudibus*, he stresses in the dedicatory letter addressed to Bishop Reginbald that his flock was still held back in a way of life that was profoundly pagan (*De eccl. disc.*, Praef., *PL* 112, c. 1191).

We are now in a position to collect together these scattered data. The reason why Rhabanus feels justified in praising a purified type of Latinity is that in his own circumstances there is no need for his own Latinity to be at all formally constrained by any need to use it to teach the illiterate. When Rhabanus considers the illiterate, he knows that they represent an imperfectly Christianized mass whose language and whose culture still have no place within written norms or Christian precepts. So he has decided to make the necessary linguistic compromises by using the *propria lingua* of the *uulgus*. That means that he has as a result to leave the areas of prescribed language and plunge into the problematic thickets of other types of speech; but that is precisely what he read Augustine encouraging him to do, taking up his well-known instructions to express himself *uulgi more* and give up the *integritas locutionis*, so that the mass of the faithful can take in and understand the evangelizing message (*De cler. inst.*, 3.30). It is the 'barbarous' language of the Germanic speakers that Rhabanus refers to with such urgency, because this has no other name than *theotisca*, that is, 'popular' (Baesecke 1943; Weisberger 1941).

THEORY AND PRACTICE OF THE NEW *SCRIPTA*

The transition of the 'popular' language towards norms that would eventually include it within the traditions of civilization is helped by being compared to the Hebrew language. On one hand, Rhabanus usually insists on the sacred nature of Hebrew, on the usefulness of knowing it, and on the benefits that have accrued to Christian learning from the work of the translators (*De inst. cler.*, 3.10). On the other hand, when teaching grammar, he puts Hebrew, when he comes to teach about syllabic quantity, in the same category as the 'Barbarian' languages: 'In *el* productam barbara, ut hic Daniel, Michael, Gabriel. . . . In *ar* correptam Latina et Graeca et barbara masculini et neutri generis, ut hic Caesar, hic bostar, hoc nectar, hoc calcar' (*Excerptio*, PL 111, c. 636–7). That does not prevent him from recalling, in a brief survey of literary history, that the Jews had a taste for poetry and song before the pagans did (he means before the Greeks), even if the latter took on ametrical forms in their case (*Excerptio*, c. 666).

It follows that for a scholar like Rhabanus, Hebrew was a 'Barbarian' language, but that even so, thanks to its role in the history of the texts of salvation, it had the right to the status of written language, and even a language of art. Since the learned abbot had already come to a similar conclusion as regards the 'Barbarian' language of the people in charge of whose souls he found himself, it is understandable that – by a kind of implicit comparison between the different elements of these two cultural and linguistic domains, separated in time but also closely allied in Christian pastoral logic – Rhabanus had the intellectual abilities that allowed him to give Germanic the status of a written language, even of a literary language.

This final stage is implied in several anticipatory hints in Rhabanus' works. He often used the word *cantilena* (*De eccl. off.*, 2.48; 3.24), whose contemporary associations are well known, both in the Germanic and the Romance fields (Delbouille 1972a: 39; 1972b: 559). In these cases the close connection between Rhabanus' implicit theoretical approach and his practical creativity becomes clear. He promoted the 'popular' language (and we must insist that this is the meaning of *theotisca*) to the level of a poetic language that he incorporated into both the biblical tradition of hymnody and the classical tradition of Alexandrine poetry; this becomes clear in his own poetry, where very often, in fact, in the notes written in classical metres that he used to send to his colleagues, he comments on the meaning of the Germanic personal names included there, and praises them on the basis of their names' etymology (*Carmen* 11, lines 40–2; 17, 21; 19, 5; 32, 4–9, *Ad Isanbertum presbyterum*: 'Nomen, quo clarus dignus honore fias: // ferrum te fortem, clarum uirtute decorum // signant'). In this way the vernacular language gains a firm foothold within the realms of civilization, that is, within *grammatica*.

I feel able now to go so far as to say that Rhabanus reflected a great deal on the problems of raising the popular language to the level of being inserted into *grammatica*. He ran into the awkward problem of the translation into Germanic of certain key words in Hebrew: 'Quae duo uerba, amen et alleluia nec graecis, nec latinis, nec barbaris licet in suam linguam omnino transferre, uel alia lingua annuntiare' (*De uniu.*, 5.9). He appreciated from experience how difficult it is to establish all the rules of a language, having grappled with the complexity of the data (*Excerptio*, c. 627; c. 663); it is worth recalling that Charles himself had been unable to get a grammar of Frankish established (Banniard 1990: Ch. 6). He understood very clearly the basic distinction between grapheme and phoneme (*Excerptio*, c. 617). Indeed, rather than leaving them on one side as having no value for the study of Latin grammar (and, as we have seen, he is entirely capable of making this kind of distinction), he became closely interested in the sounds and letters that were exclusive to Greek (*Excerptio*, c. 617). Some of these phonemes, particularly the chi and the spirantized *d* and *t*, are features of Old High German, and some of the written letters also turned up in its alphabet ('Item si fuerit *t* praeposita aspirationi pro Θ ponitur', *Excerptio*, c. 617).

It is logical, then, to conclude that it was as a result of the active influence of its abbot that the scriptorium of Fulda became, in the ninth century, a veritable experimental laboratory, in which they tried out the new written symbols that led to the elaboration first of a *scripta* and then of a *grammatica* of their vernacular language (Bischoff 1985: 107). In my view, the brief work that Rhabanus composed on the invention of alphabets is certainly not a minor appendix due only to encyclopedic curiosity and bereft of any practical purpose. In his famous passage on the invention of runes (*De inuentione litterarum*), Rhabanus recalls that the language family that includes the one that is represented in the runic alphabet is related to the *lingua theotisca* that his own compatriots speak, before he deplores the pagan state in which the speakers of the latter live (Derolez 1954: 354).

He did not confine himself, then, to the difficult but somewhat detached role of grammarian and scholar. On the contrary, his oral teaching within his monastery left traces and evidence (in the form of long lists of glosses where Latin was translated into Germanic) of his own personal investment in the task of pinning down and promoting the popular language.

THEOTISCA AND *VULGARIS LINGUA*

It was rather too soon, without doubt, for Rhabanus to be able to raise the popular language of Germania to the level of a literary language comparable to that which devised the *Artes liberales*; he was the initiator, or, if you prefer, the mediator between two cultural stages (Fleckenstein 1982), and that is why I believe, contrary to the established view (Haubrichs 1982: 192) that the Archbishop of Mainz, within his own context, was no less responsible than Otfrid for the emergence of Germanic culture.

Taking all things into account, it is legitimate to claim that there is a harmony between Rhabanus' linguistic practice and his intellectual outlook. At the very least, even if no trace had survived of his work in the vernacular, it would have been legitimate to postulate that, faithfully following Augustine's principles, he devoted himself to addressing the illiterate masses; and this, both at Fulda and Mainz, meant using Germanic.

His thoughts developed further than it might seem at first sight, in that the *lingua theotisca* is given sufficient status in his mind that gradually it becomes able to acquire a rank equal to that of the other languages of culture. The intellectual structures, within which the appearance of Germanic literature came to be possible and welcomed, were prepared in advance in people's minds. Furthermore, the general increase in the intellectual level of clerics and monks made something possible which would hardly have been possible a century earlier; the creation and edition of a 'Germanic Donatus'.

Consequently, I suggest, the reciprocal influences that existed between the Eastern and the Western Franks inevitably encouraged the intellectuals in the western area to go further themselves in accepting the culture, working out a *scripta* and grammar, and promoting the literature of their own *lingua vulgaris*.[1]

NOTE

1 The second canon of the Council of Mainz of 847, held as soon as Rhabanus became archbishop, repeated the famous Canon 17 of the Council of Tours of 813 concerning the need to consider how best to 'transferre' sermons into 'rusticam Romanam linguam aut in Thiotiscam' so that it was easier for all to understand what was being said.

BIBLIOGRAPHY

Baesecke, G. (1943) 'Das Nationalbewusstein der Deutschen des Karolingerreiches nach den Zeitgenössigen Benennungen ihrer Sprache', in T. Mayer (ed.), *Der Vertrag von Verdun 843*, Leipzig, 116–36.

Banniard, M. (1989) *Genèse culturelle de l'Europe (V^e–VIIIe siècle)*, Paris: Eds Du Seuil.

—— (1990) *Viva Voce: Communication écrite et communication orale du IVe au IXe siècle en Occident Latin*, Paris: Etudes Augustiniennes.

Bisanti, A. (1985) 'Struttura compositiva e tecnica compilatoria nel libro III del *De inst. cler.* di Rabano Mauro', *Schede Medievali* 8: 5–17.

Bischoff, B. (1985) *Paléographie de l'Antiquité romaine et du Moyen Age Occidental*, Paris: Picard (German original, 1979).

Blumenkranz, B. (1951) 'Raban Maur et Saint Augustin: compilation ou adaptation? A propos du latin biblique', *Revue du Moyen Age Latin* 7: 97–110.

Borst, A. (1961) *Der Turmbau von Babel. Geschichte der Meinungen über Ursprung und Vielfalt der Sprachen und Völker*, vol. II, Stuttgart: Hiersemann.

Brunhölzl, F. (1982) 'Zur geistigen Bedeutung des Hrabanus Maurus', in R. Kottje and H. Zimmermann (eds), *Hrabanus Maurus, Lehrer, Abt und Bischoff*, Wiesbaden: Steiner, 1–17.

Delbouille, M. (1972a) 'Tradition latine et naissance des littératures romanes', in M. Delbouille (ed.) *Grundriss der romanischen Literaturen des Mittelalters*, vol. I: *Généralités*, Heidelberg: Winter, 4–56.

—— (1972b) 'Les Plus Anciens Textes et la formation des langues littéraires', in M. Delbouille (ed.), *Grundriss der romanischen Literaturen des Mittelalters*, vol. I: *Généralités*, Heidelberg: Winter, 559–621.

Derolez, R. (1954) *Runica manuscripta. The English Tradition*, Bruges: De Tempel.

Fleckenstein, J. (1982) 'Hrabanus Maurus. Diener seiner Zeit und Vermittler zwischen den Zeiten', in R. Kottje and H. Zimmermann (eds), *Hrabanus Maurus, Lehrer, Abt und Bischoff*, Wiesbaden: Steiner, 194–208.

Hartmann, W. (1982) 'Die Mainzer Synoden des Hrabanus Maurus', in R. Kottje and H. Zimmermann (eds), *Hrabanus Maurus, Lehrer, Abt und Bischoff*, Wiesbaden: Steiner, 130–44.

Haubrichs, W. (1982), 'Althochdeutsch in Fulda und Weissenburg – Hrabanus Maurus und Ottfried von Weissenburg', in R. Kottje and H. Zimmermann (eds), *Hrabanus Maurus, Lehrer, Abt und Bischoff*, Wiesbaden: Steiner, 182–93.

Heyze, E. (1969) *Hrabanus Maurus Enzyklopädie 'De rerum naturis'. Untersuchungen zu den Quellen und zur Methode der Kompilation*, Munich: Münchener Beiträge zur Mediävistik und Renaissancen Forschung, 4.

Knöpfler, A. (ed.) (1901) *Rabani Mauri De institutione clericorum libri tres*, Munich: Ludwig-Maximilians Universität.

Kottje, R. (1982) 'Hrabanus und das Recht', in R. Kottje and H. Zimmermann (eds), *Hrabanus Maurus, Lehrer, Abt und Bischoff*, Wiesbaden: Steiner, 118–29.

Lentner, L. (1963) *Volkssprache und Sakralsprache. Geschichte einer Lebensfrage bis zum Ende des Konzils von Trient*, Vienna: Herder.

Manitius, M. (1965) *Geschichte der lateinischen Literatur des Mittelalters*, vol. I, 2nd edn, Munich: Beck.

MGH, PAC = *Monumenta Germaniae Historica, Poetae Latini Aevi Carolini*, ed. E. Dümmler, Berlin: Weidmann, 1884 (Rhabanus Maurus' poems are in vol. II).

PL = *Patrologia Latina*, ed. J. P. Migne, Paris: Teubner (Rhabanus Maurus' works are in vols 107–12, 1864–78).

Steinmeyer, E. (1879) *Die althochdeutsche Glossen*, vol. I, Berlin: Weidmann.

Weisberger, L. (1941) *Die Entdeckung der Muttersprache im europäischen Denken*, Lunebourg: Heliand.

Wolff, P. (1982) *Les Origines linguistiques de l'Europe Occidentale*, 2nd edn, Toulouse: Privat.

Part III

Latin and Romance in the Iberian Peninsula and Italy (950–1320)

There are currently two starkly contrasting views as to the metalinguistic situation in the Iberian Peninsula (outside Frankish Catalonia) before the advent of the French Ecclesiastical Reformers in the late eleventh century. Perhaps even as late as that, people envisaged their spoken–written continuum as being still just one language; on the other hand, Menéndez Pidal may have been right to envisage a bipartite or even tripartite distinction in the earlier centuries (Latin, Vulgar Latin, and Romance). This contrast of perspectives invites us to consider whether Leonese texts from before 1080 are to be interpreted, according to the first view, as being 'written Romance' (as modern written French is the written variety of French, rather than being a separate language entirely from spoken French), or on the other hand, according to the second view, as being 'barbarous Latin', or 'Leonese Vulgar Latin' (accepting that the writers learnt Latin as a separate language from their ordinary Romance, and then tried, and often failed, to write that other language). Pensado's minutely and carefully argued chapter treats this as an empirical issue, concluding from a wealth of statistics concerning mis-spellings that on balance the first view seems more likely, that here were writers trying to write acceptably the Romance language they had. Walsh, on the other hand, cannot accept the monolingual interpretation, using similar data to suggest that in many respects Romance was more different from Latin than we tend to realize, exemplifying his case here with the fricativization of secondary voiced consonants, which he argues was already phonemicized in the tenth century. Stengaard accepts the 'mono-lingual' view for the sake of argument, investigating whether such a perspective helps us understand the whole complex of the different kinds of gloss appended to the famous San Millán MS 60 and concluding that some were phonetic promptings, and others 'silent' aids, to reading aloud. Stengaard's implication that individual lexical items in the text could be read aloud as more readily intelligible synonyms, without this being a case of interlingual translation, is made explicit in two chapters. Blake proposes this in passing, while arguing that the syntactic traits of surviving documents are not counterevidence to the monolingual view. Emiliano studies thirteenth-century legal texts from the León–Portugal border area to show that the gradual emergence of unmistakeably Romance writing is merely a process of gradual removal of the traditional veneer from spellings that had existed for centuries. These five Iberian chapters collectively represent a considerable advance in the field, without reaching a consensus other than a desire to consider the data from more plausible perspectives than hitherto.

The final chapter in this part, by Danesi, returns to Italy (already considered extensively by Varvaro and Cravens in Part I) to reassess the contribution made by Dante to Romance philology, in the light of modern developments in the field. He concludes that the *De vulgari eloquentia* is essentially a synchronic classification of vernaculars made on lexical criteria, without the diachronic implications modern scholars have anachronistically tended to glimpse there. In short, in the mid-Medieval Iberian Peninsula and Italy, as in ninth-century France (and probably later), it seems that metalinguistic distinctions which we now take for granted took a long time to emerge.

14 The combination of glosses in the *Códice Emilianense 60* (*Glosas Emilianenses*)

Birte Stengaard

The *Glosas Emilianenses* are usually associated with the Romance glosses which, together with a few Basque glosses, adorn certain folios of the codex called *Códice Emilianense 60*. They were published by Menéndez Pidal (1926: 1–9), together with a few scraps of the basic Latin text.

However, most of the glossed folios contain several kinds of glosses and notes. The facsimile edition of the codex (*Glosas* 1977) and the edition by García Larragueta (1984) have facilitated the study of all the *Glosas Emilianenses*. In this chapter I try to show that information can be extracted from the lesser-known glosses, and from the combination of glosses where several kinds are present.

For the sake of convenience, I will call all additions to the basic text glosses. In the following pages, text and glosses quoted will be referred to mostly by their MP and GL numbers, MP referring to Menéndez Pidal (1926: 1–9), GL to García Larragueta (1984: 47–69), who also quotes the MP numbers.

From a formal point of view, the different sets of glosses can be divided into those consisting of words and those consisting of single letters. The latter are alphabetical sequences, preceded by the sign + which marks the initiation of a sequence. The longest sequence seems to be +*a b c d e f g h i*.

These glosses form a separate section in García Larragueta (1984: 71–7), where they are classified as 'glosas gramaticales'. They are not included in his edition of the text. Fortacín Piedrafita (1980) includes them among his morphosyntactic glosses. For the present purpose, I will refer to the signs +*abc* etc. as alphabetical glosses. They appear over words or phrases, and their obvious function is to mark word order; 'el orden lógico de las palabras', according to Menéndez Pidal (1926: 3).

The glosses consisting of words may, in their turn, be classified according to language, as in García Larragueta (1984: 45) under the heading 'Glosas latinas, romances y vascas'. These are the glosses published with the Latin text in his edition.

The Romance and Basque glosses correspond roughly to those published by Menéndez Pidal (1926: 3–9). The Latin glosses are of at least two clearly distinct types. One consists of what may be called meaningful words. They make sense as lexical items, normally within the context of the basic Latin text. In this group I include the cases where personal pronouns and nouns are added, mostly to make a subject explicit. The other group of Latin glosses is classified by Fortacín Piedrafita (1980) as morphosyntactic, together with the alphabetical glosses. These are forms of the Latin relative pronoun *qui*, sometimes combined with a preposition. I will call these glosses grammatical to distinguish them from the other sets of glosses mentioned.

The grammatical glosses have seven basic forms; *qui*, *k(e)*, *cui*, *quibus*, *cuius*, *quorum/corum*, and *quarum*. As one can see, there are no gender markers except the genitive plural, nor are there number markers in the nominative and 'accusative' cases. The ablative case is missing. Combined with a preposition, most frequently *de*, *ad*, and *in*, the form *ke*, shortened *k*, is invariably used. Fortacín Piedrafita (1980: 75) has pointed out that this reduced set of forms is the result of an attempt to create a sort of universal case–function paradigm. A very general description of it may read as follows:

qui marks any subject;
ke marks direct objects;
cui and *quibus* mark indirect objects;
cuius, *quorum/corum*, *quarum* mark nominal genitives;
de ke, *ad ke*, etc. mark the use of the prepositions *de*, *ad*, etc.

(For further detail, see Fortacín Piedrafita (1980: 72–5).)

Fortacín argues, convincingly, that the system is based on a didactic practice, well known since classical times, for the teaching of the Latin case system. From this, however, he has drawn the conclusion that the individual or individuals who marked the text in this manner were engaged in the process of learning Latin, that they were schoolboys struggling to cope with Latin nominal declension, trying to put their master's explanations into practice. Here he is close to Menéndez Pidal's view (1926: 382) and in agreement with Díaz y Díaz (1978: 26–32). These authors also seem to presume that the alphabetical glosses have the same didactic function as the grammatical glosses.

For various reasons, I find it rather difficult to accept the grammar-class theory. The grammatical glosses as a system may have their roots in the classroom, but that does not automatically confine the uses of such a system to that space. A person who has once been taught Latin in this way will, for the rest of his life, have access to the technique whenever he needs it. Furthermore, he will not be the only one who is familiar with it; he will share this knowledge with all other learners of Latin, trainees or trained.

Another argument against the grammar class is that the paradigm itself seems rather inadequate for learning the Latin case system. As I have mentioned, the paradigm lacks several forms, and all prepositions are invariably followed by the direct-object marker *ke*, as in (1) and (2):

(1) cum angelis [ke cum] (GL 413)
(2) de fructibus [ke] (GL 450)

The glossers, presuming they are several, did not need to know whether the subjects, direct objects, and nouns in prepositional complements were one or several, feminine, masculine, or neuter, but they apparently needed such distinctions in other cases. They were capable of making glosses like (3) and (4), but used markers like *qui*, *cui*, and *cuius* to understand their own correct use of the Latin cases, or for some other purpose.

(3) Dixit qui diabolus cui ebreo (GL 77)
(4) . . . dicebit qui angel[us] cuius Domini (GL 325)
(5) de ke/   fructibus
      ex   / ipsis (GL 453)

Having glossed *de fructibus [ke]* as in (2), why did they then add the correct *fructibus* to *ipsis* in (5) instead of their *ke*-case *fructus*? Probably because they knew this to be correct.

Not everything is correct, though; there are errors and mistakes, but apprentices are not the only persons who make mistakes. The grammatical glosses cannot have been designed in order to produce future masters of Latin. Díaz y Díaz (1978: 29) almost seems to indicate that his schoolmaster was teaching, not Latin, but something close to Spanish: 'a nuestro entender ya supone una fase de la enseñanza muy romanceada'.

The alphabetical glosses certainly indicate romanizing. What is being romanized is the text's word order; finite verbs are moved to precede non-finite forms, possessive adjectives are placed before the determined noun (cf. (13) and (14)), OV order is changed to VO, etc. We may conclude that this procedure adapts the basic Latin text to more vernacular habits, but I cannot see why a student of Latin should be the only possible beneficiary of this, and I find it difficult to explain what help he would find in the rather frequent inversion of SV order to VS, as exemplified by (6) (cf. (3), (4), and (13)):

(6)   qui
     ⁺Tunc ᵇanima ᶜinmunda ᵃdicit (GL 783)

This inversion, though perhaps romanizing in character, cannot be described as obeying grammatical criteria (Díaz y Díaz 1978: 29, n. 54). It is rather a question of style, as is the case with quite a few other alphabetical glossings as well.

The alphabetical and grammatical glosses can serve the same purpose only if we specify the purpose of the grammatical glosses, not as a means primarily for learning case declension, but as a tool for understanding what the different cases mean; 'who does what to whom' instead of 'how to say what about whom'. The difference between the two definitions may not seem significant. The point is, however, that if the grammatical glosses are a tool for understanding the Latin text, the glosses have been created on the basis of Romance grammar, and their purpose is primarily to romanize Latin. A theoretical desired effect of this romanizing could have been to latinize some Romance-speaking group or individual, but the situation is not *necessarily* the classroom, and grammar is not the only possible subject.

As a technique for romanizing, the grammatical glosses make more sense as a system. They provide a functional analysis of the text from the point of view of a user's language different from the Latin language of the basic text.

That would mean that the alphabetical glosses and the grammatical glosses serve the same purpose and are parts of the same system. It also means that these glosses probably have the same function as all the rest of the glosses.

If we can regard the alphabetical glosses as a documentation of the habit of turning Latin word order around to adapt it to the grammatical and stylistic habits of the vernacular (and what else can they be?), then it may be very convenient to have signs marking important syntactic functions for the reader, who is jumping back and forth in the text.

The use of a pronominal paradigm to indicate case represented a well-known practice for any literate person going through or having gone through the process of learning Latin. Here this practice has been adapted to suit its purpose, and the paradigm has been reduced to the forms needed. The system is not perfect, as we shall see, but its creator must nevertheless have been quite clever. We can also note variety in its use along the way, and this can be explained, I think, by the experimental character of these procedures.

The following analysis of the grammatical glosses is rather sketchy and generalized, as this volume is not the forum for a detailed study: *Qui* indicates where to look for the subject in a clause, but it is not necessary to explain its gender or number once located. The opposition *qui/ke* distinguishes clearly between subject and direct object, for instance not to confuse a post-verbal subject and a direct object. As to the importance of this particular distinction, Fortacín Piedrafita (1980: 72) remarks, speaking about the gloss *ke* and the graphical means by which the functions subject and direct object are indicated: 'Llama poderosamente la atención la gran diferenciación gráfica obtenida entre este signo y el anterior, eliminando cualquier posibilidad de confusión.'

The isolated *ke* normally marks a direct object. In addition, it can be described as marking an element as following some other element; the direct object in a VO or VSO sequence, the noun following the preposition, the non-finite form of a verb following a finite form, etc. This view is supported by the alphabetical glosses.

The glossers being persons trained in Latin grammar, it would be natural to distinguish the indirect object and the possessive nominal genitives from the prepositional complements glossed by *ad ke* and *de ke* respectively. It would also be practical, as these syntactic functions sometimes obey different morphological and word-order rules. In the dative and genitive cases the markers simply echo the number and gender of the glossed element. What is important is to mark these elements as indirect objects and genitive phrases respectively, and to mark them as distinct from the *ke* case.

From a Romance point of view, the ablative as a functional form has, of course, no relevance, and thus it is not included in the system. This would be one reason why we find *quibus* but not *de quibus*.

We could, perhaps, demand perfect consistency and require a single sign for the indirect object and the genitive, e.g. *cui* and *cuius*, but I think we should not expect such strictness. Although the system is based on a traditional practice, it gives the impression of being of a more experimental character than a generally used tool would be. The reductions already mentioned are one case in point; another one is the use of the relative pronoun instead of the traditional demonstrative *hic*. Fortacín Piedrafita (1980: 78–89) goes to some length to explain the substitution, and he concludes that this is what we should expect at this time and place.

The combinations *preposition + ke* have four variants: *de ke, ke de, de ke de, ke*. They all reflect exactly the same procedure, differing only in the way the basic text is incorporated into the gloss and vice versa. Putting the gloss between square brackets, this may be illustrated as follows:

de ke: de[de ke?]:   canticis –no incorporation
ke: de [ke?]:   canticis –text incorporated into gloss
de ke de:de [de ke?: de] canticis –gloss incorporated into text
ke de: de[ke? :   de] canticis –text incorporated into gloss and
                                            vice versa.

The latter type is documented quite clearly in (14) below by the split *ke / in* in lines 5–6. I interpret this variety as due to what I call the private character of the act of glossing, and not as Fortacín Piedrafita (1980: 75), who sees the repeated preposition 'como indicio de la seguridad en la determinación del *complemento*'.

The particular system may have been created by one person, as this does not exclude other persons from benefiting from it. The grammatical glosses do not need to have been put there by a group, nor does the person adding the alphabetical glosses have to be the same as the grammatical glosser in order to take advantage of these glosses. The grammatical glosses may represent a local 'school', or the invention of an individual, or both. The point is that the system is sufficiently private to show changes, minor inconsistencies and errors, and it is sufficiently general to be used for its original purpose by several persons, contemporaries or not, who have felt the need to add, correct, and explain.

Díaz y Díaz (1978: 27–8) thinks the alphabetical glosses were introduced together with the grammatical glosses. Fortacín Piedrafita (1980: 89) thinks the latter came first; on several occasions a cross or letter marks a gloss. The meaningful words in Latin, Romance, and Basque seem to have been put there at different times, and some may be contemporary with the grammatical and alphabetical ones (Díaz y Díaz 1978: 28–9).

Wright (1986) has suggested that the Romance and Basque glosses may have some connection to reading the texts aloud. I believe the alphabetical and grammatical glosses may serve the same purpose. I also believe that if the glossers were apprentices, their subject was the art of preaching.

The alphabetical and grammatical glosses would then be silent glosses, meaning that you would never hear the gloss, only its effect (e.g. word order, verbal agreement, prepositions). The other glosses may have been included in the oral version, making them audible glosses.

Some of the audible glosses which adorn the pages already dotted with silent glosses, may have been introduced in order to correct erroneous silent glosses, or to facilitate the reading of complicated passages. One passage which seems to illustrate such conditions is transcribed in (7) with alphabetical glosses:

(7) ho. * ad ke   ho. ad ke
    +qui badulterium anon facit, +qui bad aeclae/ [*fornicationem]
    siam afrecuentius uenit . . .

(MP 46; GL 444–8)

The erroneous grammatical gloss *ad ke* to *adulterium* is one of two such errors evoked by Fortacín Piedrafita (1980: 85) to refute the idea that the glosser knew enough Latin to be a preacher, as has been suggested by Prado (*apud* Olarte Ruiz 1977: 18–19). Such a person would know a word like *adulterium*, Fortacín Piedrafita argues. I agree with him, but I do not see innocence and ignorance as the only reason for adding a wrong *ad ke* to *adulterium*; such an error may be made by any tired or careless person. As one can see, the end of line 8 has a correct *ad ke* to *ad aeclae/siam*; I suggest the first *ad ke* was put over *adulterium* by mistake and was originally intended for *ad aeclaesiam*. If we follow the alphabetical glosses, after having read *frecuentius uenit* in line 9, we have to jump back to line 8 to find the prepositional complement. The gloss *fornicationem* in the right margin may have been put there to sort out the confusion created by the two *ad ke*. It should also be noted that it represents a change of meaning, substituting an excluding member of a semantic opposition by an including one. After all, we are dealing with a monastic community.

The second error referred to is a rather similar case: (GL 606) *iniuste* is erroneously glossed *in ke*, and, by coincidence (?), at the beginning of the following line there is a correct *in ke* to the phrase *in festiuitatibus* (GL 608). Here as well we have a gloss in the right margin; (MP 74; GL 607) *transtornare*, invisible in *Glosas* (1977: fol. 71r), but obviously intended for the word *subuertere*, making (fol. 71r, lines 13–14) *et causas iniuste subuerte/re* into *et transtornare causas*, allowing for the syntax indicated by the alphabetical glosses. Here the glosser has found that he could dispense with the word *iniuste* altogether.

Additions to the text, like (3) and (4) above, indicate that the glosses are not related to a word-by-word translation of the basic text. Sometimes the sense of the text is even changed completely, as illustrated in (14) and by the marginal gloss in (7). One may imagine a practice where the basic text was somehow rephrased in the vernacular, maybe with additions or omissions. For some passages the rephrasing may have been omitted, for others the vernacular version may have repeated the original text.

We know of such a text from another linguistic area, the so-called *Jonas* fragment; *Le Sermon bilingue sur Jonas*. It is probably from the first half of the tenth century and consequently older than the *Glosas Emilianenses*, dated by Díaz y Díaz (1978: 29–30) to some point well into the eleventh century. I quote a few lines in (8) from De Poerck (1955: 42–3, lines 144–8) as an illustration of the technique that may have been employed in an oral version of the sermons from the *Códice Emilianense 60*:

(8) . . . Et preparauit Dominus ederam super caput Ione
ut faceret ei umbram. laborauerat
<enim dunc> Ionas propheta habebat mult laboret e
mult penet a cel populum co dicit. e faciebat grant
jholt. et eret mult las
<et preparauit Dominus> un edre sore sen cheve
qet umbre li fecist. e repauser si podist.
Et letatus est Ionas super edera
<letitia magna. dunc fut Jonas m>ult letus co dicit.

I think the spirit and style of this text is similar to the result we obtain if we combine text and glosses in the *Glosas Emilianenses* where multiple glosses are present. I also think one should bear in mind that, like the *Jonas* fragment, most of the glossed texts in *Glosas Emilianenses* are sermons. This point did not escape Díaz y Díaz (1978: 31), speaking about the Romance glosses. To him, however, the silent glosses are irreconcilable with the idea of seeing the glosses as support for oral performance, having defined these glosses (p. 27) 'como elemento escolar para explicar gramatical-mente [los] textos'. To me, the additions and changes seem difficult to reconcile with the teaching of grammar. One can also ask why a schoolmaster should choose examples and sermons, and not, for instance, the narrative texts in the codex. Another point is that these 'grammatical exercises' always start at the beginning of a text and follow it through to the end and amen.

Of course, we cannot reconstruct an oral version of the texts in the case of the *Glosas Emilianenses*. Nevertheless, I think quite a few linguistic deductions can be made on the basis of the glosses themselves. By bringing in external sources one may learn even more. Some of my internal deductions are presented below:

As mentioned, there are inconsistencies and errors in the glosses (e.g. (7) above). One inconsistency is represented by (3) and (9):

(3) Dixit qui diabolus cui ebreo (GL 77)
(9) dicet qui populus ad ke ad ipsum sacerdotem o sacerdote (GL 632)

In (3) the indirect object has the usual marker *cui*; in (9) it is marked by *ad ke*.

If we interpret (9) as a slip, we could interpret *cui* as a way of denoting *ad* + NP in (3). A Romance gloss like the marginal (MP 48; GL 461) may show us that *quibus* could occasionally be read *alos* (or *alas*) as in (10):

(10) homo   ke   /(. . .)   *   quibus   [*qui dat alos
     +qui (. . .) ᵇdecimas/(. . .) ᶜerogandas ᵈpauperibus/ misquinos]
     ᵃreddet, . . . (MP 48; GL 451–61)

Similarly, we may use the famous gloss (MP 89; GL 687), a fraction of which is quoted in (11), to interpret *corum* and other genitives as possibly 'signifying' prepositional genitive with *de*:

(11) in   ke   corum
     in secula seculorum [. . . enos sieculos delos sieculos]
     (MP 89; GL 687)

Another general feature which supports this interpretation is the kind of glossing illustrated by (12) and (13):

(12)   corum
     ᶜstridor ᵈdentium (GL 793)
(13)   ke   / de ke   cuius
     +Et ᵃoccidit ᶜeum ᵇDominus/ ᵈgladio ᶠoris ᵉsui (GL 318–20)

In (12) *dentium* is correctly marked for the genitive plural, and the phrase is marked for a word order corresponding both to normal Latin and Romance. In (13), the phrase *gladio oris sui* has the genitive marker on the adjective *sui*, which is marked as preceding *oris*, as would be the order in Sp. *de su boca*.

As an illustration of how the glosses may be used to transform the text, I have chosen a rather straightforward passage, fol. 75r-v, 17-7, transcribed with glosses in (14). After a few comments on this passage, I present my rephrased version in (16):

```
(14)                    qui    angeli ke de    cuius
  17          +Et cantent ailli bde canticis cDauid //
             [obe][parescent]      [ena felicitudine]
                        qui angeli ke
   1         dubi manifestat        ebeatitudinem
             cuius              ke in    cuius qui angeli
   2         fanime. +Intrantes in domo Domini adicunt.
             [+O Domine]  [hominem]   [quem hominem]
                 tu    es        tu         tu
   3         aBenedictus bquem celegisti det adsum
                              [qui ipse homo]
                 +O                   ke
   4         isti. Domine. ainhabitauit bin dtaber
[*nosemplirnosamus]               O domine nos *   ke
   5              naculis ctuis. +Et arepleuimur bin
             in            cuius
   6         bonis ddomo ctue. csanctum +est btemplum
                          [est qui tuum templum]
                 qui              ke in
   7         atuum. dmirauile in equitate.
                                (MP 121–4, GL 946–72)
```

The alphabetical glosses reverse Latin word order in lines 4–5; *tabernaculis tuis* > *tuis tabernaculis*, 6; *domus tue* > *tue domus*, and 6–7; *templum tuum* > *tuum templum*, the latter repeated in the gloss to line 7. As mentioned above, the VS sequence in line 17, *cantent illi*, represents a frequent word order in the glossed text (see example (6)). In this sample one can note that the glosses *qui (angeli)* (lines 17, 1, and 2), and *qui ipse homo* (line 4) are all placed towards the end of the verb.

The combinations *preposition* + *ke* are of the type *ke* + *preposition*, except in line 4 where the gloss is *ke*. This order is typical for this part of the text.

The partitive *de* in the gloss to line 17, *de canticis*, should not be considered as a mere repetition of Latin syntax, as illustrated by (15):

(15)   de ke de
  +Et ^cpotestates ^amul / ti ^berunt (GL 207)

In connection with (11)–(13) above I have commented on the location and possible interpretation of *cuius* (lines 17, 2, and 6). The relation between alphabetical and grammatical glosses is also illustrated by the location of *qui* to *(templum) tuum* in line 7. In line 17 *angeli* is separated from *qui* and is put over *illi*, signifying, I presume, that *angeli* is an audible gloss; *cantent illi* <*angeli*>.

The atypical concordance error made in line 1, *qui angeli*, could be due to fatigue or carelessness. *Angeli* has been a very frequent subject in this sermon and it is the subject of *cantent* in the main clause. The glosser has then inadvertently read *manifestant*; at least, a transitive verb is indicated by *ke* to *beatitudinem*.

The error may also be intentional. The glosser may have found it more suitable to continue to speak about 'angels' instead of introducing 'David' as a subject at this point. Thus he changes the meaning, but only slightly; singing the song, the angels will manifest what the song manifests, and, thus, what David wrote.

In my view, the Romance glosser has taken advantage of the wrong *numerus* in the gloss *qui angeli*, changing the text completely, making a new clause; *obe parescent* <*angeli*> *ena felicitudine*. He has not let his imagination run wild; as we can see, his inspiration is close at hand: *parescent* is semantically close to *manifestat*, and the distance is not far between *felicitudine* and *beatitudinem*. The way this passage is quoted in Menéndez Pidal (1926: 8), it looks as if the Romance glosser fetched the third person plural out of thin air, translating directly *manifestat [parescent]* and *beatitudinem [ena felicitudine]*. Even if the Romance glosser did not understand the construction *manifestat beatitudinem*, which I think he did, he could have consulted the grammatical gloss to the accusative, which marks it as a direct object.

Using the glosses for improvisations is not uncommon, and can be related, I think, to the technique of preaching, where the point is not to translate the text, but to transfer it into another linguistic context, as illustrated by the *Jonas* fragment quoted above in (8).

In (14) another change of meaning is represented by the glosses to the clause in lines 3–4 which add to it the phrase *O Domine, tu benedictus es*. This change seems an obvious embellishment.

Expansions of the text like line 3 *Benedictus quem [hominem] [tu] elegisti et [quem hominem] [tu] adsumisti* and the repetition of subject and verb in line 7; *mirauile [est tuum templum] in equitate* seem to me to adapt the text to the oral medium, making it easier for the listener to follow the spoken words.

Quem instead of *ke* in line 3 is, as far as I know, the only occurrence of *quem* in these glosses. This *quem* is probably meant as an audible gloss, and thus distinguished from the silent *ke*. It could, perhaps, be read **qual huamne* or **elo huamne ke*, forms attested in the Romance glosses (MP 68, 89; GL 578, 689) except for the relative *ke*, attested as a grammatical gloss and as the homophonous conjunction *ke* in (MP 89; GL 689).

The following 'reading' of the text in (14) is based on the arguments and comments presented above. Apart from the substitution *de (+art.)* for *cuius*, and the change of the following nouns to denasalized accusatives, I have not attempted to romanize the Latin forms not attested as such in (14), as this would need a much ampler commentary than I have been able to present here.

(16) Et cantent illi [angeli] de canticis <de> Dauid // ubi manifesta<n>t [angeli] beatitudinem <dela> anim<a>. (var.: [obe parescent [angeli] ena felicitudine].) Intrantes in domo <de> Domin<u> dicunt [angeli]:[O Domine tu] benedictus [es]. Benedictus quem [hominem tu] elegisti et [quem hominem tu] adsumisti. [O] Domine; inhabitauit [ipse homo] in tuis tabernaculis. [O Domine nos emplirnosamus] in bonis <de> tu<a> dom<u>. Est sanctum tuum templum! Mirauile [est tuum templum] in equitate!

BIBLIOGRAPHY

De Poerck, G. (1955) 'Le Sermon bilingue sur Jonas du ms. Valenciennes 521 (475)', *Romanica Gandensia* 4: 31–66.

Díaz y Díaz, M. C. (1978) *Las primeras glosas hispánicas*, Barcelona: Universidad Autónoma.

Fortacín Piedrafita, J. (1980) 'Glosas morfosintácticas en el códice emilianense 60', *Revista de Investigación* (Soria), 67–89, + illustrations.

García Larragueta, S. (1984) *Las Glosas Emilianenses, edición y estudio* (Biblioteca de Temas Riojanos, 54), Logroño: Instituto de Estudios Riojanos.

Glosas Emilianenses, Las (1977) Madrid: Ministerio de Educación y Ciencia.

Menéndez Pidal, R. (1926) *Orígenes del Español* (8th edn, 1976), Madrid: Espasa-Calpe.

Olarte Ruiz, J. B. (1977) 'En torno a las "Glosas Emilianenses"' in *Glosas Emilianenses*, 11–30.

Wright, R. (1986) 'La función de las glosas de San Millán y de Silos', J. C. Bouvier (ed.), *Actes du XVIIe Congrès International de Linguistique et Philologie Romanes*, vol. IX, Aix-en-Provence: University of Provence, 209–19.

15 How was Leonese Vulgar Latin read?*

Carmen Pensado

It is a highly debatable issue whether Medieval Latin and Early Romance were – as traditionally considered – two independent entities (I will refer to this as the 2L hypothesis) or were instead a single entity (Early Romance) with an archaic spelling and two different registers, as contended by Wright (1982). I will refer to the latter position as the SL hypothesis. It may actually boil down to the *vexata quaestio* of how different must language varieties become in order to be considered independent. Unfortunately, this can have more than one answer. Our contribution to this controversy intends to be mostly methodological, i.e., we will try to devise a procedure to test both alternative hypotheses. Our conclusions will only be tentative. As we shall see, the picture drawn by the data is extremely complicated. I shall be concerned with mis-spellings involving phonological innovations and completely ignore morphological phenomena. Our study is based on a corpus of mis-spellings involving intervocalic obstruent voicing in documents in Visigothic script mostly from the Leonese area.[1]

Leonese Vulgar Latin (LVL) – as Menéndez Pidal labelled the barbarous Latin that was written in León and Portugal in the tenth and the eleventh centuries – is an excellent case in favour of Wright's (1982) SL hypothesis. The number and quality of errors is such that Menéndez Pidal (1950: section 95) was forced to admit that those texts could not possibly be read as Classical Latin. As Wright (1982: 165–73) has shown, Menéndez Pidal's alternative explanation – viz. that LVL was not contemporary Romance, but an archaic preservation by Mozarabic notaries of the language spoken in the fifth or sixth centuries – is completely unnecessary. However, as will become apparent later on, LVL cannot be equated with the spoken language.

To begin with, we may classify mis-spellings into three categories:

(a) mere errors which may be psycholinguistically significant but are irrelevant to the historical linguist: e.g. *quomomo* 'quomodo', *OD* doc. 42 (1001); (b) errors stemming from a mismatch between the spelling system and the spoken language: e.g. *sibit* 'sive', *OD* doc. 42 (1001); and (c) errors due to changes in progress: e.g. *flauinicz, flauinici, OD* doc. 39 (1001) with loss of final -*e*, still a variable process in thirteenth-century Spanish. Both the second and the third kind of errors will be relevant for our purposes.

Spelling deviations from the classical norm in Late Latin texts may be alternatively interpreted as either the result of Romance interference, if we start from the 2L hypothesis, or as simple misspellings, if we presuppose an archaically spelled language (SL hypothesis; see Figure 15.1).

> 2L hypothesis:
>
> (a) Latin → spelling
> (b) Romance → latinization rules → spelling
>
> SL hypothesis:
>
> Romance → spelling rules → spelling

Figure 15.1 Alternative hypotheses for spelling deviations

I shall speak of Latin and Romance as convenient labels without any *a priori* commitment to the 2L hypothesis. According to the 2L hypothesis scribes either wrote in Latin (a), or they strove to latinize Romance words (b). According to the SL hypothesis, scribes spelled their native Romance following highly elaborate spelling rules. Both the hypothetical latinization rules and the spelling rules were more or less equivalent. For instance, Sp. *lado* would be latinized by changing -*o* into the appropriate case suffix and -*d*- into -*t*- and read as e.g. /látus/. Alternatively, if the SL hypothesis were true, Sp. *lado* would be spelled e.g. *latus* and read /ládo/.[2] Unfortunately, we can expect similar errors under both hypotheses. For instance, by rule over-application: *atrianum*, which involves a false generalization starting from the equivalence Sp. *lado* = Lat. *latum*, can be alternatively interpreted as spoken /atriánum/ according to the 2L hypothesis, or as /adriáno/ according to the SL hypothesis.

But there is a great difference in the predictions made by the two hypotheses regarding the treatment of non-Romance elements. If the SL hypothesis were true, non-inherited Latin words would be subject to the same kind of orthographic rules as Romance ones.

Conversely, if the spelling system fit the pronunciation (2L hypothesis), then purely Latin words did not have to pass through any deliberate orthographic filters. In our case, this hypothesis predicts that, while in Romance words which are latinized both voicing and hypercorrect devoicing should occur, in those Latin words which were not preserved in Romance, we should expect at most hypercorrect devoicing, but never voicing. In spite of this, we do find instances of voicing in our data (see Table 15.1).

Table 15.1 Some instances of voicing in Latin words

<b> for <p>	abut, cribidine, nun(c)cubata, obificis, particibium, probe, probinquis, prosabia;
<d> for <t>	adrium, comudare, condide, Dadan, -dur < -TUR, -ider < -ITER, ida, licidum, perpedim, posteridas, podestatem, prodidore, quader, quodidie, sicudi, anagorida;
<g> for <c>	apligavimus, catoligorum, celiga, degrebi, edifigata, indigatum, iurigabit, obsegramus, paupertagula, siguti, spiragulum, veridigum;
<v> for <f>	amplivicavit, edivicia, iurivicavi, opivicem, pontivice, prolivigare, salmograbus, verivigo.

In our corpus 393 instances of voicing in Latin words occur in 94 different lexical types, i.e. 15.1 per cent of all the tokens showing voicing (2,604) and 26.85 per cent of all the lexical types (350). At first sight, the low frequency of voicing in non-inherited Latin words relative to that in Romance words would seem to argue for the 2L hypothesis. However, on closer inspection, we observe that non-inherited words occur only in formulae, while voicing, like all other mis-spellings, is most frequent in non-formulaic passages: e.g. proper names alone account for 131 types (37.42 per cent of all the voiced types) and 868 tokens (33.33 per cent of all the voiced tokens). Leaving out proper names, voicing in non-inherited words goes up to 42.92 per cent of the types and 22.63 per cent of the tokens. Given the approximate running-text frequency of non-inherited words (15.50 per cent of the total of lexical items), we conclude that the treatment of Latin and Romance words is very much the same after all. It was this Romance 'flavouring' of Latin which forced Menéndez Pidal (1950: section 45.6) to admit that these texts could not possibly reflect a Classical Latin pronunciation.

Now let us turn to a phenomenon of a different kind. In our sample we also find attested voicing and hypercorrect devoicing of post-consonantal obstruents, even though obstruents in this context

Table 15.2 Voicing in post-consonantal position

2(a) Hypercorrections

	Source
concampio, -iamus, -iavi, -iata, -ionis	*Crr.* 265, 266 (1121 2 x), Sm. 171 (1050 4 x), *Elz.* 73 (1080), 80 (3 x), 81 (1089), Vc. 85 (1078), *OD* 44 (1007), 49, 50 (1002 2 x), *Stg.* 227 (1015), 228 (1015 3 x)
palumpa	*DEPA* I 160 (854)
melantjz	*OD* 53 (1003)
Fagunto	*Vc.* 105 (1085)
Gontesalbes	*Shg.* 52 (933)
Gontesaluo, -iz	*Vg.* 5 (946)
iscalta	Sm. 168 (836)
Leanter	*Shg.* 80 (941)
vulco	*COv.* 217 (1075)

2(b) Abnormal voicing

predido	Br. 219 (964)
spondania	*OD* 62 (1008)
aquadudiles	*Shg.* 233 (965 2 x)
faculdate	*Shg.* 351 (996)
Gundina	*Stg.* 240 (1026)
ingendi	*Shg.* 351 (996)
podesdatem	*Shg.* 268 (973)
sebtendrio(n)	*Shg.* 341 (989), 264 (971)
arbusgula	*Vc.* 32 (1028)
episgopi	*Shg.* 351 (996)
Liengres	*Oñ.* 19 (1011)
porciungula	*Vp.* 322 (940)
propinguis	*DEPA* II 45 (SMillán 869)

were not affected by the diachronic process of voicing (see Table 15.2).

Once again, the 2L hypothesis is at odds with such data. In order to account for the abnormal voicing of /p, t, k, f/ (in Table 15.2b), Menéndez Pidal (1950: sections 45, 6; 55) is forced to postulate – against the evidence of present-day Leonese – that post-consonantal voicing was a feature of LVL. He tried to relate this phenomenon to the voicing of obstruents after continuants in Basque and Aragonese and explained the case of *aquadudiles* < DUCTILES as a specific development of LVL. Mis-spellings with <p, t, c, f> (Table 15.2a) would be hypercorrections due to syncope (1950: section 45, 6–7, 110, 2). It is true that contexts of syncope favour hypercorrection: cf. *Melcare, Shg.* 260 (972), *Adca, Vc,* 134 (1103), *Sescutiz,* Br. 246 (1102), *Sescudus, Stg.* 227 (1015) < SISEBUTUS. But this explanation is unnecessarily complicated and has to have recourse to *ad hoc* phonological changes. An explanation in terms of graphic phenomena is both more likely and economical.

Hypercorrect <p, t, c, f> (in Table 15.2a) are not problematic for the SL hypothesis: the intervocalic voiced value of <p, t, c, f> has been overgeneralized. On the other hand, the SL hypothesis cannot account for post-consonantal <b, d, g, v> in place of <p, t, c, f> in (Table 15.2b) any better than the 2L hypothesis: if <b, d, g, v> never stood for voiceless obstruents in voicing contexts, why use them to spell /p, t, k, f/?[3] Notice that if we admit that, at least sporadically, intervocalic <p, t, c, f> could still be read as voiceless obstruents, we have an explanation for the complete confusion of orthographic <p, t, c, f> and <b, d, g, v>. If intervocalically both series of letters could represent phonetic /p, t, k, f/ as well as /b, d, g, v/, then they could be taken as fully equivalent symbols. That this orthographic equivalence had no effect on reading can be inferred from instances of confusion between <c, qu, k> and <g> before front vowels (see Table 15.3).

Table 15.3 Some instances of confusion between <c, qu> and <g> before front vowels

<g> = /ts/	*iudigio, Shg.* 264 (971), *uindigetis, Shg.* 264 (971), *salges,* *DEPA* II Liébana 86 (873), *Giprianus* (for *Ciprianus*);
<qu> = /dʒ/	*quermanos* (for *germanos*), *Vc.* 292 (1200), 291 (1200, 4 times), *subroquita* COv170 (1046);
<c> = /dʒ/	*Eucenius DEPA* Liébana 166 (827, fourteenth-century copy).

It is highly unlikely that these forms were read as /dʒudídʒo/, /kermános/, or /tsermános/. The mis-spellings only imply that <ge>, <ce>, and <que> were misinterpreted as equivalent orthographic symbols for the same set of values, much in the same way as in the equivalence between <k>, <c>, and <qu>.

For a parallel, consider the case of present-day Gran Canaria Spanish, where a variable process of voicing of intervocalic /p, t, k, tʃ/ has been detected (Oftedal 1985). Symptomatically, Lecuona's (1987) corpus provides instances of mis-spelled obstruents not only intervocalically, but also post-consonantically (see Table 15.4).

Children who pronounce orthographic *bonita* either /boníta/ with /t/ as in *toro* or /bonída/ with /d/ as in *donde*, are led to interpret <t> and <d> as equivalent graphemes, and then generalize this equivalence to other environments, where there is no phonological

Table 15.4 Mis-spelled obstruents by eleven-year-old children in Gran Canaria

4a Mis-spellings indicative of intervocalic voicing

\<b\> for \<p\>	albacera 'aparcera', abarceros, abbacero 'aparcero, -s'
\<d\> for \<t\>	bonidas, contandode, escondide
\<g\> for \<c\>	aganchas 'canchas', chiguo 'chico', bicigleta

4b Hypercorrect spellings

\<p\> for \<b\>	gapón 'jabón', pueplo, tampién
\<t\> for \<d\>	catetral, cuatro, recoto
\<c\> for \<g\>	amicos, gucar, dico, recresamos, soca, vertico

4c Orthographic confusion in post-consonantal position

\<b\> for \<p\>	embiesa, conbra, culba
\<d\> for \<t\>	gende, tarda, divierdo, vido 'visto'
\<g\> for \<c\>	blangura, esgapa

4d Hypercorrect spellings in post-consonantal position

\<t\> for \<d\>	grante, cuanto, deste
\<c\> for \<g\>	ponco, puca 'pulga', salco, salca

variation.[4] Thus – contrary to Menéndez Pidal's interpretation – there is no reason for postulating *ad hoc* phonetic phenomena in order to account for the above-mentioned mis-spellings in LVL. In my judgement, in the case of Gran Canaria Spanish the key factor is the fact that both voiceless and voiced obstruents actually occur as synchronic variants so that \<p, t, c, f\> and \<b, d, g, v\> are misinterpreted as fully equivalent.[5] But can we postulate such a situation for eleventh-century Leonese?

Table 15.5 Some instances of geminate- and cluster-reduction

geminate reduction	vaka, sica, uacas, ata, metemus, mata
cluster reduction	fico, fiquo, autoricare, netjbus, setember

To be sure, we find in the latter some instances of \<p, t, c\> in intervocalic position standing unambiguously for /p, t, k/, i.e. those resulting from geminate or cluster reduction (see Table 15.5). There are also hypercorrections which are to be interpreted as representing voiceless pronunciations rather than as a telescoping of the equivalences \<d\> = \<t\> = \<tt\>, e.g.: *quodque* 'quoque', *adput* 'apud', *dupplada, trippata* 'triplata', *committe*. We can thus admit that – in case orthographic awareness includes the possibility of mis-spellings – intervocalic <p, t, c> could actually represent both a voiced and a voiceless pronunciation.

All this would be indirect evidence for a voiceless value of intervocalic <p, t, c>. But we can even find instances where intervocalic <b, d, g> stand for voiceless sounds, thus showing that, in fact, there was phonetic variation. This is what we can infer from the half-learned words shown in Table 15.6. All these words preserve voiceless consonants in their modern forms. We cannot explain them away as loans from Latin after the Carolingian Renaissance because they show Romance developments. The spellings in Table 15.6 imply that such words could have voiced variants. But it is obvious that voiceless forms must have coexisted with them in order to account for the modern results. And if this is the case in half-learned words, how can we deny the possibility that there was in fact a wavering between voiced and voiceless pronunciations in the Latin words we saw in Table 15.1?

Table 15.6 Voicing in half-learned forms (number of tokens)

episcobus, -i, -o, -orum (cf. MnSp. obispo)	14	*Crr., COv, Shg., Vc., Vg.*
probrium, -o, -a, -as, -ium, -iis (cf. MnSp. propio)	27	*OD,* Br., *Crr., DEPA* II León, *Vg., Elz., Shg., Vc., DEPA* Huerta An., *COv., Ply.*
abostoli (cf. MnSp. apóstol)	1	*Shg.*

Wright's (1982) solution to this problem is lexical diffusion. Being at the end of the diffusion queue, learned words would have preserved their voiceless obstruents. Lexical diffusion seems to be a satisfactory explanation for many of the problems connected with half-learned forms (see also Pensado 1983: 188–92). Differences in the distribution of phonological changes between medieval and modern forms are not a serious problem for a diffusionist interpretation: each word must have passed through a variation stage. In our case we must admit that, in fact, intervocalic voiceless obstruents were produced in some words, at least in reading styles. But is it possible for voicing to be a variable process as late as the eleventh century? And, given that voicing is just one of the many processes that show variation in these texts, are we to suppose that all those processes were still alive? This is, in fact, what the traditional interpretation postulates. Variation in spelling would mirror a similar variation in the spoken language (Menéndez Pidal

1950: sections 107–8). This idea is hardly surprising. After all, historical linguists are used to finding changes in progress in mis-spellings. This would be the third type of mis-spelling we mentioned above (p. 191).

Now we have completed the whole circle. One of the conclusions of the SL hypothesis is that variation in Late Latin texts must not be taken as a clue for linguistic change. The intention of writing correct Latin deprives archaisms of any value and so, *a priori*, it precludes any significant generalization based on orthographic variation. We started by dismissing variation as only apparent and we have ended up conceding that it is genuine. But let us try to see whether our orthographic variation shows any of the characteristics of a change in progress. I shall start with the purely phonological aspects and then go on to lexical diffusion.

Even though there are wide divergences among scholars as to its dating, our first attestations of voicing reach back to the first century AD. No author seems to date it later than the seventh century (cf. Pensado 1984: 202–4). At any rate it would be much earlier than the eleventh century. It is doubtful whether changes with a century-long implementation can qualify as genuine sound changes, or are rather of an analogical nature (cf. Hock 1986: 651–2). But even if they were genuine, for purely internal reasons voicing could not be one of them. Once geminate reduction took place (at the latest in the eighth century; cf. Pensado 1984: 214–15), a new series of voiceless intervocalic obstruents arose, to which voicing was never applied. This implies that either voicing no longer existed, or – less probably at such a late stage – that degemination and voicing applied in counterfeeding order.

In order to strengthen our viewpoint, let us check whether we can discover any of the characteristics of a living phonological change in our data. Although our texts represent the most formal style, if a living phonological change shows a uniform distribution across styles, as claimed by Labov (1981: 296), we should still be able to reconstruct its diffusion pattern. It has been repeatedly observed that /k/ is more prone to voicing than the other obstruents both in Late Latin (see already Richter 1934: 136) and in the Romance languages (see Oftedal 1985 for the higher voicing rate of -*k*- in Gran Canaria Spanish). We could expect to find a consistent difference in relative voicing rates across documents.

But the data do not meet our expectations. We can see (Table 15.7) that relative voicing rates do not keep constant; this fact is enough to show that they cannot be interpreted as an effect of the spoken language. Leaving aside corpora where the relevant items are few, we see that, when the number of errors is large enough to yield statistically significant results, relative voicing rates tend to coincide with the relative frequency of intervocalic voiceless obstruents as shown on Table 15.8.

However, in some corpora there seems to be a preference for the voicing of -*k*-, and in others for -*t*-. There can be non-phonological factors for the high voicing rate of -*k*- in spite of its being much less frequent than -*t*-. First, orthographic rules involving /k/ and /g/ were intrinsically more complex due both to the existence of three symbols for /k/ (i.e. <k, c, qu>) and to the fact that <c, g> were also used for the outcomes of palatalization. Second, the high frequency of -*t*- is due to its occurring in many inflectional and derivational suffixes. Apparently, highly frequent suffixes tend to be

Table 15.7 Relative voicing rates (total number of tokens in parentheses)

Relative voicing rate	Collection	% v	% b	% d	% g
t > p > k > f	*Crr.*	2.12	25.53	51.06	21.27
t > k > p > f	*OD*	2.07	15.02	52.84	30.05
	Br.	7.35	8.088	57.35	34.55
	Stg. (251)	6.77	7.96	50.19	35.05
	Vc. (596)	3.35	11.57	53.85	31.20
k > t > p > f	*Shg.* (327)	4.28	8.56	24.77	62.38
	Elz. (104)	0.96	8.65	20.19	70.19
	COv. (439)	4.32	9.79	15.03	63.26
k > t > f > p	*Vg.* (88)	6.81	3.40	15.90	73.86
k > t > p	*Blm.* (44)	0	9.09	34.09	56.81
k > f > t	*Cvr.* (35)	14.28	0	5.71	80
t > k > f	*Oñ.* (32)	12.5	0	56.25	31.25
k > t > f	Vp. (24)	12.5	0	37.5	50
t > p > k	Ctñ. (21)	0	14.28	76.19	9.52
k > p > t	*Ply.* (9)	0	33.33	22.22	44.44
t, p	*Cdñ.* (2)	0	50	50	0

Table 15.8 Estimated frequency for intervocalic voiceless obstruents*

estimated frequency for -f-	2.52%
estimated frequency for -p-	12.45%
estimated frequency for -t-	65.69%
estimated frequency for -k-	19.32%

* Based on their average frequency in *Crr.*, *OD*, and Br.

correctly spelled, as I infer from Lecuona's (1987) corpus. This is confirmed by our data: while suffixes account for an estimated 54 per cent of all occurrences of *-t-*, only 29.15 per cent of the instances of <d> for <t> occur in suffixes. Third, and more important, each specific school of scribes has its own spelling habits. If we compare original documents signed by the same notary, we observe a high consistency in mis-spellings: e.g. mis-spelled *Stevanus* and *artigulo* are characteristic of Stevanus (Br. docs 8 and 11); Vermudus (*Crr.* docs 13 and 18) spells VERMUDUS; Velasco (*Crr.* docs 5, 7, 12, 17, and 18) writes *episcobo* and *domidio* < DOMITU; and Cidi (*OD* docs 48, 49, and 50) writes *probria*. This tendency to standardization is most apparent in large corpora: in *COv*, out of a total of 311 tokens of voicing of *-k-*, 50 correspond to *eglesia*, 20 to *sexiga* < SESSICA, and 45 to *deganea* < DECANEA. In *Shg.* out of 204 tokens, 101 correspond to *eglesia*. This specific spelling is so frequent (215 instances in our corpus) that we can consider it as an alternative orthographic norm.

Variation in relative voicing rates and the tendency to standardization imply that spelling does not correspond to any systematic phonological variation in speech. Therefore our data do not confirm the productivity of voicing.

Let us now consider lexical diffusion. Even though consonant lenition typically diffuses with neogrammarian regularity (see Labov 1981: 302), once restructuring has begun, change in lexical entries will obviously take place word by word (see Labov 1981: 276, and especially 1987: 150–5). Since our indexes for lack of voicing are only indirect, we cannot ascertain which words *did not* voice. It is still possible to analyse those words that *do* voice and see whether they show any of the characteristics suggestive of anticipated evolution.

In the first place, we should expect a given lexical item to exhibit a consistent behaviour across texts. What we find instead is a complete lack of consistency: while the lexicon remains fairly stable across corpora, up to 56 per cent of the mis-spelled words show voicing only in one source. This suggests that the distribution of voicing errors across the lexicon is not significant.

Regarding specific lexical items, it can be safely assumed that restructuring will take place first in the most common words which are subject to strong phonetic erosion. We will try now to re-examine our data taking word frequency into consideration. A frequency count based on the number of occurrences of these words in our texts would not be significant, due to their formulaic nature.

We have had recourse to Sala (1988) as a means of indirectly calculating their probable frequency in actual speech. Out of 350 lexical types which show voicing only 55 (15.71 per cent) appear on Sala's list. And, what is more important, some of the most basic lexical items (*pater*, *mater*) never show voicing. This further corroborates our conclusion that mis-spellings involving voicing are just that: simple mis-spellings.

Of course, this does not imply that lexical diffusion never occurred or that half-learned words are not to be explained as a result of lexical diffusion, but only that the variation which we have inferred from our texts does not seem to result from a change in progress. Most probably, voicing was already restructured by that time, although some words were able to change class again. We have arrived again at Wright's (1982) conclusions, but at the expense of having no explanation for the variation in voiceless stops.

The only possible explanation would be to suppose that even if, for instance, intervocalic <t> was regularly pronounced as /d/, its etymological value could have been recoverable for literates. The spelling system provided speakers with clues for inferring a 'basic' (and etymological) value of letters. Those persons who were able to read may have captured the 'correct' values of letters by a default rule. On the one hand, Latin <t> was still read /t/ word-initially and after a consonant. On the other hand, there was also a specific letter <d> to cover the voiced value. All this could lead literates to the 'etymological' reasoning that /t/ was the 'true value' for <t> even in intervocalic position. That is, variation might have been due to spelling pronunciation. For instance, even if <t> may sound in various ways in English (*tea* [t], *action* [ʃ], *future* [tʃ], and even Am. Eng. *better* [ɾ]), literate speakers still have the feeling that /t/ is its proper value. Spelling pronunciation is directly proportional to the degree of phonetic inadequacy of a spelling system (see Wells 1982: 106–9 for English). That /t/ was considered as the primary value for intervocalic <t> in LVL is shown by the high degree of consistency in writing /p, t, k/ resulting from geminates or clusters as <p, t, k>, as we have earlier observed. If this were true, at least some words could have variable pronunciations due to the influence of spelling. This implies that at least some half-learned forms may be just inherited forms reshaped by the influence of an archaic spelling.

Only the small minority who was able to read and write could be influenced by spelling, but these forms could be borrowed by other speakers for reasons of prestige. Supposing that all people who used latinisms were literate would be as ill founded as deducing that nowadays people who use English loanwords or calques in other languages have some knowledge of English. The influence of writing upon the spoken language has been observed even in mostly illiterate societies (see Goody 1987: 268).

But the presence of spelling pronunciations presupposes consciousness of the superiority of the written norm, and this is hardly compatible with deliberate vulgarization. Obviously, whether scribes were doing their best or they were trying to vulgarize will always be a highly controversial issue. But let me add a brief argument in favour of the first hypothesis. The reader who is confronted for the first time with these documents is surprised by their lack of coherence. The technique of writing involved copying formulae from a repertoire, but the notaries' mastery of the written language was not enough to enable them to conjoin formulae in a meaningful way. 'Ideo placuit nobis adque conuenit . . . , which implies a rhetoric preamble (as in *Formulae Wisigothicae* x; see Zeumer 1886), is systematically used after the initial formula. Some notaries were not even able to substitute shifters consequently (formulae repertoires give only third persons). At the same time formulae were degenerate to the point of becoming nonsensical: e.g. 'nullus quoque gentis' or 'nulius quoque agentis inperio nec suadentis articulo', which is a corruption of 'nulli coagentis imperio' as in *Cartae senonicae* or 'nulli cogenti imperio' in *Formulae Marculfi* II, 20; Zeumer (1886). Its correct version is not even attested in corpora such as Br., *OD*, and *Crr*. *Nec per vim nec per metum* becomes 'nec per vinum nec per metum' in, e.g., Br. doc. 12. *Claro animo et spontanea mea voluntate* becomes 'caro animo . . .' in, e.g., *Crr*. doc. 21. These are obvious signs that scribes could not fully understand their models. But they show even more about their attitude to their texts. If they intended to be faithful to their models and to stylistic elegance to the point of producing incoherent and even meaningless texts, it is plain that their main intention was not that of vulgarizing (as assumed by Wright 1982: 62), but to be as conservative as possible.

Now I come to my conclusions. According to the evidence provided by obstruent mis-spellings, LVL was most probably read as Romance. But this does not imply that no awareness of a distinction between spoken Romance and the written norm was felt. Both initial hypotheses are partly true: LVL was read as Romance, but it was probably felt as Latin.

ABBREVIATIONS

Unless otherwise stated numbers refer to pages. Dates are in parentheses:

Blm.   A. C. Floriano Cumbreño (1960) *Colección diplomática del Monasterio de Belmonte*, Oviedo: IDEA.

Br.   J. M. Fernández Catón (1973) 'Documentos leoneses en escritura visigótica. Fondo M. Bravo del Archivo Histórico Diocesano de León', in *León y su Historia, Miscelánea Histórica 2*, Leon: Fuentes y Estudios de Historia Leonesa: 203–95.

Cdñ.   L. Serrano (1910) *Fuentes para la historia de Castilla. III. Becerro gótico de Cardeña*, Valladolid: Tipografía y Casa Editorial Cuesta.

cj.   J. Guallart (1946) 'Documentos para el estudio de la condición jurídica de la mujer leonesa hace mil años', *Cuadernos de Historia de España* 6: 154–71.

COv.   S. García Larragueta (1962) *Colección de documentos de la Catedral de Oviedo*, Oviedo: IDEA.

Crr.   J. M. Fernández Catón (1982) 'Documentos leoneses en escritura visigótica. Fondo del archivo del monasterio de Carrizo', *Archivos Leoneses* 72: 195–291.

Ctñ.   A. Rodríguez González (1966) 'El tumbo de San Martín de Castañeda', *Archivos Leoneses* 20: 181–354.

Cvr.   L. Serrano (1907) *Fuentes para la historia de Castilla*, vol. II: *Cartulario del Infantado de Covarrubias*, Valladolid: Tipografía y Casa Editorial Cuesta.

DEPA   A. C. Floriano Cumbreño (1949–51) *Diplomática española del período astur*, Oviedo: IDEA.

Elz.   V. Vignau (1885) *Cartulario del Monasterio de Eslonza (primera parte)*, Madrid: Imprenta de la Viuda de Hernando.

evc.   A. Millares Carlo (1973) 'Consideraciones sobre la escritura visigótica cursiva', in *León y su Historia. Miscelánea Histórica*, vol. 2, León: Fuentes y Estudios de Historia Leonesa, 297–391.

OD   J. M. Fernández Catón (1974) 'Documentos leoneses en escritura visigótica. Fondo Otero de las Dueñas (años 1000 a 1009) del Archivo Histórico Diocesano de León', *Archivos Leoneses* 55–6: 31–83.

Oñ.   J. Alamo (1950) *Colección diplomática de San Salvador de Oña*, Madrid: CSIC.

Ply.   F. J. Fernández Conde, I. Torrente Fernández, and G. Noval Menéndez (1978) *El monasterio de San Pelayo de Oviedo. Historia y fuentes*, Oviedo: Monasterio de San Pelayo.

Shg.   J. M. Mínguez Fernández (1976) *Colección del Monasterio de Sahagún (Siglos IX y X)*, León: Fuentes y Estudios de Historia Leonesa.

Sm.   C. Sánchez Albornoz (1946) 'Documentos de Samos de los reyes de Asturias', *Cuadernos de Historia de España* 4: 147–60.

Stg.   M. P. Yáñez Cifuentes (1972) *El monasterio de Santiago de León. Estudio histórico-documental*, León: Fuentes y Estudios de Historia Leonesa.

Vc.   L. Serrano (1929) *Cartulario de San Vicente de Oviedo, 781–1200*, Madrid: Centro de Estudios Históricos.

Vg.   L. Serrano (1927) *Cartulario del Monasterio de Vega*, Madrid: Centro de Estudios Históricos.

Vp.   L. Barrau-Dihigo (1900) 'Chartes de l'église de Valpuesta du IXe au XIe siècle', *Revue Hispanique* 7: 273–389.

NOTES

* I wish to dedicate this paper to my father, José Luis Pensado, who first called my attention to the peculiarities of voicing in Leonese Vulgar Latin. My thanks go also to Julián Méndez Dosuna for his encouragement and his help with the manuscript, and to Jorge Guitart who made helpful comments on an earlier version and checked my English style.

1 All sources will be cited in abbreviated form (see Abbreviations list).

2 Slashes indicate a broad phonetic transcription. I presuppose for eleventh-century Leonese a phonological system with a single series of voiced obstruents (see Pensado 1984: 183–8).

3 Although evidence is scant, Romance /b, d, g, v/ were probably devoiced in word-final position. Since mis-spellings conditioned by syllable- or word-final neutralization processes do not seem to spread to syllable-initial position (e.g. Castilian Sp. *saluz* 'salud' does not generalize to **zato 'dato'), it does not seem probable that final devoicing contributed to the use of <b, d, g, v> for voiceless obstruents in syllable-initial position.

4 Notice that orthographic errors occur in spite of the fact that there is a phonetic difference between primary voiced obstruents, which are fricatives or continuants, and secondary voiced consonants, which are stops. This shows that our argumentation for LVL would also obtain in the case that LVL had two series of voiced obstruents (see n. 2).

5 If, against our contention, there was no variation between voiced and voiceless intervocalic plosives, our mis-spellings would involve the

unexpected error of misusing unambiguous signs (i.e. <b, d, g> biuniquely representing /b, d, ɡ/). Such errors do not seem to occur. At first sight, z standing for /k/ in *OD* doc. 53 (1008), *zlara, artjzulo, zuntjs* and *Shg.* doc. 261 (971), *fruztuosis, magnivizarat,* could seem to be such a case. But a free variation between /k/ and /ts/ is attested at least in the words *mihi, nihil* which show both the expected velar variants (*niquil*) and affricate ones (cf. *mizi Shg.* doc. 257 (970), *micz(i) OD* doc. 36 (1000)).

BIBLIOGRAPHY

Goody, J. (1987) *The Interface between the Written and the Oral,* Cambridge: Cambridge University Press.

Hock, H. H. (1986) *Principles of Historical Linguistics,* Berlin: Mouton de Gruyter.

Labov, W. (1981) 'Resolving the Neogrammarian controversy', *Language* 57: 267–308.

—— (1987) 'The interpretation of zeroes', in W. U. Dressler, H. C. Luschützky, O. E. Pfeiffer, and J. R. Rennison (eds), *Phonologica 1984,* Cambridge, Cambridge University Press: 135–56.

Lecuona Naranjo, M. P. (1987) *La ortografía. Una experiencia en Gran Canaria,* Salamanca: Amarú Ediciones.

Menéndez Pidal, R. (1950) *Orígenes del Español,* 3rd edn, Madrid: Espasa-Calpe.

Oftedal, M. (1985) *Lenition in Celtic and in Insular Spanish,* Oslo: Universitetsforlaget.

Pensado, C. (1983) *El orden histórico de los procesos fonológicos,* Salamanca: Ediciones Universidad de Salamanca.

—— (1984) *Cronología relativa del castellano,* Salamanca: Ediciones Universidad de Salamanca.

Richter, E. (1934) *Beiträge zur Geschichte der Romanismen,* Halle: Max Niemeyer.

Sala, M. (ed.) (1988) *Vocabularul reprezentativ al limbilor romanice,* Bucharest: Editura Ştiinţifică şi Enciclopedică.

Wells, J. C. (1982) *Accents of English,* 1: *An introduction,* Cambridge: Cambridge University Press.

Wright, R. (1982) *Late Latin and Early Romance in Spain and Carolingian France,* Liverpool: Cairns.

Zeumer, K. (1886) *Formulae merowingici et karolini aevi* (Monumenta Germaniae Historica. Legum Sectio V, Formulae), Hanover: Impensis bibliopolii Hahniani.

16 Spelling lapses in early medieval Latin documents and the reconstruction of primitive Romance phonology

Thomas J. Walsh

The central thesis of Roger Wright's 1982 book, *Late Latin and Early Romance in Spain and Carolingian France*, stated succinctly in the opening sentence, was 'that "Latin", as we have known it for the last thousand years, is an invention of the Carolingian Renaissance' Prior to the end of the eighth century in France and the end of the eleventh century in Spain (when Roman liturgy replaced the Visigothic), according to Wright, no conscious distinction was drawn between Latin and Romance. Latin was regarded as the written mode of the spoken vernacular of each locale. Accordingly, the literate, when reading, gave each Latin word its vernacular pronunciation, much as English speakers today articulate *knight* as [nájt] or as Francophones reproduce *doigt* 'finger' as [dwá]. Wright flatly rejected the possibility of distinct Latin and vernacular pronunciation norms, whose existence had been taken for granted by many Romanists, including some of the giants of our discipline.

While I admire Wright for the originality and boldness of his stance and, in fact, agree with many of his interpretations, I suspect that, perhaps out of a desire to take a position diametrically opposed to the traditional one, he pushed the point a little too far, at times even ignoring the thrust of his own evidence. True, one can almost imagine some of the legal and notarial documents he cited, along with numerous others of the period, being read with vernacular phonetics and being understood even by illiterate speakers as a slightly pompous form of their own dialect. By way of illustration, consider the following sentence, which appears in a mid-eleventh-century document from Toro (prov. Zamora):

Et quando dedit domno Migael Citiz illa caſa ad illo abbate, ille jacente jn ſuo lectu, uenit filio de Rodrigo Moniiz et ſuo uaſſallo et prendiderunt ſuo clerigo ad ſua uarua et ſouarunt illum et jactarunt eum jn terra ad te ʃuoʃ pedeʃ de illo abbate.

(Menéndez Pidal 1950: 26)

A word-for-word rendition even into Modern Spanish, such as the following, would, with minor morphological adjustments, be largely comprehensible to any native speaker:

Y cuando dio dueño Miguel Cídez la casa al abad, él yacente en su lecho, vino el hijo de Rodrigo Moniz y su vasallo y prendieron su clérigo a su barba y sobáronlo y echáronlo en tierra ante [?] los pies del abad.

Few sentences, however, even in the most humdrum legal charters lend themselves quite so smoothly to literal vernacular paraphrases. But the idea that writers of such sentences deemed them the written versions of strings they might well utter in informal conversation hardly exceeds the bounds of the conceivable. By contrast, consider the following sentence, excerpted at random from a perfectly ordinary ninth-century manuscript from the monastery of San Millán – a manuscript which, by chance, forms part of the same codex as the one containing the famous glosses:

Quoniam necdum homines sciunt quod soror mea es, parum de uia secede donec transeant. Et post transgressos illos, vocat eam: Eamus, soror, uiam nostram. Illa autem non respondente perquirens invenit eam mortuam et vestigia pedum eius plena sanguine.

(García Larragueta 1984: 97)

I contend that, even if read with vernacular pronunciation, such a passage would have been indecipherable to the native speaker of tenth-century Hispano-Romance who lacked specialized training in Latin. Even the simplest everyday notions were habitually expressed in writing in such a way as to be incomprehensible to the unlettered. It seems safe to speculate that 'Let us enter the house, he said' was, in tenth-century north-central Spain, uttered as [entrémoz en (e)la káza, díʃo]. None the less, in that same unremarkable manuscript, one reads, 'Ingrediamur, inquid, domum' (García Larragueta 1984: 100). Even if one conjectures – as seems altogether probable – that such a sentence were read [eŋgreðjámor, íŋkið, dómu], it would still have been unfathomable to the untrained listener. If, on the other hand, 'Ingrediamur, inquid, domum' was rendered orally as [entrémoz en (e)la káza, díʃo], then we shall have to admit that the reader simply translated from Latin into vernacular, an act which itself presupposes the awareness of distinct codes.

In short, I fully agree with Wright that vernacular phonetics must have been employed in the reading of Latin in pre-Carolingian times. In a certain sense, it could not have been otherwise, since speakers of the period, unlike us, had no access to first-century BC pronunciation of Latin. But even we, who can easily consult the work of fellow twentieth-century linguists who have reconstructed Classical Latin phonology, persist in pronouncing Latin through our native systems. I have no doubt but that Latin as articulated by the average English, French, or Spanish university student (or, for that matter, professor) bears far more resemblance, on the strictly phonological level, to English, French, or Spanish than to Vergil's pronunciation of the classical tongue. But we must not forget that Latin pronounced with English, French, or Spanish phonetics is still Latin, and not English, French, or Spanish. The exception, of course, is Latin so faulty as to exhibit outright predominance of vernacular morphology, syntax, and lexicon over strictly Latin elements. Wright generalized from that sort of Latin to all levels – an unjustifiable leap, in my judgement (see Walsh 1986: 212).

Two types of Latinity were, broadly speaking, current in the period under discussion, as presumably also in subsequent centuries, namely notarial and ecclesiastical. The former was used by legal practitioners who required a smattering of Latin grammar and vocabulary – largely stock phrases – to draw up the documents for which they were daily responsible. Such individuals were perhaps never exposed to correct Latin, say, in literary works or scripture. They must have relied largely on memory, rather than on reference books, for their grammar, a risky approach even for those of us with advanced degrees in Romance philology. Dependence on memory as chief resource in matters of vocabulary would also explain the presence of numerous strictly vernacular words in such documents. With Wright, I can easily envision such individuals feeling that Latin – their brand of Latin, to be sure – was an elaboration on their spoken vernacular.

Monks living and working in monasteries, however, must have enjoyed an altogether different experience of Latin. To begin with, they would have come into daily contact with works composed centuries before, such as scriptural, patristic, liturgical, and hagiographic writings, which, while perhaps never exhibiting the stylistic polish and refinement of the great classical authors, were nevertheless couched in respectable Low Latin. Certain monks may even have glimpsed the great classics of the Augustan Age.

Exposure to such ancient texts must have caused those monks to realize that the language in which they were composed was equally ancient – one that pertained to another time and place. If Dante's notion of Latin as a sort of koiné artificially created to facilitate communication among scholars from different parts of the world was original with him, then the conventional thinking must have been that Latin was an ancient language, quite distinct from the vernaculars current in the various parts of ROMANIA. Moreover, the famous list of cheeses (transcribed in Menéndez Pidal 1950: 24–5, and discussed in some detail in Wright 1982: 173–5), if written out by a monk, i.e., someone who presumably knew that the accusative plural of 'cheeses' was spelled *caseos* or *casea* in Latin, bears witness to the perception by at least some members of the literate community that Latin and vernacular were distinct languages. While that document is by no means a phonetic transcription, it may come fairly close to being a phonemic one.

Wright was justified in doubting that Classical Latin was ever employed alongside vernacular as a normal medium of informal discourse in monasteries, as some scholars had believed (though even Menéndez Pidal alluded to a 'romance corriente . . . hablado por todos en su conversación diaria' (1950: 454)). But while accepting Wright's argument, we may still assume that literate clerics were at least subliminally conscious of speaking one language and writing another. Spoken Latin in this period was probably limited mainly to liturgical celebrations. In those instances, processes of speakers' native phonology would surely have impinged on their pronunciation of Latin, just as they do today. But frequent non-vernacular lexical items, inflections, and word order would still have made all but the most dreadful Latin bewildering to the uninitiated. With all due respect for Wright's originality and impressive ability to marshal evidence in support of his opinions, I feel that he swept certain serious problems under the rug by claiming, e.g., that 'Outdated word order is of no consequence' (1982: 168). His suggestion (1982: 168–70) that Latin inflections were considered silent letters like the *gh* in Eng. *knight* and never pronounced overlooks the fact that if fairly correct Latin is read aloud without declensional suffixes, it promptly becomes gibberish, since, as everyone knows, those endings signal the relationship of nouns to other nouns and also to verbs in any given sentence. Under the assumption that monks who had spent years studying Latin knew what those endings meant, it simply makes no sense to think that they should not have pronounced them when reading.

Having made those general observations regarding the status of Latin in the Early Middle Ages, I wish now to focus attention on a hypothetical language – or, rather, register – postulated by Menéndez Pidal (1950: 454–60), whose thinking on the subject was submitted to a searching critical assessment by Wright (1982: 165–77), namely 'Leonese Vulgar Latin'. The great Spanish scholar, in his study of tenth- and eleventh-century documents from Leon, identified two sharply distinguishable strains of Latin. Certain documents – the vast majority – were couched in what one might label 'standard scholastic Low Latin', of the sort current throughout western Europe in the High Middle Ages. Such documents, which routinely exhibit a sprinkling of grammatical errors and orthographic lapses of various sorts, were written for the most part in fairly correct Latin. Another, smaller, group of documents offers a Latinity so shot through with vernacular features that one is inclined, with Wright, to interpret it as the written mode of local vernacular, with the thinnest veneer of Latinity superimposed. Documents belonging to the latter group are invariably legal/ notarial – never ecclesiastical – in content. The most baffling feature of such documents is that, despite the pervasive orthographic slips, which seem to betoken an advanced state of phonetic evolution, numerous archaic (i.e., correct Latin) morphological features are preserved; e.g., synthetic passive (*cingidur* for CINGITUR 'it is surrounded'), future participle (*avidura* for HABITURA 'having' (fut.)), case endings, and many vocabulary items – both lexical and grammatical – that had doubtless fallen out of spoken usage centuries earlier.

To account for the unusual language of such documents, with no known parallels in other parts of Spain, Menéndez Pidal postulated a spoken register intermediate between scholastic Low Latin and vernacular. For him, pervasive orthographic blunders denoted not a low level of Latinity, but rather a deliberate decision by certain scribes to write in a more spontaneous, less artificial, and less solemn language than that which characterized liturgy and official state chronicles. That language was said to represent a 'precious survival' of the spoken Latin current in all of ROMANIA in the closing centuries of the Roman Empire – a language which, though quite advanced on the phonetic level, none the less preserved certain morphological and syntactic features of the classical tongue. The existence of a similar brand of Latinity in Merovingian France simply confirmed its wide currency as a spoken language in the late Empire. As for why such a language, doomed in France by the

Carolingian Reforms, should still have been written by a minority in León in the tenth and eleventh centuries, Menéndez Pidal conjectured that the group at issue was constituted by Mozarabic immigrants who, owing to isolation after the Islamic conquest, perpetuated the written usage of the Late Empire and very early Middle Ages. Elsewhere in Spain, according to him, such a register, which would have continued to serve as a means of oral communication among the cultivated, was no longer employed for writing. With the decline of Mozarabic influence in León in the late eleventh century and the suppression of the Mozarabic liturgy, such a language came to be felt as inappropriate for writing. But even after its demise as a written medium, it remained in spoken use, supplying the numerous semi-learned words observable in the earliest Romance documents.

Wright's explanation (1982: 165–73) for the poor Latinity of those documents is far simpler and, to my way of thinking, infinitely more plausible: as the vernacular evolved ever farther away from the classical model, and as educational standards – especially for the laity – declined, many scribes simply failed to achieve proficiency in Latin. If we view the learning of a language closely related to one's own as consisting largely in mastering, through the exercise of memory, contrasts between the native and target codes, we may infer that the scribes who wrote in Leonese Vulgar Latin had not, for whatever reason, spent the time necessary to accomplish that task. Otherwise stated, their errors merely betray gaps in their knowledge of written Latin, stemming, no doubt, from educational deficiencies.

While accepting Wright's view that some of those documents may have been read aloud as vernacular and were felt by their authors to represent spoken vernacular, I also believe that he overstated his criticism of Menéndez Pidal, in some respects staking out for himself a position every bit as naive as the Spanish master's had been. Reproaching Menéndez Pidal for interpreting such texts as phonetic transcriptions of their writers' speech, Wright insisted that 'We have no direct access to the nature of tenth-century Old Leonese speech' and that 'Surviving texts tell us little about speech' (1982: 166). He argued further that 'The practical purpose of writing words on a page is to indicate the right lexical item to the reader; originally semi-phonetic spellings can achieve this even if they have in time become distant from evolved phonetics' (1982: 168). Since the written form of a word served only to signal that lexical item to the reader, a word's spelling (or mis-spelling) bears, according to

Wright, no more relation to its pronunciation than the English orthographic sequence *knight* does to [nájt] or the French sequence *chantent* does to [ʃãt].

While I grant that such texts must not be analysed as straightforward phonetic transcriptions of speech, I believe that they afford us direct access at least to certain aspects of tenth-century Leonese speech and that, in general, they reveal a great deal about the vernacular phonology of those who wrote them. If we assume – as common sense dictates – that those writers were not intentionally composing in a barbaric style, but rather that their target was correct scholastic Low Latin, then errors should systematically reflect divergences between the target language and writers' native linguistic systems. Careful analysis of those errors should yield detailed information on – in the present case – tenth-century Leonese Romance.

Before scrutinizing those charters with an eye to extracting specific information regarding tenth-century Leonese vernacular phonology, it is worth asking why scribes who had a passing knowledge of Classical Latin morphology and syntax and who routinely used terms (albeit often mis-spelt) that had almost surely fallen into desuetude centuries before (e.g., *pulchritudo* 'beauty', *amaritudo* 'bitterness', *pontifex* 'high priest, pope', *secus* 'following', *sicut* 'as'; see Menéndez Pidal 1950: 247) should have been such poor spellers. Their writings leave the odd impression that the grammatical and lexical sophistication of a university student and the spelling ability of a child in the third year of elementary school have been combined in a single individual.

The only credible explanation which suggests itself to me for such a paradoxical state of affairs is that those individuals' study of Latin must have been almost entirely oral. After learning the general phonetic value of the letters of the Roman alphabet, they must have assimilated morphology and lexicon through auditory, rather than visual, stimulation. Their language-learning experience must have consisted largely of rote repetition of paradigms and word lists. The predictable result was a far stronger auditory than visual image, something which would have caused few problems were not the chasm separating Latin orthography from Old Leonese phonology so wide. When in doubt about the spelling of a particular word, given the likely unavailability of dictionaries, the only solution was to attempt to 'sound it out', something you may recall being forced to do in elementary school, with predictably poor results, at least for those of us who were raised in an Anglophone context. Those words that we now know how to spell, we have largely memorized, by dint of seeing them in written form hundreds of times, an experience doubtless denied to people living outside monasteries in the tenth century.

When speakers of a modern tongue attempt the pronunciation of a 'dead' language for which native-speaker models are in principle unavailable, one anticipates that they will fall back on their own phonological patterns. Specifically, two broad categories of processes will come into play, both operating, of course, at the subconscious level. First, learners will apply the allophonic rules and phonotactic constraints peculiar to their native speech. Thus, in pronouncing Latin, English speakers will predictably aspirate pretonic voiceless stops, pronounce simple vowels as falling diphthongs, and reduce certain unstressed vowels to schwa. French speakers may decline to observe the Latin stress rule, preferring to follow their own native rule of word- or phrase-final stress. Hispanophones will spirantize postvocalic voiced stops, pronounce -M as [n] or [ŋ], and render R- as a trill.

Second, and far more importantly for our purposes, such learners will almost never reproduce phonemic contrasts characteristic of the target language but alien to their native parlance. Thus, while Italians – at least those hailing from south of the La Spezia–Rimini line – are quite adept at enunciating Latin geminate consonants, Anglo-, Franco-, and Hispanophones virtually never distinguish Latin geminates from their simple counterparts. Spanish speakers, when pronouncing Latin routinely equate B with consonantal V, pronouncing both as stops or fricatives according to phonetic environment. We Americans, often chided by speakers of a certain insular dialect of English for confounding intervocalic *t*'s and *d*'s (e.g., *latter* and *ladder* are homophones) in our futile efforts to speak their language, may fall prey to that same vice when pronouncing Latin, equating, e.g., CREDAM 'I shall believe' with CRETAM 'grown' (fem. acc. sg.) or even CRETAM 'Crete' (acc. sg.). Finally, in no country that I know of are Latin vowel-quantity distinctions consistently observed, even by classical scholars, who are free to check the length of any orthographic vowel in Ernout and Meillet's etymological dictionary, the most reliable guide on this point. There is no reason to believe that speakers in tenth-century Leon – or anywhere else for that matter – should have succeeded where we consistently fail.

Of interest in the present context is the effect that this apparent inability of speakers to reproduce target-language phonemic distinctions absent from the native system may have on their efforts to write in the target language, in this case Latin. In highly literate cultures such as ours, those foreign phonemic distinctions will be reinterpreted as orthographic quirks to be committed to memory, under pain of receiving a D or even an F on a midterm or final examination. Given our ready access to all manner of textbooks, bilingual dictionaries, and literally hundreds of editions of the classics, we simply have no excuse for forgetting that, say, [míɾəɹej]] 'to send' is written with two *t*'s rather than one, that [víɾə] 'life' contains a *t* rather than a *d*, or that [məmóɹijəm] 'memory' ends in -AM rather than -UM.

Those tenth-century Leonese notaries, who no doubt pronounced Latin through the prism of their own phonological system, differed from us in having little, if any, access to the materials just enumerated, let alone to a Latin spell-checker on floppy disk – something which I understand will soon be available. The point is that many, if not most, of their orthographic gaffes resulted from phonemic mergers and deletions that had taken place during the millennium separating them from Cicero and thus provide us with precise information on both their native phonemic pattern and the distribution of phonemes in lexical items.

Restricting our attention for the moment to the four short documents from late tenth- and eleventh-century Leon transcribed by Menéndez Pidal (1950: 24–9), we find strong evidence for the following changes:

1 Raising of /a/ to /e/ by influence of yod: *keʃos* for CASEOS 'cheeses'; *lexauit* for LAXAUIT 'he left', *benfectria* for BENEFACTORIA (recorded in Late Latin of Spain) 'free town'.
2 Monophthongization of /ej/ and /ow/: *kesos*, *lexauit*; *ouiʃti* for HABUISTI 'you had'.
3 /ɔ/ > /u/ by influence of /w/: *puʃeron* for POSUERUNT 'they put'.
4 Raising of /e/ to /i/ (or /j/) in hiatus: *vinia* (alongside *uenea*) for UINEA 'vineyard'.
5 /i/ > /e/: *Feleʃ* for FELIX (anthroponym), *entrequidate* for INTEGRITATE 'soundness', *tiue* for TIBI 'to you'.
6 Monophthongization of /aj/ and /aw/: *hec* for HAEC 'this', *etate* for AETATE 'age'; hypercorrect *audie* for HODIE.
7 Diphthongization of /ɔ́/: *puablo* for POPULO 'district'.
8 Prothetic /e-/: *escr[i]psi* for SCRIPSI 'I wrote'.
9 Syncope: *cadnato* for CATENATUM 'padlock', *cargatura* for

CARRICATURA 'load', *domno* for DOMINO 'lord', *-eblis* for -IBILES '-able', *benfectria* for (Low Latin) BENEFACTORIA.

10 Merger of /b/ and /w/: *lebaron* for LEUARUNT 'they raised', *ſalbatore* for SALVATORE 'saviour', *cauallo* for CABALLU 'horse', *ceuata* 'barley' (deriv. of CIBUS), *uarua* for BARBA 'beard', *tiui/-e* for TIBI, *uouis* for VOBIS 'to you (pl.)', *nouis* for NOBIS 'to us', *auitacione* for HABITATIONE 'dwelling', *uocauatur* for UOCABATUR 'he was called', *migrabit* for MIGRAUIT 'he migrated'.

11 /-nt/ > /-n/: *lebaron, taliaron* 'they cut'.

12 Merger of /-t/ and /-d/: *aput* for APUD 'at', *aliut* for ALIUD 'other'.

13 Merger through palatalization of /tj/ and /kj/: *uendiciones* for UENDITIONES 'sales', *porcione* for PORTIONE 'part', *donacioniſ* for DONATIONIS 'of giving', *populacione* for POPULATIONE 'population'.

14 Deletion of intervocalic /d/: *Freinandici* 'Fernández', deriv. of *Fredinando* (anthroponym).

15 Deletion of /g/ before /j/: *Lejone* for LEGIONE 'Leon'.

16 Deletion of /h/: *abuimus* for HABUIMUS 'we had', *abeatis* for HABEATIS 'you might have', *auitacione* for HABITATIONE, *ereditauerunt* for HEREDITAUERUNT 'they inherited'.

17 Deletion of /-m/: dozens of examples throughout documents.

18 Deletion of /n/ before /s/: *leoneſiſ* for LEONENSIS 'Leonese'.

19 Replacement of intervocalic *p, t, c* by *b, d, g*: *abidura* for HABITURA 'having (fut.)', *abut* for APUD 'at', *acebit* for ACCEPIT 'he took', *artigulo* for ARTICULO 'article', *ederna* for ETERNA 'eternal', *episcobus* for EPISCOPUS 'bishop', *eredidade* for HEREDITATE 'inheritance', *excomunigatus* for EXCOMMUNICATUS 'excommunicated', *exido* for EXITO 'gone away', *mader* for MATER 'mother', *nebotes* for NEPOTES 'grandchildren', *nodicia* for NOTICIA 'notice', *pacifigas* for PACIFICAS 'you pacify', *plaguit* for PLACUIT 'it pleased', *prado* for PRATO 'meadow', *probria* for PROPRIA 'own', *rodundo* for ROTUNDO 'round', *confirmada* for CONFIRMATA 'confirmed', *semedarium* for SEMETARIUM 'of footpath', *Stebano* for STEPHANO 'Stephen', *suber* for SUPER 'above', *subra* for SUPRA 'above', *teridorio* for TERRITORIO 'territory', *tidulus* for TITULUS 'title', *uindigare* for VINDICARE 'to venge onself', and *uolumtade* for VOLUNTATE 'will'.

I hope through the foregoing enumeration of features to have demonstrated that even if we do not take those documents as phonetic transcriptions, we may still extract from them a wealth of information directly relevant to the synchronic phonology of tenth-

and eleventh-century Leonese. Moreover, they may also help us to establish the absolute chronology of certain important sound changes. Thus, while Hispanists may not be thrilled to find evidence for, say, loss of /h/ and /-m/, monophthongization of Lat. /aj/, merger of /b/ and /w/, etc., changes known to have occurred centuries – if not a full millennium – earlier, they may well be tickled to chance upon – in a Leonese document dated 980 – definitive evidence for metathesis of /s/ and /j/, closing of /a/ in contact with tautosyllabic /j/, and monophthongization of /ej/ (*keʃoʃ* for CASEOS).

I wish to devote the remainder of this paper to the last feature cited in the above list, namely pervasive replacement of letters representing the Latin voiceless stop phonemes by their voiced counterparts. Curiously enough, on the interpretation of this feature at least, Wright seems to have been in complete agreement with Menéndez Pidal, for whom recurrent use of *b*, *d*, or *g* in lieu of correct *p*, *t*, or *c* was a sure sign that intervocalic voicing was under way in León by the late tenth century. Though Wright declined to address the issue directly, his transcriptions (1982: 167) of *salutem*, *placuit*, *probria*, *suber*, *domniga*, *lloco*, *rrodundo*, *abut*, *Iudigare*, *potestatem*, and *dubplata*, from an early tenth-century Leonese document as [salúde], [plógo], [próbrja], [sóbre], [ðoníga], [ʎwégo], [rodóndo], [ábo], [ʒulgáre], [podestáde], and [ðobláda] make his adherence to Menéndez Pidal's position explicit. To my way of thinking, however, such mis-spellings suggest more than just voicing.

To understand why this should be so, we must keep two important considerations in mind. The first, hinted at above, is that, while non-contrastive use of previously discrete graphemes constitutes all but conclusive proof of phonemic merger, strictly allophonic changes will not as a rule be represented in writing (see Penzl 1957: 200–1; 1971: 23; and 1982; and Puentes Romay 1986). This important principle follows logically from Sapir's observation (1933) that speakers are not consciously aware of allophonic alternations in their native systems; the only distinctions they 'hear' are those with contrastive value in their own phonemic systems. If speakers fail to 'hear' and are not cognizant of subphonemic variation, a necessary consequence is that such variation will not be reflected in orthography.

The second consideration, specific to the history of Hispano-Romance, is that prior to voicing of intervocalic surds, intervocalic voiced stops were spirantized and – in some instances – deleted. Spirantization of /b/ and that phoneme's subsequent merger with

/w/, datable on epigraphic evidence to the early Empire (see Grandgent 1908: 134–5), are reflected in all Romance languages, while evidence for spirantization of /d/ and /g/, which probably occurred a century or two later, is present in all Neo-Latin tongues save Rumanian and, perhaps, Tuscan Italian. There can be no doubt, in the light of such mis-spellings as *peones* for PEDONES 'splay-foot', *Diago* for DIDACUS (anthroponym), *Araon* 'Aragon', and *pao* for PAGO 'country district', that spirantization (and deletion) pre-dated the documents studied by Menéndez Pidal.

The key is that mere voicing of intervocalic /p/, /t/, and /k/ would have occasioned no phonemic merger, in so far as voiced stop phonemes in that same position would invariably have been pronounced as spirants at that time. Otherwise stated, the phonemic distinction of voiceless vs voiced stop would have been realized phonetically as voiced stop vs voiced spirant. In this scenario, speakers would have been completely unaware of such voicing and would consequently have had no conceivable motivation for writing /p/, /t/, and /k/ as *b*, *d*, and *g*.

What I am proposing is that massive confusion of the Latin voiceless with voiced stop graphemes constitutes unassailable proof that the corresponding phonemes had merged prior to the composition of the documents in Leonese Vulgar Latin. To put it in another way, the transition from the Classical Latin three-term system of occlusive contrasts (i.e., geminate voiceless vs simple voiceless vs voiced stop phonemes) to the two-term system characteristic of Modern Spanish, whose voiceless stop phonemes contrast only with voiced stop phonemes (realized as spirants in postvocalic position), had been fully accomplished – at least in Leon – prior to AD 980. The precise phonetic mechanism responsible for the merger must have been a second round of spirantization, this time affecting phonetic voiced stops derived from 'underlying' voiceless ones by the voicing rule. Schematically represented, the relative chronology is as follows:

1 spirantization of Latin voiced stops;
2 voicing of Latin voiceless stops;
3 spirantization of voiced allophones of Latin voiceless stops (i.e., the output of 2 above).

If this analysis is correct, then we may suppose, with Alarcos Llorach (1965: 264), that the phonemic contrast of voiced stop vs voiced spirant, assumed by many historians of Spanish (see, e.g., A. Alonso 1967: 63) to have persisted throughout the medieval period, had in fact been lost before the appearance of the earliest vernacular documents. In fact, that merger may have pre-dated the debut of Hispano-Romance written vernaculars by a margin of centuries, given the two instances of 'voicing' (*felgarias* < FILICARIA 'covered with ferns' and *sebaratus* for SEPARATUS 'severed') present in the earliest original Asturian document studied by Menéndez Pidal (1950: 240–1), traceable to AD 775. The earliest reliable evidence from other parts of Spain dates from roughly a century before (see Menéndez Pidal 1950: 253–6; and Castellani 1955, who discredited Carnoy's attribution of IMUDAUIT to the second century AD).

Finally, we recall that Menéndez Pidal's prime motivation for viewing Leonese Vulgar Latin as a 'precious survival' from the remote Middle Ages was the prior attestation of a similar brand of Latin in Merovingian France. Consulting Menéndez Pidal's source of information on Merovingian Latin, namely J. Pirson's 1909 study, we read the following descriptions of the treatment of intervocalic stops: 'Entre deux voyelles, *b* et *p* sont transcrits par *v*' (p. 892); 'Entre deux voyelles . . . la dentale sonore prend souvent la place de la dentale sourde' (p. 896); 'Les scribes ne font pas plus de distinction entre les explosives palatales [i.e., 'velar'] intervocaliques qu'ils ne font entre les dentales' (900); and, finally, 'Les copistes de l'époque mérovingienne et carolingienne font de la dentale sonore et de la dentale sourde un emploi tout à fait arbitraire, sans aucun rapport avec la prononciation de l'époque' (897). Unlike Pirson, I maintain that such orthographic anarchy has everything to do with the (vernacular) pronunciation of the period. As in Leon, such confusion provides conclusive evidence of merger of the Classical Latin simple voiceless and voiced stop series. We are thus free to interpret spelling lapses characterizing both Merovingian and Leonese Vulgar Latin as the effects on orthographic usage of similar developments in the respective vernacular phonological systems, predictable during periods of relatively low educational standards.

BIBLIOGRAPHY

Alarcos Llorach, E. (1965) *Fonología española*, 4th edn, Madrid: Gredos.
Alonso, A. (1967) *De la pronunciación medieval a la moderna en español*, 2nd edn, vol. 1, Madrid: Gredos.
Castellani, A. (1955) Note in 'Cronaca' section of *Archivio Glottologico Italiano* 40: 81–3.
Ernout, A., and Meillet, A. (1959) *Dictionnaire étymologique de la langue latine: Histoire des mots*, 4th edn, Paris: Klincksieck.

218   *Thomas J. Walsh*

García Larragueta, S. (1984) *Las Glosas Emilianenses: edición y estudio*, Logroño: Comunidad Autónoma de La Rioja.
Grandgent, C. H. (1908) *An Introduction to Vulgar Latin*, Boston MA: Heath.
Menéndez Pidal, R. (1950) *Orígenes del español: Estado lingüístico de la península ibérica hasta el siglo XI*, 3rd edn, Madrid: Espasa-Calpe.
Penzl, H. (1957) 'The evidence from phonemic changes', in E. Pulgram (ed.), *Studies Presented to Joshua Whatmough on his Sixtieth Birthday*, The Hague: Mouton, 193–208.
—— (1971) *Lautsystem und Lautwandel in den althochdeutschen Dialekten*, Munich: Hueber.
—— (1982) 'Schreibungsumwertung und die Methoden der historische Phonologie', in A. Alqvist (ed.), *Papers from the 5th International Conference on Historical Linguistics*, Amsterdam: Benjamins, 249–55.
Pirson, J. (1909) 'Le Latin des formules mérovingiennes et carolingiennes', *Romanische Forschungen* 26: 837–944.
Puentes Romay, J. A. (1986) 'Acerca de la grafía del latín altomedieval', *Euphrosyne* 14: 97–112.
Sapir, E. (1933) 'La Réalité psychologique des phonèmes', *Journal de Psychologie Normale et Pathologique* 30: 247–65. (Reprinted in D. Mandelbaum (ed.), *Selected Writings of Edward Sapir in Language, Culture and Personality*, Berkeley and Los Angeles: University of California Press, 46–60.)
Walsh, T. J. (1986) 'Latin and Romance in the Early Middle Ages', *Romance Philology* 40: 199–214.
Wright, R. (1982) *Late Latin and Early Romance in Spain and Carolingian France*, Liverpool: Cairns.

17 Syntactic aspects of Latinate texts of the Early Middle Ages

Robert Blake

In 1982, Wright published *Late Latin and Early Romance*, in which he claimed, among other things, that the Latinate forms of many Peninsular writings before the eleventh century belie their actual purpose of representing one or more registers of Hispano-Romance. According to Wright, the abrupt appearance of Romance-looking documents after the eleventh century resulted from a new adherence to a Carolingian orthographic principle of one letter to one sound, which was part of a greater educational reform designed to improve the Latin skills of the day.

For writings before the eleventh century, Wright posits a series of correspondences for reading aloud: for example, intervocalic voiceless stops become voiced fricatives, as in *vita* > [biða]; tonic mid vowels are realized as falling diphthongs, as in *terra* > [tjera]; or an accusative ending such as *-um* is pronounced [o], as in *manum* > [mano]. In order to read materials written in these older, more traditional spellings, only simple word-recognition was required.

While these types of modifications when reading aloud rely on simple word-recognition, syntactic reprocessing is another matter. Archaic syntactic patterns present the reader with a more formidable cognitive task which significantly complicates, if not makes altogether impossible, a successful reading performance.

And reading aloud is the key issue when considering the Peninsular documents that are available from the eighth to the eleventh century. In the main, they are Church records whose legalistic nature leaves little doubt that they were intended to be read aloud and understood by literate and illiterate citizens alike.[1] The performance aspect is often explicitly acknowledged in the text, as the following late ninth-century fragment clearly shows (Ubieto Arteta 1976: 12): 'Ego Vitulus, cum fratre meo Erbigio legente, audivimus.'

If Peninsular Latinate documents are, in fact, a textual representation of some (presumably, high) register of Hispano-Romance clothed in traditional spellings, as Wright has claimed, then the syntactic patterns should, at the very minimum, closely parallel those of Medieval Spanish. In accordance with this assumption, the present study seeks to add more weight to Wright's thesis by examining the word order of a small sample of Peninsular documents from the ninth, tenth, and eleventh centuries. But first some idea of Spanish word order is required.

Modern Spanish word order has traditionally been described as SVO, having evolved from Latin, a non-rigid SOV language (Wanner 1987: 380).[2] In spoken Spanish, however, there is little doubt that VSO – or, more simply, VO, with an unexpressed Subject – is the most common pattern, for both Modern (Green 1976: 10) and Medieval Spanish (England 1980, 1983, 1984; Bossong 1984).[3]

Theoretical analyses of Modern Spanish word order increasingly stress a base structure which is also VO in nature. The VSO order is preferred by those who use Greenberg's typological approach (Greenberg 1963; Green 1976), while a VOS order is assumed by the generativists who adhere to a strict interpretation of VP-constituency (Contreras 1987; Westphal 1986; Groos and Bok-Bennema 1986).[4] Despite formal differences, both these theoretical accounts would interpret the traditionally championed SVO pattern as merely one manifestation (granted, the most frequent one) of several possible preverbal, topicalized constructions in Modern Spanish, as outlined in (1):[5]

(1) Topicalized Structures in Modern Spanish
a. Unmarked order: V(S)O
    Le escribe (Juan) la carta a Lola.
b. Topicalized subject: SVO
    Juan le escribe la carta a Lola.
c. Topicalized direct object: $O_1V(S)O_2$
    La carta se la escribe (Juan) a Lola.
d. Topicalized indirect object:[6] $O_2V(S)O_1$
    A Lola le escribe (Juan) la carta.

Returning again to the point of departure, many scholars seem to agree that Latin was originally an SOV language. Whatever the actual mechanism, then, which induced the shift from Latin SOV to Romance VO (cf. Harris 1976; Green 1976; Vincent 1976; Wanner 1987), a rather radical syntactic change did occur and should manifest itself at some point in the written tradition. But if England's (1980, 1983, 1984) results are correct, there is no discernible Peninsular word-order development between twelfth and fifteenth century which might testify to an OV–VO switch. In other words, Spanish has always exhibited a basic VO pattern ever since its sudden textual appearance in the eleventh century. What about the word order of texts written before the eleventh century? If Latinate writing represents Romance speech, then a dominant VO pattern should also surface in these earlier texts.

Following this line of reasoning, the present study will examine the syntactic patterns found in the ninth-, tenth-, and eleventh-century documents from the *Cartulario de San Millán de la Cogolla* (Ubieto Arteta 1976). Notwithstanding the obvious formulaic portions of these legalistic charters, their basic syntactic nature will be shown to reflect that of Hispano-Romance.

This particular chartulary was chosen because the famous eleventh-century *Glosas Emilianenses*, one of the first known examples of distinctly phonetic writing in Hispano-Romance, was produced at San Millán.[7] The *Cartulario* itself is also one of the best-preserved corpora of Peninsular writings from the period in question. It offers the researcher a fairly uniform linguistic domain of legal transactions, bills of sale, property donations, depositions, and minor charters of privileges, as transacted and overseen by the clerics at San Millán. In other words, the *Cartulario* provides a fixed slate of scribal parameters.

In a previous study (Blake 1987), I briefly examined the grammatical 'errors' (i.e. deviations from the norms of Classical Latin) contained in eleventh-, twelfth-, and thirteenth-century documents from another Castilian chartulary, *El Cartulario de San Pedro de Arlanza* (Serrano 1925). For manuscripts before the eleventh century, this type of comparative approach is best exemplified by Bastardas y Parera's (1953) meticulous study of Early Medieval Peninsular Latin. With respect to case endings, for instance, Bastardas y Parera (1953: 16) states 'de una simple lectura de nuestros documentos [del VIII al XI] parece deducirse que los escribas usan cualquier caso en cualquier función'.

The morphological confusions described by Bastardas y Parera are well known to Hispanic philologists and, traditionally, have been cited as proof that *bajo latín* was actually spoken by at least part of the Castilian speech community. In other words, a segment of the community was diglossic, speaking a degenerate form of Latin known as *bajo latín* (or *latín bárbaro*) alongside a Hispanovernacular, for which there is no written record until around the eleventh century.[8] The logical implication is that these early Latinate texts provide phonetic transcriptions for the *bajo latín* that coexisted with the Romance vernacular.

This traditional interpretation runs contrary to two linguistic facts: first, that few writing systems are strictly phonetic representations of speech (because phonetics is only marginally necessary for reading and tradition often plays a more influential role in determining scribal conventions); and second, that true diglossic speech communities, as described by Ferguson (1959), are relatively uncommon.

These contradictions can be avoided, however, by supposing that these Latinate documents were meant all along to convey at least one register of the vernacular using the only available literary tools of the day, an archaic morphological and orthographic system loosely based on Latinate conventions. This interpretation concords well with what Hoenigswald (1960: 7) has described as 'the conservatism of an uninterrupted scribal tradition . . . [where] language continues to be represented as though it had not changed'. Deviant spellings then become important indications of attempts to readapt the script to the changed state of the spoken language (Hoenigswald 1960: 8). This new interpretation of Latinate writing not only squarely addresses the problem of spelling evolution and morphological confusions, but also obviates the need to imagine a diglossic community in Spain during the early medieval period. This interpretation in no way rules out the existence of different registers within the Medieval Castilian speech community located along a normal sociolinguistic continuum.

There are some precedents for this new viewpoint. Many philologists have been struck by the similarities between these early texts and Old Spanish, although they have been unable to make that final deductive leap that these scribes were actually writing in Romance using Latinate conventions. For example, Jennings (1940: 314) describes the documents from the *Cartulario de San Vincente de Oviedo* in the following terms:

> In the phonology only one characteristic is almost completely lacking: diphthongization of *e* and *o*. In the morphology we see clear signs of Romance endings in the nouns and adjectives. In the syntax of the cases, the prepositions, the demonstratives, and the verbs we see what Old Spanish *is to be*. (my emphasis)

Bastardas y Parera (1953: xxv) has a similar impression as a result of his study of other documents from this same period: 'Se admite en ellos [los documentos], por ignorancia o por una decidida intención de acercarse al lenguaje corriente, gran abundancia de construcciones correspondientes al romance coetáneo'.

Phonological and morphological evidence has primarily fuelled this debate; word order is rarely referred to. Syntax, however, as I have previously explained, cannot be manipulated or reconstructed as easily while reading aloud and, therefore, would serve well in the task of evaluating the linguistic status of these early medieval texts.

The present study must begin, however, by looking at Latin word order as found in the writings from Plautus (second century BC) to the *Peregrinatio ad loca sancta* (fourth century AD). Although different research methods make comparisons difficult, I offer a summary distilled from Wanner (1987) and Adams (1976, 1977) in Table 17.1, which lists the proportional VO patterning for Latin prose found in main clauses.[9]

Table 17.1 VO order in main clauses of Latin texts[*]

Source (by centuries)		Wanner (% VO)	Adams (% VO)
−II	*Twelve Tables*	·	0
−II	Plautus	·	38
I	*Cena Trimalchionis*	49	·
II	Terentianus	85	74
III	*Itala*	87	·
IV	*Peregrinatio*	75	82

[*] The symbol '·' means results are unavailable.

The results from Table 17.1 make it strikingly clear that VO was the favoured syntactic pattern for whatever was being spoken (Vulgar Latin?) by the fourth century. After the *Peregrinatio*, researchers generally jump to the post-eleventh-century documents, which are remarkably similar to the syntactic patterns of Modern Spanish, as discussed above (England 1980, 1983, 1984).

The gap I wish to fill lies in between the eighth and the eleventh century. Compare the results of Table 17.1 with those of Table 17.2 derived from the present study of the *Cartulario de San Millán de la Cogolla*. In Table 17.2, the percentages have been computed from documents concerned with small legal transactions, excluding royal decrees and charters where the style tends to be excessively ceremonial. Tables 17.1 and 17.2 can only indicate gross trends, but

Table 17.2 Word-order patterns in the *Cartulario**

Word order	IX	X	XI
% SOV	12	19	13
% OV(S)O	6	1	11
% SVO	38	38	45
% V(S)O	44	37	38
Total % VO	82	75	83

Sources: Ubieto Arteta (1976).
* Royal charters not included.

even so, the percentage of VO sentences in the early medieval period is not significantly different from the basic patterns found in the *Peregrinatio*.

Yet there certainly are major differences in the vocabulary and phraseology between a fourth-century Latinate text, such as the *Peregrinatio*, and ninth-century one, such as the fragment from the *Cartulario* given in (2). In order to read (2) successfully as Hispano-Romance, the reader must occasionally perform a few low-order syntactic operations, such as inserting functor words like articles or possessive markers, but nothing more.

(2) No. 19 (899–912)[10]
a. Ego Oveco Nunnuz trado ad ipsa regula in valle
   (Yo Ovego Muñoz doy a esa regla en el valle)
b. de Fridas una vinea, latus de Val Nuni.
   (de Frías una viña, lado [sito] del Valle de Muñoz)
c. Ego Albura et uxor mea Gutina tradimus
   (Yo Albura y mi mujer Gudina damos)
d. ad ipsa regula de salceto uno agro in Salgoa,
   (a esa regla de Salcedo un campo en Salgoa,)
e. ad VI modios seminatura.
   (a [cambio de] 6 moyos de sembradura.)
f. Comite Monnio Nunniz in Castella.
   (Conde Muño Núñez en Castilla.)

The text, from a syntactic point of view, appears very readable to contemporary speakers of Spanish. The few unfamiliar words, such as *agro*, *uxor*, *tradere*, and *regula*, do not contradict this statement. In fact, it becomes even more recognizable as Romance after having applied a few of Wright's correspondences. For example, the *t* of *seminatura* (2e) is voiced; and the nasals, brought into contact through syncope, dissimilate and strengthen to [m·br], the expected result in Castilian (e.g. *nomine* [nom·bre]).

Romance syntactic patterns, like those of (2), tend to cluster in the main body of each document in the *Cartulario*. Other portions of the text, especially the beginnings and ends, are often crafted in petrified Latin phrases, similar to the examples given in (3). These formulae are repeated over and over again throughout the different legal transactions recorded in the *Cartulario*.

(3)
a. No. 10 (871: first two lines)
   In nomine ingenite, prolisque ac procedentis, conexa unius semper natura Deitatis.
b. No. 13 (872?)
   Si quis vero homo extraneare voluerit, sit anathematizatus et percusus et infernum voragine sit dimersus, amen.

Sections like (3) tend to be highly formulaic, as befits the opening or closing of a public ceremony, and help create the overall impression that the text was actually read aloud to the populace in some form of Late Latin. But even highly formulaic sections seem to follow a Romance word order in some *Cartulario* documents. Compare the OV syntax of (3b) above with that of (4) below, written a century later:

(4) No. 139 (1009)
Si quis homo voluerit traere de hac regula, de Domino Deo sit excomunicatus et confusus, anathematus permaneat cum Iuda traditore in inferno inferiori, amen.

The syntactic pattern of (4) is clearly V(S)O and can be read easily with the aid of a few Old Spanish glosses: *voluerit* from *velle* 'querer', *tra(h)ere* 'retardar', *permanere* 'permanecer'.

Without question, some scribes were more adept than others in writing not only true Latin prose but also Latinate prose, especially if royal parties were involved, as shown by (5), a document drafted by the royal scribe of King García Sánchez I.

(5) No. 30 (943)
Igitur divina inspirante clemencia, qui sepe gratis beneficium prestat indignis, de bonis quod ipse nobis benigne largitus est, ad laudem nominis eiusdem creatoris et ob honorem sanctissimi Emiliani, presbiteri et confessoris, *offerimus* et *concedimus* ex toto corde et tota voluntate villam in confinium Naiele positam, antiquo usu

Villar de Torre dictam, integra et sana, cum omnibus hominibus, terris, vineis, ortis, pomariis, molinis, domibus, cum exitu et regressu, et pascuis, cum montibus ac defesis, cum omnibus mobilibus et inmobilibus, quicquid ad eandem villam pertinet vel aliquando pertinuit . . . (emphasis mine)

The complex single sentence shown in (5) is a run on, which begins with a formulaic invocation and ends with a detailed list of personal property. Nevertheless, the declarative parts of it are still VO.

The same VO pattern holds true for the example given in (6), written by a tenth-century scribe who scrupulously maintains Latin case markers and avoids the use of prepositions to assign Case. The text can still be read aloud in Romance in a straightforward manner with only a basic knowledge of Latin case endings. In fact, the reader does not really need to possess even this basic morphological knowledge since fixed word order and semantic features (e.g. [± animate]) carry the major burden of determining the grammatical roles. Consequently, a modern reader has no trouble assigning the role of 'indirect object' to *Deo* or that of 'direct object' to *villam*.

(6) No. 110 (996)
. . . damus et confirmamus *Deo* et *Sancto Emiliano*, Christi confessori, et tibi patri spirituali Ferrutio abbati ceterisque fratribus ibidem Deo regulariter servientibus, *unam villam* que dicitur Terrero que est sita inter . . . (emphasis mine)

For other non-royal texts, the level of writing skill is understandably less impressive. In this case, differences in writing skill show up in small degrees. Compare the fragments given in (7) and (8). The scribe in (7) seems to command a slightly surer hand with case endings than his contemporary. Still, both texts can be read, without special syntactic modifications, by the modern reader versed in Wright's phonetic algorithms and familiarity with a few vocabulary items such as *poniferis* 'frutales' or *ferragine* 'herrén'.

(7) No. 18 (912)
Ego Apre presbiter sic me trado, pro remedio anime mee, cum omnibus rebus meis et que ad me pertinent, ad ecclesia Sancti Emeteri et Celedoni et tibi abbati Sisenando, presbitero de Taranco, illa quarta racione in terras, in mazanares, in omnibus poniferis, in casares, una cetera hereditate, de illo Arco usque ad agro de Venze malo, et iuxta termino de Lieto; de alia pars, termino de Senioredo presbitero; in Lizinio, in illa ferragine, inter ambas vías, illa quarta racion.

(8) No. 21 (932?)

Ego Eita Hoco de Salinas dono ad Sancti Felicis quatuor eras. Et ego domna Momadona de Cereso, quatuor eras que comparavi de ita Hacurio, et alias quatuor eras de Mer Nunnu. Et alias tres eras comparatas de Mer Galindo iuxta de Oveco Manero.

Finally, the passages given below in (9)–(13) all mix Latinate morphology with a thoroughly Romance word order, complete with clitic pronouns and prepositions. The example given in (10) is particularly striking in its similarity to Modern Spanish.[11]

(9) No. 11 (872?)

Hanc ergo nos hedificavimus hunc atrium Sancti Martini, fecimus domus et excalidavimus ecclesias per manibus nostris. . . . Istam totas rem iam dicta ego Paulus abba et Iohannes presbiter et Nunno clerico nos *illa* tradimus *ad patrono nostro* sancti Martini episcopi pro remedio animarum nostrarum in ipsa regula deservientium. (emphasis mine)

(10) No. 99 (986)

Ego Ionti presbiter de Sancti Felicis de Auca illo die quando *me saccaron* de capivitate de terra de mozlemes, abbates et fratres de Sancti Felicis dederunt in mea redemptione C.L. solidos argenti. Et ego Ionti presbiter sic roboro duos meos agros in territorio de villa Domino Assur *ad Sancti Felicis*. Uno agro est iuxta villa, latus serna de Sancti Felicis; de alia pars, carrera. Alio agro in lomba, iuxta limite de Amuna. (emphasis mine)

(11) No. 197 (1032)

Placuit nobis et *vendimus ad vos germanos Oveco Belascoz et Citi Belascoz* vinea nostra propria qui est in viniarum de Granione: . . . Et dedistis precium quamtum [sic] *nobis placuit*, id est quinquaginta III solidos de argento; in roboratione, XXV panes, et argenzata et media de vino, et uno ariete, et tozino. Et nos accepimus totum. . . . (emphasis mine)

(12) No. 198 (1033)

. . . et crepantavi occulum *at meum congermanum* de Aquilare, et proinde debebam calumniam. Similiter habebam in ortu meo puteum aque, et cecidit in eum unus puer, et mortuus est; et *tenebant me* pro illo homicidio, et non potui pactare tam grande calumniam, et pactavi pro me domna Oneca CCCC solidos; *et solvit me* de isto pecto. Unde ego *mitto illam* et corroboro totam meam hereditatem quam habeo in Eclesiasilena, tam domos quam etiam terras et vineas et quantum invenire potuerit meo pertinente, totum ab integro, et *confirmo illud sibi* et filiis suis, quietum et sine ulla

inquietudine possidendum in perpetuum. (emphasis mine)
(13) No. 217 (1040)
Et accepi de te in precio caballo castaneo, valente D solidos,
Persigna nominato, illo qui fuit que *tibi dedit* comite Fredinando
Munnioz, et *abeo illum* aput me, et nichil contra *te remansit*
precium. (emphasis mine)

Looking at these five examples as a whole, I find it disconcerting
that they exhibit no dramatic orthographic evolution from the ninth
to the eleventh century. In fact, the tenth-century document shown
in (10) strikes me as slightly more Romance-looking than (11) or
(12), both eleventh-century documents. If this writing were to
reflect a *bajo latín* spoken in a diglossic speech community,
according to the traditional view, it must have been a very stable
speech community indeed, judging from samples like (9)–(13). But
why should such a stable diglossia, maintained for over three
centuries, die out so rapidly, in a textual sense, after the
implementation of Carolingian writing practices? Moreover, it
seems implausible to say, on the one hand, that scribes used
phonetic principles to write *bajo latín*, but, on the other, needed
over three centuries to learn how to accomplish the same trick with
the Romance vernacular. Why should scribes take so long to
consolidate Romance orthographic conventions after the eleventh
century, if phonetic writing were already commonplace? The variety
among Old Spanish registers and dialects alone cannot explain the
variations that plagued the first attempts to write Romance,
including the glosses of San Millán and Silos. These quandaries, in
conjunction with the aberrant case morphology already widely
observed by philologists (Bastardas y Parera 1953), make the
traditional interpretation of these Latinate texts unsatisfactory.

If phonetic writing was, however, an entirely new enterprise
spurred on by the Carolingian reforms, no further explanation
is necessary. A variety of Hispano-Romance registers would
provide the common element lurking beneath these earlier documents from the *Cartulario*. The more proficient the scribe was, of
course, the greater variety of written forms he could pen and later
read aloud at public ceremonies – from styles that were ornately
Latinate to semi-Latinate. That is what literacy must have meant in
the Peninsular context during this early medieval period: different
individual proficiencies in Latin and Latinate writing, which would
account for the divergent forms found throughout the *Cartulario* as
a whole.

If diglossia – Latin (High) and Hispano-Romance vernacular (Low) – did exist at some former moment in time, perhaps at the end of the Roman Empire, surely it had faded away by the early medieval period in question. Ferguson (1959: 339) describes the fate of all H dialects that do not become the standard as becoming 'a learned or liturgical language studied only by scholars or specialists and not used actively in the community'. In the Peninsular case, the Latinate orthographic practices used by scribes into the eleventh century and beyond simply obfuscated the reality of the linguistic situation in the community.

The intent of this study, then, is not to deny that some early medieval scribes on certain occasions wrote impeccable Latin – this is self-evident, and examples abound – but, rather, to show that Latinate texts like those of the *Cartulario* were read aloud and understood by people who only spoke Hispano-Romance.[12] If the chartulary's orthographic appearance does not immediately alert us to the vernacular base, I have endeavoured to show that their consistent VO syntactic patterning should. A crude attempt was begun here to develop new syntactic tests that can be used to determine whether a particular text is Latin in substance or merely Latinate in appearance. Admittedly, the study of syntax enjoins special difficulties, which might explain its minor role up to now as a diagnostic tool in Romance philological studies. Nevertheless, syntactic analysis can help focus scholarly attention on a largely unexploited body of literature from the eighth to the eleventh century and, in turn, make a valuable contribution to the history of the Spanish language.

NOTES

1 There are no Latinate documents ('textos vulgares') in Spanish before the eighth century, according to Bastardas y Parera (1953: xxv).
2 Wanner (1987: 378) seems to recognize implicitly the relevance of a VSO typology for Spanish, but only as part of its evolution: 'If Latin is of the SOV type, then Romance is SVO, perhaps closer to VSO in Old Romance, but definitely of a different type from the Latin base.' Wanner (ibid.) also asserts that VSO in Classical Latin was a stylistically marked type used for verbal emphasis and contrast, a fact which might explain its origin and eventual implementation in Hispano-Romance.
3 Green (1976: 9) states that morphology has an inherent bias towards VSO order since, even when S is dropped, the verb morphology indicates S in verbal-final position.
4 Remember that Greenberg himself (1966: 79) predicted that VSO

languages will have an SVO stylistic alternative, but the reverse is not true.

5 Note that only one preverbal topicalized NP is allowed in Spanish. The term 'topicalization' is used here in the strictly grammatical sense. Pragmatic topicalization – such as theme/rheme or old/new information contrasts – are discussed by Silva-Corvalán (1981). Her data suggest that SVO order is strongly favoured in discourse when S maintains the same reference (i.e. old information). According to Silva-Corvalán, preverbal subjects are especially favoured by intransitive verbs.

6 In Medieval Spanish, the indirect object occurs preverbally less frequently than does the direct object (cf. England 1983). This observation was confirmed in the present study as well.

7 The dating of the *Glosas Emilianenses* and *Glosas Silenses* remains somewhat controversial. See Wright (1986) for a brief discussion of this question.

8 Menéndez Pidal (1926: para. 95) postulates a trilingual situation for the kingdom of Leon: the Romance vernacular, *bajo latín*, and *latín popular leonés*.

9 I have tried to limit the data to main clauses to avoid the syntactic complications introduced by subordinate clauses. For instance, VO order is obligatory in relative clauses: e.g., *El hombre [que vio a Jorge/*que a Jorge vió] ya salió* 'The man who saw George already left.'

10 The numbering is that used in Ubieto Arteta's edition of the *Cartulario* (1976). The document's date is given in parentheses, followed by a question mark when a precise dating is unavailable.

11 With a few of the eleventh-century documents, the Latinate façade seems to crumble almost completely, as in the case of the following example (no. 231, 1044). The case morphology is restricted to the accusative, with the genitive function being supplanted by the preposition *de*; digraphs such as *nn*, *gn*, and *gg* are employed for the corresponding palatal sounds of the vernacular; the sequence *in illa* has assimilated to the common vernacular form *enna*; there are occasional lapses in verb morphology (*ficiesse* without '-t', and *matod* with a hypercorrected 'd' at the end); main-clause word order is strictly SVO; and pronominal verbs like *irse* (e.g. *et ibat se*) have also appeared.

> In Aventinus habent duas defesas: una de los labradios usque ad semdero qui exit per serum et vadit ad Valleziello. . . . Et si fillaren aliquem de Villa Gundissalvo facientem ligna, pro asino duos arienzos donet; et pro homine, uno arienzo. . . . Et in diebus regis Garsie si ganato ficiesse dannum in sernas aut in vineas de rege, aut de Sancti Emiliani, por bovem uno argenzo; et si non, apreciatura. . . Et in dias de rege Garsia, Sancho Lopez fuit custiero, et in serna de rege matod I puerco de Villa Gunzalo. Et rex Garsia mandavit peggare et serna apreciare et peggare. Et in dias de rege Garsia enna villa ubi uno germano aut tres oviesset uno alzariez mano por facendera; et alteros ibant se ubi volebant. Et si non abiet que alzasset manum, dimitebat totam suam hereditatem, et ibat se.

12 A good example from the *Cartulario* of Latin prose comes from text no. 361 (1067), composed at the Council of Bishops at Nájera. The

audience is a select group of highly educated clerics. This type of text clearly lies outside of the scope of the present study.

Quidam episcoporum nostre provintie contra nos insurrexerunt, census et tertias non sibi debitas ab ecclesiis nostris accipere voluerunt, quos omnes episcopos, nos ostensis prvilegiis nostris et canonicis sententiis in generalibus conciliis, superavimus, et nostrum monasterium ab omni episcopali censu liberavimus.

BIBLIOGRAPHY

Adams, J. N. (1976) 'A typological approach to Latin word order', *Indogermanische Forschungen* 81: 70–99.

—— (1977) *The Vulgar Latin of the Letters of Claudius Terentianus*, Manchester: Manchester University Press.

Bastardas y Parera, J. (1953) *Particularidades sintácticas del latín medieval: Cartularios españoles de los siglos VIII al XI*, Barcelona and Madrid: Gredos.

Blake, R. (1987) 'New linguistic sources for Old Spanish', *Hispanic Review* 55: 1–12.

Bossong, Georg (1984) 'Diachrony and pragmatics of Spanish word order', *Zeitschrift für Romanische Philologie* 100: 92–111.

Contreras (1987) 'Small clauses in Spanish and English', *Natural Language and Linguistic Theory* 55: 225–43.

England, J. (1980) 'The position of the direct object in Old Spanish', *Journal of Hispanic Philology* 5: 1–23.

—— (1983) 'Word order of Old Spanish prose: the indirect object', *Neophilologus* 67: 385–94.

—— (1984) 'Word order in Old Spanish prose: the subject complement', *Neuphilologische Mitteilungen* 85: 385–400.

Ferguson, C. A. (1959) 'Diglossia', *Word* 15: 325–40.

Green, J. (1976) 'How free is word order in Spanish?, in M. Harris (ed.), *Romance Syntax: Synchronic and Diachronic Perspectives*, Salford: University of Salford, 7–32.

Greenberg, J. H. (1963) *Universals of Language*, 2nd edn 1966, Cambridge, MA: MIT Press.

Groos, A. and R. Bok-Bennema (1986) 'The structure of the sentence in Spanish', in I. Bordelois, H. Contreras, and K. Zagona (eds), *Generative Studies in Spanish Syntax*, Dordrecht: Foris, 67–80.

Harris, M. (1976) 'A typological approach to word order change in French', in M. Harris (ed.), *Romance Syntax: Synchronic and Diachronic Perspectives*, Salford: University of Salford, 33–53.

Hoenigswald, H. M. (1960) *Language Change and Linguistic Reconstruction*, Chicago: University of Chicago Press.

Jennings, A. C. (1940) *A Linguistic Study of the Cartulario de San Vincente de Oviedo*, New York City: S. F. Vanni.

Menéndez Pidal, R. (1926) *Orígenes del Español*, 3rd edn 1950, Madrid: Espasa-Calpe.

Serrano, L. (1925) *El cartulario de San Pedro de Arlanza*, Burgos: Rafael Ibáñez de Aldecoa.

Silva-Corvalán, C. (1981) 'Subject expression and placement in Mexican–American Spanish', in J. Amastae and L. Elías-Olivares (eds), *Spanish in the U.S.: Sociolinguistic Aspects*, Washington, DC: Center for Applied Linguistics, 93–120.

Ubieto Arteta, A. (1976) *El cartulario de San Millán de la Cogolla*, Valencia: Anubar Ediciones.

Vincent, N. (1976) 'Perceptual factors and word order change in Latin', in Martin Harris (ed.), *Romance Syntax: Synchronic and Diachronic Perspectives*, Salford: University of Salford, 54–68.

Wanner, D. (1987) *The Development of Romance Clitic Pronouns*, New York: Mouton de Gruyter.

Westphal (1986) 'On the expansion of S in Spanish', in S. Choi, D. Devitt, W. Janis, T. McCoy, and Z. Zhang (eds), *ESCOL 85: Proceedings of the Second Eastern States Conference on Linguistics*, Columbus OH: Department of Linguistics, Ohio State University, 264–75.

Wright, R. (1982) *Late Latin and Early Romance in Spain and Carolingian France*, Liverpool: Cairns.

—— (1986) 'La función de las glosas de San Millán y de Silos', in J. C. Bouvier (ed.), *Actes du XVIIᵉ Congrès International de Linguistique et Philologie Romanes*, vol. IX, Aix-en-Provence: University of Provence, 209–19.

18 Latin or Romance? Graphemic variation and scripto-linguistic change in medieval Spain

António Emiliano

To L. F. Lindley Cintra

Examination of the mixed spelling of twelfth- and early thirteenth-century notarial Latinate texts from Spain such as the long legal codes known as *Foros* or *Costumes* (Sp. *Fueros extensos*), and comparison of their varying Latinate character with the fully romanized orthography of later Romance versions, raise two interesting questions:

1 Is the language represented in those texts Latin or Romance? And what is the exact nature of the apparent language mixture?

2 Was the change from Notarial Latin to Romance in the thirteenth-century Romance versions of the *Foros* a matter of translation or of orthographical change?

The first question, concerning the general problem of the degree of Latinity or Romanicity of notarial texts, has been traditionally put in terms of correctness, as the depreciatory expression *Latim bárbaro* (Ptg.)/*Latín bárbaro* (Sp.), still current among philologists and historians, eloquently shows; it refers to the supposed ignorance and 'unletteredness' of medieval notaries. If we ignore this traditional and culturally biased view, which can no longer be seriously considered, we can identify two basic approaches to Notarial Latin:

1 Notarial Latin is Latin: i.e., it is a vernacularized variety of Medieval Latin, 'latín arromanzado' (Menéndez Pidal 1980: 458; Lapesa 1981: 160), written with an admixture of vulgar forms (Vasconcellos 1966: 15);

2 Notarial Latin is Romance: i.e., it is a vernacular tradition of writing on which a 'camouflage of Latin' (Elcock 1975: 424) or a 'veneer of Latinity' (Wright 1982: 240) was superimposed.

Both these concepts of a *romanized Latin* or a *latinized Romance* are ambiguous and misleading, in that they suggest or imply the existence of an established autonomous Romance tradition of writing that the scribes knew and used, but consciously and obstinately tried to disguise.

As regards the translation of the *Foros* into Romance in the thirteenth century, this question was never considered as a problem by traditional philologists (see Cintra 1959: xcvii), given the two-norm conception of the relation of Latin and Romance throughout the Middle Ages.

I would like to propose a strictly graphematic and scripto-linguistic approach to these questions, by considering Notarial Latin as a complex system for the written representation of a Romance Vernacular. Its mixed character results from the coexistence and interaction of different principles of graphemic mapping; these principles define different sets of Latin and Romance written forms within the orthographical repertoire. Variation between Latin and Romance indicates that Latin and Romance spellings were synchronically and functionally equivalent and that the predominant Latin element could be easily converted (at all levels of graphemic representation) into vernacular phonetics, morphology, and lexis.

I will first present a brief outline of the development of Romance Writing in relation to the Latin tradition. Second, I will consider the phenomena of graphemic variation and alternation, referring to data from a group of genetically related Leonese *Foros*.

LATIN ORTHOGRAPHICAL TRADITION AND THE DEVELOPMENT OF ROMANCE WRITING

The existence of Latin orthography as the sole available tradition of writing throughout the Early Middle Ages is the single most important fact in the early history of Romance writing. The beginnings of a romanized tradition of writing lie ultimately in the complex scripto-linguistic situation of Medieval Romance-speaking nations, where the conservative orthography of Latin served as the basis for the written representation of the vernaculars.

As a consequence of its conservatism, Latin spelling, which was originally a phonographic system of writing, became increasingly opaque and logographic: morphological categories which had become obsolete in the spoken language were fully represented and preserved in the written code; the same happened to word forms, idioms, and formulae that survived only in their written form. In other words, Latin spelling, which had been conceived as an orthography based on grapheme–phoneme correspondence (GPC), had by Late Antiquity and the Early Middle Ages become a mixed system, where some sequences of graphemes could relate directly to morphemes and meaning, rather than being mapped to an intermediate phonic level.

The processes of conversion involved in the *transcription* of spoken utterances and in the *oralization* of written texts became complex and difficult to master. Medieval notaries faced their most demanding and challenging problems when they had to transcribe vernacular items that did not have an accepted written form within Latin tradition, and particularly, when reading a document aloud, they had to oralize archaic written forms; i.e. spellings that were phonologically, morphologically, and even lexically outdated had to be converted into vernacular phonetics, morphology, and lexis. It was especially in situations such as these that innovations, deviations, and re-elaborations were likely to arise, leading to the development, as Sabatini has put it, of 'una tradizione di lingua scritta intermedia, che costituisce un vero preannuncio delle scriptae romanze' (Sabatini 1968: 349).

The basic principle behind the creation and development of Romance Writing, as opposed to unreformed Latin tradition, was phonemicization. Romance spellings aimed at transparency and consistency of grapheme–phoneme (GP) mapping; they were based on simple 'romanizing' rules such as:

1 avoid 'silent' letters;
2 avoid unpredictable GP-mappings;
3 reduce and restrict multiple choice in GP-mapping.

The scripto-linguistic change from Latin to Romance which came about in the Iberian Peninsula in the thirteenth-century involved a general extension of regular and transparent GP-mapping and the drastic reduction of inconsistent phonography and logography: it consisted in a gradual process of *de-latinization*.

GRAPHEMIC VARIATION, SCRIPTO-LINGUISTIC CHANGE AND THE EMERGENCE OF ROMANCE ORTHOGRAPHY: THE EVIDENCE OF THIRTEENTH-CENTURY LEONESE FOROS

The following discussion is based on data from a group of four genetically related Leonese legal codes known collectively as the *Foros de Riba-de-Coa*, from a north-eastern area of Portugal which was part of the kingdom of León.[1] Two are written in 'Foral' Latin

– the *Foros de Alfaiates* (FA), from the late twelfth or early thirteenth century and the *Foros de Castelo Bom* (FCB), from the mid-thirteenth century; and the other two in Romance – the *Foros de Castelo Rodrigo* (FCR) and the *Foros de Castelo Melhor* (FCM) (both from the late thirteenth century). These texts illustrate different stages in the evolution of Romance writing in the thirteenth century, by presenting diverse orthographical solutions for the adaptation of the same textual material.

The peculiar and inextricable mixture of Latin and Romance in twelfth- and thirteenth-century texts like the Latin *Foros* can be better described and interpreted in terms of a varying and changing orthography rather than as a mixture of two orthographies or of two languages: this mixture results from graphemic variation and intra-textual graphemic alternation between Latin and Romance variants. Notarial Latin was not a different language from Romance, but a way of writing Romance before vernacular orthography was available. Consequently, the replacement of Latin by Romance in late thirteenth-century versions of the *Foros* can be explained as a change in spelling rather than as translation of Latin into Romance. This is borne out by the fact that patterns of cross-textual substitutions of Romance for Latin are very similar, if not identical, to patterns of intra-textual graphemic variation found in the Latin *Foros*; both cases are instances of romanization *qua* orthographical change.

Graphemic variation means that when writing the scribes were able to switch between different sets of orthographical forms: the writing system allowed them to use in the same text (sometimes in the same line) different interchangeable forms with an equivalent representational content. In this perspective Latin and Romance are no more than orthographical labels with no relation whatsoever to the degree of 'Latinity' or 'Romanicity' of the language of the text.

Variation could occur at all levels of graphemic representation, and a single written word-form could exhibit variation at several levels. Three types of variation can be found in Notarial Latin:

1 *grapho-phonemic variation*: alternations in the written representation of *phonemes*, e.g. <iu*di*care : iu*dg*are : iu*zg*are> → [dʒulgár];
2 *grapho-morphemic variation*: alternations in the written representation of *morphemes* (see Table 18.1), e.g. <andau*erit* : and*aret* : and*are*> → [andár];
3 *grapho-lexemic variation*: alternations in the written representation of *lexemes* (see Table 18.2), e.g. <*percuss*erit : *feri*re> → [firiér].

Alternations and substitutions at the latter level have traditionally been treated as instances of lexical conversion or translation, justifying implicitly or explicitly a two-norm theory of Latin and Romance as conceptually distinct languages and orthographies in pre-thirteenth-century Spain.

A good example of a grapho-morphemic variable with Latin and Romance allographic variants is the written representation of the future subjunctive third person singular, which is overwhelmingly the most frequent verbal category in the *Foros* (due to their prescriptive character). Table 18.1 shows the Latin (LAT) and Romance (ROM) variants of the Leonese verbs *mandar*, *fazer*, and *auer*. In the last two verbs there is also grapho-phonemic variation in the written representation of the root. The Romance *Foros* present of course no LAT-variants.

The perfect and free interchangeability of Latin and Romance forms, as a matter of pure orthographical choice, is shown in examples (1–4) below, where different variants (italicized) of the same verb occur side by side in the same paragraph:

(1) FA 54 Totus homo qui infermare et *mandare* pro sua anima et post alia uice *mandauerit*, ipsa manda postremera ualeat.

(2) FA 465 Per tota nemiga aut forzia que *fezieren*, aut aueres que se enprestarent aut habuerint ad dare, si in las ferias fuerit facto, respondant illos qui lo *fecerint*.

(3) FCB 220 Totus iudeus qui pescado *comparare* in uernes pectet I morabitinum a los alcaldes: et si christianus *comparauerit* pora iudeus, pectet I morabitinum a los alcaldes.

(4) FCB 229 Qvolibet homo qui pignus *reuelaret* in uilla aud in aldea . . .;
Hoc est dictum, si *reuelauerit* pignus a los andadores . . .;
et qui *reuelare* pignus a los VI^ex pectet IIII morabitinos. . . .

The fact that the Romance versions show only ROM-variants means that LAT-variants were cross-textually replaced by corresponding romanized forms. Examples (5)–(9) illustrate the replacement of forms with LAT-endings:

(5) FA 59 Manda que *mandauerit* uir mulieri sue aut mulier uiro suo usque ad medietatem cum ipsa manda et

Table 18.1 Intra-textual alternations and cross-textual substitutions of grapho-morphemic and grapho-phonemic variants in the *Foros de Riba-de-Coa* (thirteenth century)

	FA	FCB	FCR	FCM	phonetic transcription
mandar					
LAT:	\<mandauerit\> \<mandaret\>	\<mandauerit\> \<mandaret\>	--------	--------	[mandár]
ROM:	\<mandar(e)\>	\<mandar(e)\>	\<mandar(e)\>	\<mandar(e)\>	
fazer					
LAT:	\<fecerit\> \<fezier(e)\> \<fizier(e)\>	\<fecerit\> \<fezier(e)\> \<fizier(e)\>	--------	--------	[fidziér̨]
ROM:			\<fezer(e)\>	\<fezier(e)\>	
auer					
LAT:	\<habuerit\>	\<habuerit\>	--------	--------	[oviér̨]
ROM:	\<ouier(e)\>	\<ouier(e)\> \<ouuiere\>	\<ouer(e)\> \<ouuer(e)\>	\<ouer(e)\> \<ouier(e)\> \<ouyere\>	

alias mandas prestet; et lo demais non prestet.

FCR 12iv   Manda que *mandare* marido a moller ou moller a marido, fasta la meetad preste; e de mas non preste.

(6)   FA 102   Qui dampno *fecerit* in lino per la entrada pectet I solidum et por quanto dampno *fecerit* adprecienlo quasi sano et pectet alius tanto.

FCR 22i   Qvi dano *fezere* [FCM *feziere*] en lino, porla entrada peyte I soldo e quanto dano *fezere* [FCM *feziere*], aprecienno assi como sano e peyte otro tanto.

(7)   FA 32   Qvi ad morador *habuerit* a firmare, firmet cum moradores aut cum uiçinos quales *habuerit*.

FCR 24ii   Qvi a morador *ouer* [FCM *ouier*] a firmar, firme con moradores o con uizinos, quaes *ouer* [FCM *ouier*].

An important fact here is that, when autonomous Romance orthography emerged in the thirteenth century, ROM-forms were already available in the Notarial Latinate tradition; they were not created from scratch expressly for writing documents in a completely vernacular fashion.

Moreover the change from Latin to Romance seems to have involved no more than a change in the number and type of graphemic variants: the use of ROM-variants was extended, while LAT-variants were simply dropped. Complete romanization was achieved by a gradual and protracted process of de-latinization. Perhaps the real discovery or invention in the development of Romance orthography was the possibility of dropping LAT-variants altogether, and that if LAT-variants were dropped, the written language of documents would look very different from traditional Latin writing and could perhaps be regarded as functionally and conceptually distinct.

The gradual reduction of the Latin element is found in the different incidence of LAT-variants in Latin *Foros* written with an interval of some decades. Comparison of the percentual incidence of LAT- and ROM-variants in FA and FCB reveals a significant decrease of Latin and increase of Romance in FCB (see Figure 18.1). FCB is more romanized than FA but still more latinized than FCR. Latinity and Romanicity *qua* orthographical labels are not fixed discrete points in a scale, but rather overlapping categories whose balance within a scribal tradition changes with time.

But reduction of LAT-variants is not only found between texts

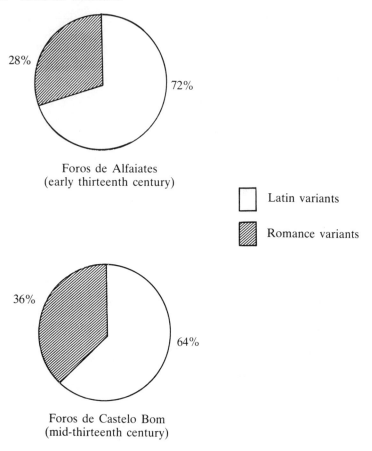

Foros de Alfaiates
(early thirteenth century)

☐ Latin variants

▨ Romance variants

Foros de Castelo Bom
(mid-thirteenth century)

Figure 18.1 Graphemic variable: future subjunctive. Foros de Alfaiates vs Foros de Castelo Bom

written at different dates, but also, and perhaps more revealingly, between different textual zones of the same text. In fact, a pattern of intra-textual reduction of Latin variants clearly emerges when the rubrics and paragraphs of FA and FCB are considered separately. Each paragraph is headed by a rubric which contains either a transcription or an adaptation of the first words of the corresponding paragraph. The rubrics were a kind of a quick and easy reference system inside the text. Not surprisingly, rubrics show a greater degree of romanization than the paragraphs; in some cases this involves substitutions just like in the Romance texts, as examples (8)–(11) show:

(8) FA 50   rubric: Qui *demandar* adforciadura
               para: Qui *demandauerit* aforciadura de muliere

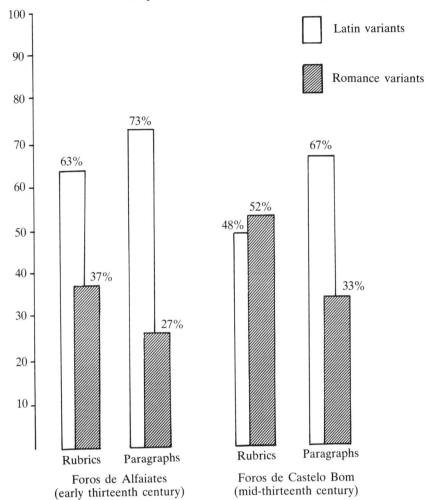

Figure 18.2 Graphemic variable: future subjunctive. Rubrics vs paragraphs

(9) FA 414   rubric: Quando *uinier* el rege a la uilla
              para: Quando *uenerit* el rege a la uilla . . .
(10) FCB 89   rubric: Qui *cogiere* uuas in uinea
              para: Qvi *colligeret* uuas in uinea . . .
(11) FCB 127   rubric: Qui *intrare* cum alio
              para: Totus homo qui *intrauerit* cum alio . . .

These substitutions are particularly interesting, because they occur in the same textual and orthographical environment and within the same text. The rubrics exhibit a significant increase of ROM-variants and decrease of LAT-variants (see Figure 18.2), particularly in FCB with a remarkable difference of 20 points. These cases of intra-textual orthographical vernacularization mirror in all respects the process of cross-textual substitutions referred to above, and are also instances of ongoing scripto-linguistic change.

That Latin forms like <mandauerit>, <fecerit>, and <habuerit> in Table 18.1, were easily converted into vernacular [mandár], [fidziér], and [oviér] when read aloud, is indicated by the high occurrence values of the LAT-variants, the existence of phonemically transparent and functionally equivalent ROM-variants, ánd the universal replacement in Romance texts by forms that are structurally identical to intra-textual ROM-variants.

Phonemic and morphemic conversion of Latinate spellings seems relatively straightforward when there is a historical link between the written forms of Latin and the spoken forms of Romance vernaculars.

On the other hand, phonemic conversion of Latin written forms with no lexical equivalents in Romance, and with no romanized variants, presented different and more complex problems. Reading aloud obsolete forms like, for instance, <uoluerit> or <occiderit> by using letter-to-sound correspondences would result in nonsense words to the majority of twelfth- and thirteenth-century Leonese speakers.

Only for those few people acquainted with *litterae*, was orthography a way of relating sounds to letters and letters to sounds in a linear and consistent fashion, at least in principle (Wright 1982: 105 *et passim*). Only for people trained in the 'New Latin' of the Roman Liturgy would straight grapho-phonemic conversion of Latin forms make any sense. But this in turn meant that reading aloud Notarial Latin as if it were Medieval Latin would result in a strange and nonsensical mixture of scholarly Latin and Romance forms from various historical stages.

Oralization in the context of unreformed Latin and Notarial Latin was more than matching vernacular phonetics to outdated spellings. Reading aloud of texts was not just a matter of applying GPC-rules, but of giving to the written signs possible vernacular signifiés. If not, there is no reason why <uoluerit> or <occiderit> could not have had a Romance pronunciation. But as it is, if written forms like <uoluerit> and <occiderit> have no romanized variants in the *Foros* and notarial documents in general, it is because there was no phonetic input to generate phonemically transparent forms.

The absence of grapho-phonemic variants of opaque Latin forms supports the view that these would have to be oralized via *rules of grapho-lexemic conversion*, i.e. they would have to be read aloud like logograms through *letter-to-meaning correspondences*, where sequences of letters would bear no meaningful relation to sequences of sounds. <uoluerit> would be read as [kiziér], <noluerit> as [no(n) kiziér], and <occiderit> as [matár].

Although this may seem a bit farfetched, especially to a modern user of a GPC-based orthography, Latin opaque forms *did* occur in patterns of intra-textual variation and cross-textual substitution alongside more transparent but totally unrelated variants, a fact that bears the above interpretation out. Examples (12)–(14) show some alternations and substitutions of this type in FA, FCB, and FCR:

(12) FA 64   ... Et postquam acceperit hoc et id *dimiserit* uel maritum *acceperit* de lo dupplato.

     FCB 69   ... Et postquam acceperit hoc et lo *delexauerit* aut uirum *acceperit* de lo duplado.

     FCR 8iv   ... E de poys que tome aquesto e sio *lexare* e marido *tomare* delo dublado.

(13) FA 27   rubric: Qui *percusserit* aut messauerit
                 para: Qui *percusserit* aut messauerit uicinum ...

     FCB 40   rubric: Qui messare aut *ferir*
                 para: Qvi *percusserit* aut messauerit ad uicinum ...

     FCR 2iii   rubric: Qui *firir* uizino
                 para: Qvi *firir* o mesare a uizino ...

(14) FA 271   Alcaydes qui a ad bolta aut baraia uenirent et *ferire* aut messare et lo uiderint alcayde sua pesquisa de alcayde sit hata V morabitinos et pectet ille qui *percusserit* aut messauerit ...

     FCB 268   Alcaldes o uozeros que a bolta o a baraia super-uenerint et uiderint *ferir* o messar e lo uiere alcalde o uozero firme usque V morabitinos et pectet el que *ferire* o el que messare ...

     FCR 11viii   Alkaldes o iurados que a bolta o baralla sobre-ueneren e uiren *ferir* o mesar e lo uire alkalde o iurado firme fasta en V morabitinos e peyte el que *firire* o messare ...

Cases of cross-textual substitutions like these in the Romance *Foros* could at first sight be considered as instances of translation of Latin into Romance, were it not for the fact that similar patterns of substitution and alternation also occur intra-textually, as examples (13) and (14) show, and in texts written down prior to the emergence and generalized use of Romance orthography. The relation of synchronic equivalence in Notarial Latin between <percusserit> and <ferir> is the same as between <fecerit> and <feziere> with the difference that the latter are diachronically related. <percusserit> and <ferir>, as their free interchangeability in Latinate texts tells, are *grapho-lexemic variants* with the same representational status. The excerpt in example (13) would then be pronounced as something like [ki firjér o mesár a vidzíno], regardless of the more or less latinized character of its written representation.

This means that replacement of Latin opaque forms by more transparent ones involved only substitution of orthographical variants, without entailing translation (see the list of grapho-lexemic variants in Table 18.2). <uoluerit> and <occiderit> would be simply regarded as written representations of [kizjér] and [matár], and would be equivalent to <quesierit> and <mactauerit>, and to <quisier(e)> and <matar(e)>. As for the ROM-variants, they did not form an autonomous orthographical system before complete de-latinization was achieved; Romance forms were as much part of the scribal tradition as the Latin forms, from which they were not conceptually distinct. The way to translation, resulting from a clear separation between Latin and Romance, was paved by the gradual reduction of Latin forms. When Latin forms ceased to be interchangeable with Romance variants in the same text, they could be considered as belonging to another system, not only a writing system but a distinct linguistic reality.

The grapho-lexemic correspondences in Table 18.2 look very much like a fragment of a lost Medieval Latin–Romance Glossary. Such a glossary, whose existence Ramón Menéndez Pidal assumed as the basis for the *Glosas Emilianenses* and the *Glosas Silenses*, existed only in the scripto-linguistic competence of medieval scribes, as a list of equivalent heterographs. The correspondences do, in fact, resemble many of the glosses in the *Glosas Silenses* (one or two are identical). A graphemic assessment of the *Glosas* in the light of patterns of alternation shown by the legal codes might provide an interesting insight to their still controversial function and purpose.

To conclude, the adoption of Hispanic orthographies in notarial texts did not necessarily involve at first a process of language substitution, a change from Latin to Romance: Latin and Romance had existed side by side for centuries in the notarial written

Table 18.2 Intra-textual alternations and cross-textual substitutions of grapho-lexemic variants in the *Foros de Riba-de-Coa* (thirteenth century)

Latin	FA	FCB	FCR	FCM
ACCEPERIT	acceperit	acceperit	---------	---------
	tomauerit	tomar(e)	tomar(e)	tomar(e)
	tomaret			
	tomar(e)			
DIMISERIT	dimiserit	dimiserit	---------	---------
	delaxare	delexauerit	dexar(e)	leygar
	lexare	laxaret	lexar(e)	leyxar
		dexare	leyxar(e)	
EIECERIT	eiecerit	eiecerit	---------	---------
	iactauerit	iactaret	echare	echar(e)
	iactaret	iectaret	geytar(e)	geytar(e)
	iactare	iectare		ieytare
	iectar			
INUENERIT	inuenerit	inuenerit	---------	---------
	falaret	falare	achar(e)	fallar(e)
	falare			
OBIERIT	obierit	obierit	---------	---------
	morierit	morierit	moriere	moriere
	moriere	moriere	morir(e)	
	morir(e)	morire		
	murier(e)			
	murir(e)			
OCCIDERIT	occiderit	occiderit	---------	---------
	mactauerit	mataret	matar(e)	matar(e)
	mactare	mactare		
	matar(e)	matare		
PERCUSSERIT	percusserit	percusserit	---------	---------
	feriret	ferire	ferire	ferier(e)
	feriere		firir(e)	ferire
	ferir(e)			
	firiere			
	firire			
UOLUERIT	uoluerit	uoluerit	---------	---------
(NOLUERIT)	quesierit	quisiere	queser(e)	queser
	quisier(e)			quesier
	quesier			quessier
				quisier(e)

tradition, which was like an *orthographical palimpsest* where forms relating to diverse scripto-linguistic layers could exist simultaneously in the same 'scripto-graphic synchrony'.

The 'coscienza linguistica del volgare', to use Sabatini's expression, probably did not arise before the completion of a complex and protracted process of orthographical restructuring and experimentation, which finally gave the vernaculars a distinct written appearance. The introduction of Medieval Latin in Spain contributed from the late eleventh century on to this process of vernacularization of the written code, accelerating the establishment of the awareness of the vernacular and consequently the distinction between Latin and Romance as different languages, each with its own written medium. When the vernacular orthographies emerge Notarial Latin disappears: only pure Latin and pure Romance orthographies exist.

NOTE

1 The codes are preserved in single copies in thirteenth-century codices kept at the Arquivo Nacional da Torre do Tombo in Lisbon, and belong to the family of *Foros* granted by Alfonso IX of León (1188–1230). This group of municipal legal codes includes the *Foros* from Riba-de-Coa (now Riba-Coa), a north-eastern area of Portugal which was repopulated by Alfonso IX and his father, Fernando II (1157–88), and was part of Leonese Extremadura until 1296, when it was annexed by Portugal. This family of *Foros* (studied in Cintra 1959), which includes three other Leonese *Foros*, the *Foros de Cáceres*, the *Foros de Coria*, and the *Foros de Usagre*, had as its source a lost Latin archetype, which can be identified with certainty with the lost *Foros de Ciudad Rodrigo* (Cintra 1959: lxxxv). The *Foros de Riba-de-Coa* were published in the documental collection *Portugaliae Monumenta Historica*. The *Foros de Castelo Rodrigo* were the object of a diplomatic edition and linguistic study in Cintra 1959.

BIBLIOGRAPHY

Cintra, L. F. L. (1959) *A linguagem dos Foros de Castelo Rodrigo*, Lisbon: Publicações do Centro de Estudos Filológicos.
Elcock, W. D. (1975) *The Romance Languages*, London: Faber & Faber.
Lapesa, R. (1981) *Historia de la lengua Española*, 9th edn, Madrid: Gredos.
Menéndez Pidal, R. (1980) *Orígenes del Español*, 9th edn, Madrid: Espasa Calpe.
Portugaliae Monumenta Historica. Leges et Consuetudines I, Lisbon: Academia das Ciências, 1856.

Sabatini, F. (1968) 'Dalla scripta latina rustica alle scriptae romanze' *Studi Medievali* 9: 320–58.

Vasconcellos, J. L. (1966) *Lições de Filologia Portuguesa*, 4th edn, Rio de Janeiro: Livros de Portugal.

Wright, R. (1982) *Late Latin and Early Romance in Spain and Carolingian France*, Liverpool: Cairns.

19 Latin vs Romance in the Middle Ages: Dante's *De vulgari eloquentia* revisited

Marcel Danesi

INTRODUCTION

A common tendency among authors of textbooks in historical linguistics, especially among those working in the Romance field, is to trace the origins of their craft to Dante Alighieri's intriguing 1305 treatise, the *De vulgari eloquentia* (*DVE*). I quote from Robins (1967: 100) as an illustrative case in point: 'The serious study of the neo-Latin (Romance) languages can be said to have been instituted by Dante's *De vulgari eloquentia* in the early fourteenth century.' If the notions of genetic relationship and of evolutionary change form the basis upon which the scientific study of language change is implanted, then, from the perspective of our post-Darwinian mindset, it would indeed seem that Dante did put forward observations that fall within the perimeter of this conceptual model of language evolution: i.e. of change which is analysable in genetic terms and which is perceived as being adaptive to environmental flux and influence.

The purpose of the present study is to call into question this mindset, given that it is based on a textual exegesis of a specific excerpt in the *DVE* (I, 8). The relevant points in the controversial passage are the following ones (see Chiappelli 1965; 661–2): (1) Dante briefly surveys the speech of Europe and establishes a tripartite division of languages (essentially the Greek, Germanic, and Romance families), using the term *ydioma tripharium*. (2) He then alludes to a further tripartite division – a lower-scale *ydioma tripharium* – to account for the observed lexical similarities in speakers of Italian (*Latini*), French (*Franci*), and Provençal (whom he calls *Yspani*). This division is based on the different lexicalizations of the particle of affirmation: 'Totum autem quod in Europa restat ab istis, tertium tenuit ydioma, licet nunc tripharium videatur; nam alii *oc*, alii *oil*, alii *si* affirmando locuntur; ut puta Yspani, Franci et Latini.' (3) These languages contain lexical cognates: 'Signum autem quod ab uno eodemque ydiomate istarum trium gentium pregrediantur vulgaria, in promptu est, quia multa per eadem vocabula nominare videntur, ut Deum, celum, amorem, mare, terram, est, vivit, moritur, amat, alia fere omnia.'

It is Dante's utilization of the term *ydioma tripharium* that leads historical linguists to see in the *DVE* a blueprint of a genetic theory for the origins of the Romance languages. But it can be legitimately asked if we are not really reading the *DVE* through the conceptual lens of a model of language change that we have inherited from the nineteenth century: i.e. a model based on an arboreal image of linguistic parentage and genealogy. Certainly no one prior to the previous century has interpreted the *DVE* in such a way. And there exists no documentary evidence to suggest that anyone writing in the Late Middle Ages – including one of the greatest poets of all time – was aware of the conceptual distinction between Latin and Romance.

The modern interpretations of the *DVE* can be categorized in terms of three general hypotheses:

Hypothesis 1: Dante was aware of the Latin vs Romance distinction.
Hypothesis 2: Dante may not have been aware of this distinction, but he did understand the genetic relationship among languages.
Hypothesis 3: Dante's *ydioma tripharium* reflects no more than an attempt at classification, in line with the scholastic practices prevalent in the Middle Ages.

Clearly, each hypothesis is derived from a reading of the same text – a chronologically determined and culturally embedded artifact. Therefore, the method for examining each hypothesis that immediately suggests itself is the one which may be characterized as 'philological semiotics'. The main procedure is to evaluate the hypotheses in the light of the cultural context in which the *DVE* was written.

THE CONCEPT OF GENETIC KINSHIP IN HISTORICAL LINGUISTICS

Before examining each hypothesis, it is crucial to the analytical task at hand to locate the historical origins of the concept of genetic kinship in the scientific study of languages. The idea that change in language is the process responsible for what may be called the 'genetic splitting up' of a single language into filial languages surfaces tentatively in the revitalized intellectual *Zeitgeist* of the Renaissance. Poggio Bracciolini (1380–1459) and Leonardi Bruni (1370–1444), for instance, saw in the Romance languages a pattern of descent from a spoken, or popular, version of Latin (e.g. Hall 1974: 231). But it is not at all clear, from the historiographical evidence, that the full-fledged notion of genetic kinship, as we know it today, had crystallized in the mentality of pre-Darwinian linguistic science, despite the fascination for etymology shown by ancient, medieval, and Renaissance philosophers and grammarians. As Robins (1967: 7) perceptively suggests, this 'may be linked with the failure of ancient historians to envisage the fact of change as no more than the revelation of what was innately present at the time in a political system or in a person's character'.

This does not mean that pre-Darwinian scholars were not aware of language filiation; but, rather, that they had not struck upon the idea of language change as analogical to adaptive change in biological organisms. It is the Darwinian nineteenth century that awaits the formulation of this powerful metaphor.

Actually, the stage was set at the end of the eighteenth century when the historical approach to language study became the dominant one, being enriched by insights coming out of the biological sciences. It is also at this time, of course, that the discovery of Sanskrit, and of ancient scholarship on this language, came forward to transform the scientific study of language in a permanent way. Shortly thereafter, in 1860, Augustus Schleicher introduced the tree diagram into linguistics. This iconic device became the crucial conceptual *Gestalt* that made the notion of genetic kinship and evolutionary descent a firmly entrenched one in the *modus operandi* of historical linguistics, shaping all subsequent thinking in the field.

Tree-like representation is, needless to say, one of the oldest graphic techniques known in western culture. Medieval scholastic philosophers, for instance, continually devised tree diagrams to model all kinds of taxonomies. But never before Schleicher was this device used to represent a genetic relationship among languages. As Stewart (1976: 15) has astutely observed, ever since Schleicher linguists have invariably tended to portray, and thus to understand, the notion of genetic relationship in accordance with his graphic suggestion. The semiotic features of this iconic technique are explained by Stewart as follows:

The vertical dimension represents time – 'real' time, that is, historical time, time through which change occurs. Units for the vertical axis are therefore things that occupy the same time, that are not mutually exclusive with respect to time. Conversely, units on the horizontal axis are things that occupy the same time, that are not mutually exclusive with respect to time. To put units on the same horizontal says of them nothing more than that they do not succeed each other directly.

There is some disagreement as to whether or not Schleicher was directly influenced by Darwin (e.g. Greenberg 1957: 56–65; Hoenigswald 1963; Maher 1966). Actually, it was Schleicher himself – taken by the *Origin of Species* – who drew a parallel between biological and linguistic evolution. As Harris and Taylor (1989: 166) have recently remarked, there is no doubt that the 'arrival of Darwinism on the linguistic scene was announced by the publication in 1863 of August Schleicher's *Die Darwinische Theorie*, in which sound change is held to take place in accordance with fixed laws, which are assimilated to natural laws'. This analogy became a powerful one indeed, spawning neogrammarian theories of regular change and providing a conceptual framework for developing glottochronological and lexico-statistical techniques in this century. Schleicher also made liberal use of the tree diagrams that had been employed in human genealogy for centuries before. Terms like *mother*, *daughter*, and *sister* languages figure prominently in the development of Schleicher's theories.

The Darwinian mind-set, portrayed iconically by Schleicherian tree diagrams, has become the conceptual template through which the *DVE* is interpreted by those who subscribe to the first two hypotheses *vis-à-vis* the *DVE*. Thus it is that both can essentially be seen to be victims of a mind-set, and anachronistic with respect to the culturally embedded concepts of language that prevailed in the Middle Ages.

HYPOTHESIS 1

The hypothesis that Dante was aware of the Latin vs Romance distinction (H1) is the least plausible of the three. A typical articulation of H1 is the one by Mario Pei (1976: 226):

> Dante Alighieri's *De Vulgari Eloquentia* of 1305 marked, on the one hand, the beginning of Romance philology in the narrow sense (specific study and comparison of the Romance languages).

It also marked the beginning of modern linguistic thought.

According to this hypothesis, the *DVE* constitutes the first conscious attempt at language derivation and comparison, tracing the origins of Italian, French, and Provençal to a Latin source. It also holds that, in correctly enumerating and classifying the Italian dialects, the *DVE* gets linguistic geography off to an early start.

Nothing reflects the projection of a post-Darwinian and post-Schleicherian mode of thinking onto textual interpretation more than does H1. It is, of course, true that Dante's statements in the *DVE*, if taken at face value, can be made to fit the Schleicherian conceptual grid. But in so doing such an interpretation ignores the ideological and cultural context which furnished the themes of the *DVE*. Among other things, it behoves the proponents of H1 to show that Dante was consciously aware of the Latin vs Romance (or Vulgar Latin) dichotomy. The available evidence suggests that he was not. A conceptual understanding of this dichotomy would mean that Dante saw a horizontal genetic link among the three *volgari* that pointed vertically towards Vulgar Latin. This, in turn, would imply that Dante would have had the extraordinary insight and foresight to separate Vulgar Latin from its ordinary speech contexts and to put it into a conceptual frame that would allow readers of the *DVE* to see it as 'the ancestral speech out of which the Romance languages developed,' to use Hall's (1963: 8) accurate characterization of Vulgar Latin. (On the term *Vulgar Latin* see the excellent discussions by Lloyd 1979 and Holtus 1987.) But Dante did no such thing. If Dante had indeed developed such an insight, then he would have been rather explicit in pointing out to his audience the nature of the historical continuity between Latin and the Romance languages in his text, given the privilege and authority accorded to Latin in the Middle Ages. This would have made Dante's argument in favour of the use of 'vulgar' tongues for literary purposes – the theme of the *DVE* – an even more persuasive one.

The main piece of evidence used in making the case for H1 is Dante's use of the ambiguous term *ydioma tripharium* to relate the lexical similarities found in the three *volgari*. But is Dante's term really to be understood as a kind of medieval synonym for the nineteenth-century concept of *Ursprache*? Joseph Cremona (1965: 155), a staunch supporter of H1, thinks that it is: Dante's *ydioma tripharium* 'is the direct ancestor of what we now call the Romance languages'. But, given that Dante never equates his *ydioma tripharium* to any version of Latin in the *DVE*, there really is no textual reason for reaching such a conclusion. It is more likely that

Dante was describing what was felt to be a conventionalized, common koiné that manifested itself differentially (i.e. as Italian, French, or Provençal) as it moved along a geopolitical axis. The words of Maurizio Vitale (1978: 19) are germane to this point:

> Occorre notare che alla nozione di *ydioma tripharium*, che non è da Dante identificato con il latino grammaticale, che resta nella concezione del *De Vulgari Eloquentia* tuttavia lingua di creazione convenzionale, è sottointesa l'idea acutamente intuita da Dante, di 'comunione linguistica' . . . secondo la quale si spiega la stretta affinità e parentela, la sostanziale unità di lingue concretamente e storicamente differenziate.

In a nutshell, there is nothing in the *DVE* to suggest that Dante saw a connection between Latin and what he calls an *ydioma tripharium*. The evidence in other texts suggests the opposite. As Cecil Grayson (1965: 112) points out, in the *Vita nuova* it can be seen that Dante 'non vede tra loro nessun rapporto se non quello di maggior e minor antichità e riputazione; presenta latino e volgare come due entità separate, quasi statiche, e non fa nessun accenno a dipendenza o ad affinità linguistica'. This is also true of the *Convivio*. As Pagani (1982: 112) perceptively remarks, the view that Dante saw a diachronic relation among the three *volgari*, as descendants of a proto-language, is a modern one. As such it had no conceptual locus in the medieval mind-set. As she aptly puts it, such a view unconsciously projects 'i termini danteschi nel grafico di analisi della linguistica moderna'.

HYPOTHESIS 2

The second hypothesis (H2) holds that Dante may not have conceived of a specific parentage between the three *volgari* and Latin, but he did understand the genetic nature of linguistic change. So, it is claimed, Dante may not have been the father of Romance philology, but he was the father of historical linguistics. One of the staunchest supporters of H2 is Antonino Pagliaro (1947: 490), who attributes to Dante the notion of the 'modificarsi delle lingue nel tempo'. Pagliaro admits that Dante's *ydioma tripharium* is not equatable to Latin, but it does allude to the 'elemento genetico comune alle tre lingue romanze, considerato in rapporto al latino letterario'.

H2 is clearly as untenable as H1 for virtually the same reasons. There is nothing in the text of the *DVE* to lead one to extrapolate from it, as does Cremona (1965: 156–7), a precursory genetic theory of change: 'Dante had a clear conception of the genealogical or family-tree view of the origin and genesis of language, very similar to the one current among nineteenth-century linguists.' As Hall (1974: 228) appropriately remarks, the 'intellectual basis of Dante's theories was primarily mediaeval theological speculation concerning language'. And, indeed, the *DVE* starts off with an abstract scholarly discussion of the nature of language and of the history of its development as set forth in the Old Testament. The crux of Dante's linguistic epistemology is the existence of a fundamental dichotomy: (1) a *locutio vulgaris naturalis*, which Dante describes as an abstract, universal, noble code given to humans directly by God; and (2) a *locutio secundaria artificialis*, which Dante envisages to be a specific, concrete artifact, made by humans. Not surprisingly, he identifies Hebrew as the human *Ursprache*. This is, of course, completely in line with medieval theology. It is hard indeed to see in this characteristic medieval philosophical scenario anything to suggest a Schleicherian-type theory of linguistic change.

The question of why the *DVE* is seen by many to be a precursory text in historical linguistics is an intriguing one. Perhaps the only way to explain H1 and H2 is in terms of a kind of philological Heisenberg's principle: i.e. the modern reader of the *DVE* tends to interpret it through the conceptual lens of a post-Schleicherian mentality.

It is interesting to note that in his study of Darwin's early notebooks (1837–40), Howard Gruber (1974) discovered the constant use of a tree image as an analogue for evolution. He concludes that Darwin needed this iconic *Gestalt* in order to comprehend the nature of change in organisms. But once such a device is made available to cognition it starts to exert a powerful influence on perception as a thematic organizer. This is why Schleicherian trees have become fixtures in any discussion of change in linguistics. Supporters of H1 and H2 seem to be unconsciously projecting such conceptual fixtures onto the reading of the *DVE*. In interpreting the *DVE* in essentially Schleicherian terms, these scholars have unconsciously translated Dante's words into patterns of thought that fit in with their stored Schleicherian notions. As Cole (1984: 67) aptly puts it, 'what we learn to see is culturally conditioned'. (A detailed discussion of the cognitive role played by models and metaphors in mental organization can be found in Hoffman 1980.)

HYPOTHESIS 3

The hypothesis that Dante is attempting no more than a suitable classification of vulgar tongues, on the basis of which he can argue for a *volgare illustre* (H3), is the only really plausible and contextually synchronized one. In fact, the theme of the *DVE* is about rhetorical matters, as Marigo (1957: xxii) accurately observes:

Al vanto di sommo poeta morale, vuole aggiungere quello di primo teorizzatore dell'arte del dire in volgare. . . . E si presenta come maestro che . . . movendo dalla dottrina tradizionale e da una raffinata esperienza di lingua, di stile, di verso e, in modo speciale, di tecnica strofica, può esprimere una compiuta teorica di eloquenza volgare.

Dante's classification of French, Italian, and Provençal under the single category of *ydioma tripharium* reflects the scholastic practice of taxonomic description. The *DVE* is, in effect, a *summa linguistica*; i.e. a synthesis of all that was known about language in the Middle Ages. The criterion Dante uses for classifying his *volgari* under the same rubric is that of lexical similarity. All three vernaculars use the same etyma for certain basic concepts – DEUM, CELUM, AMOREM, MARE, TERRAM, EST, VIVIT, MORITUR, AMAT. The main point of his argument is that these *volgari*, as manifestations of a *locutio vulgaris naturalis*, are more suitable for literary expression than Latin – an example of a *locutio secundaria artificialis*. His argument is, essentially, that Latin is a static code that cannot possibly express the feelings of an emerging new society. As Nardi (1922: 227) wrote during the early part of this century, 'Il latino è, per Dante poeta, una lingua morta e incapace, per ciò stesso, di esprimere adeguatamente i sentimenti sempre nuovi ed originali che fremevano nell'anima di un popolo nuovo.' Of the three *volgari*, he selects Italian as the superior one, because of what he sees as its grammatical proximity to Latin (see also Vinay 1959 and Pazzaglia 1967 on this point).

Then, turning to his specific situation, he argues for the need of a *volgare illustre*. He does this, essentially, in a way that foreshadows modern geographical dialectology. Dante may not have been the first historical linguist; but a strong case can be made that he anticipated the synchronic study of dialects. For instance, he accurately describes Lombard as having words ending in consonants, Sardinian as being too conservative, and Veronese as having truncated nouns and participles (see also Gensini 1982: 171). He ends up listing fourteen dialects which he discards as being unfit for literary usage. Therefore, he does not locate his *volgare illustre* in any one of the local dialects of Italy, but over and above all of them. In his view this *volgare* must be 'illustre, cardinale, aulicum et curiale . . . quod omnis latie civitatis est et nullius esse videtur, et quo municipalia vulgaria omnia Latinorum mensurantur et ponderantur et comparantur (*DVE*, I, 6). The rhetorical characteristics of this *volgare* are summarized concisely by Migliorini (1966: 173):

> *Illustre* lo chiama Dante, cioè fulgido perché sublimato per magistero d'arte, e atto a commuovere col suo potere; *cardinale*, perché intorno ad esso, come la porta sul suo cardine, si muovono i dialetti; *aulico*, perché degno della reggia, se l'Italia avesse una reggia; *curiale*, perché degno di supremo tribunale, se anche questo l'avessimo.

H3 is the most plausible one, because it fits in with Dante's stated purpose in the *DVE* and with the specific cultural modes of thinking and writing which are characteristic of the Middle Ages. Specifically, Dante intended to argue for the use of vulgar tongues for literary purposes. His method was to classify and synthesize the existing knowledge on language in general and on vulgar tongues in particular. This scholastic technique became the ideological platform on which he constructed his rhetorical model of an appropriate language of poetry, which he called *illustre*. What we have in the *DVE* is not a proto-textbook in Romance philology (H1) or historical linguistics (H2), but an 'eloquently' argued treatise (and appropriately in Latin) on poetic language. It is a book that both reflects the medieval mentality, but also looks forward to current literary theories on the relationship between form and content in poetic expression. As such, it is an isolated monument. That most of his contemporaries probably did not understand it, is borne out by the fact that there are no contemporary discussions of Dante's thesis.

CONCLUSION

If nothing else, this exercise in philological semiotics has proven to be an instructive one on what can only be characterized as the mindset of post-Schleicherian linguists. The modern linguist, like any scientist, works within a specific cultural system of thought. This system becomes a powerful shaper of the linguist's perceptions. Those who support H1 and H2 are really reading the *DVE* with a modern mind-set. The lesson to be learned from such an exercise in self-analysis is an obvious one. Authors of textbooks of Romance philology and of historical linguistics who trace the origins of their science to the *DVE* will have to rethink this historiographical practice. By way of conclusion, it ʻis interesting to note that Dante's conceptual separation of the vernacular languages from Latin was based on his observation that *grammatica*, as Wright (1982: 262) aptly portrays it, 'was an invented international language'. As modern work on the nature of grammatical systems has shown, Dante was absolutely right. The *Latin vs Romance* dichotomy is, actually, at the core of a vigorous debate on the meaning of the *DVE* – a debate, incidentally, which started only in this century in the 1930s (see Pagani 1982 for a detailed assessment of this debate). But the greatness of the *DVE* lies not in any one of its separate thematic components. Like Euclid's *Elements*, or Saint Thomas' *Summa Theologica*, the *DVE* puts forward a catalogue of ideas which can be arranged in infinite ways to generate continually new insights, and to chart new ideological landscapes. As Alberto Varvaro (1968: 17) appropriately characterizes it:

> Così, mentre per la sua impostazione retorico-stilistica l'opera tocca solo in parte temi propriamente linguistici, d'altro canto l'ampiezza della prospettiva e l'acutezza fuori del comune dell'autore ne fanno il libro più originale che in questo campo ci abbia dato il medioevo.

BIBLIOGRAPHY

Chiappelli, F. (ed.) (1965) Dante Alighieri, *De Vulgari Eloquentia*, Milano: Mursia.

Cole, K. C. (1984) *Sympathetic Vibrations: Reflections on Physics as a Way of Life*, New York: Bantam.

Cremona, J. (1965) 'Dante's views on language', in A. Limentani (ed.), *The Mind of Dante*, Cambridge: Cambridge University Press, 138–62.

Gensini, S. (1982) *Elementi di storia linguistica italiana*, Bergamo: Minerva Italica.

Grayson, C. (1965) 'Nobilior est vulgaris', *Centenary Essays on Dante*, Oxford: Oxford University Press, 101–21.

Greenberg, J. H. (1957) *Essays in Linguistics*, Chicago: University of Chicago Press.

Gruber, H. (1974) *Darwin on Man: A Psychological Study of Scientific Creativity*, New York: Dutton.

Hall, R. A. (1942) *The Italian Questione della lingua: an interpretive essay*, Chapel Hill: University of North Carolina Press.

258   *Marcel Danesi*

—— (1963) *Idealism in Romance Linguistics*, Ithaca, NY: Cornell University Press.

—— (1974) *External History of the Romance Languages*, New York: Elsevier.

Harris, R. and Taylor, T. J. (1989), *Landmarks in Linguistic Thought*, London: Routledge.

Hoenigswald, H. H. (1963) 'On the history of the comparative method', *Anthropological Linguistics* 5: 1–11.

Hoffman, R. R. (1980) 'Metaphor in science', in R. P. Honeck and R. R. Hoffman (eds), *Cognition and Figurative Language*, Hillsdale NJ: Lawrence Erlbaum Associates, 393–423.

Holtus, G. (1987) 'Zur Sprach- und Wortgeschichte von "latino" und "volgare" ', in W. Dahner, G. Holtus, J. Kramer and M. Metzeltin (eds), *Latein und Romanisch*, Tübingen: Narr, 340–54.

Lloyd, P. M. (1979) 'On the definition of "Vulgar" Latin', *Neuphilologische Mitteilungen* 80: 110–22.

Maher, J. (1966) 'More on the history of the comparative method: the tradition of Darwinism in August Schleicher's work', *Anthropological Linguistics* 8: 1–12.

Marigo, A. (ed.) (1957) Dante Alighieri, *De Vulgari Eloquentia*, Firenze: Le Monnier.

Migliorini, B. (1966) *Storia della lingua italiana*, Firenze: Sansoni.

Nardi, B. (1922) 'Il linguaggio', *Giornale Storico della Letteratura Italiana* 19–20: complete supplement.

Pagani, I. (1982) *La teoria linguistica di Dante*, Naples: Liguori.

Pagliaro, A. (1947) 'I "primissimi signa" nella teoria linguistica di Dante', *Quaderni di Roma* 1: 485–501.

Pazzaglia, M. (1967) *Il verso e l'arte della canzone nel De Vulgari Eloquentia*, Firenze: La Nuova Italia.

Pei, M. (1976) *The Story of Latin and the Romance Languages*, New York: Harper & Row.

Robins, R. H. (1967) *A Short History of Linguistics*, London: Longman.

Schleicher, A. (1860) *Die deutsche Sprache*, Stuttgart: J. G. Cotta'schen.

Stewart, A. H. (1976) *Graphic Representation of Models in Linguistic Theory*, Bloomington: Indiana University Press.

Vinay, G. (1959) 'Ricerche sul *De Vulgari Eloquentia*', *Giornale Storico della Letteratura Italiana* 136: 236–74.

Viscardo, A. (1942) 'La favella di Cacciaguida e la nozione dantesca del latino', *Cultura Neolatina* 2: 311–14.

Vitale, M. (1978) *La questione della lingua*, Palermo: Palumbo.

Varvaro, A. (1968) *Storia, problemi e metodi della linguistica romanza*, Naples: Liguori.

Wright, R. (1982) *Late Latin and Early Romance in Spain and Carolingian France*, Liverpool: Cairns.

Index